REVOLUTION IN SEATTLE

REVOLUTION
IN SEATTLE

A Memoir

Harvey O'Connor

Haymarket Books
Chicago, Illinois

Originally published in 1964 by Monthly Review Press, New York
© Harvey O'Connor

This edition published in 2009 by
Haymarket Books
P.O. Box 180165,
Chicago, IL, 60618
773-583-7884
www.haymarketbooks.org
ISBN 978-1-931859-74-5

Trade distribution:
In the U.S. through Consortium Book Sales and Distribution, www.cbsd.com
In the UK through Turnaround Publisher Services, www.turnaround-psl.com
In Australia through Palgrave MacMillan, www.palgravemacmillan.com.au
In all other countries through Publishers Group Worldwide,
www,pgw.com/home/worldwide.asp

Cover design by Ragina Johnson.

Published with the generous support of the Wallace Global Fund.

Printed in Canada by union labor on recycled paper containing 100 percent
post-consumer waste in accordance with the guidelines of the Green Press
Initiative, www.greenpressinitiative.org.

The 1964 edition of this book is cataloged by the Library of Congress under
Catalog-in-Publication card number 64–16129.

Bliss was it in that dawn to be alive,
But to be young was very heaven!

—*Wordsworth*

Foreword

There was a time in this country when radicals openly advocated abolition of the capitalist system — not merely reform of its most glaring abuses. There was a time in this country when workers learned class consciousness from these radicals, and from their own experiences in militant struggles against their profit-hungry employers. *Revolution in Seattle* is the story of such radicals and trade unionists who preached and practiced class consciousness and direct action and solidarity, and so won shorter hours, better conditions, and higher wages for the workers of America, at the cost of beatings, imprisonment, and death.

Since class consciousness and solidarity and devotion to principle are almost extinct in the United States — they quickly go out of fashion in corrupt, "affluent" societies — much of what appears in these pages will seem incredible to many readers, particularly the younger generation. How could it be otherwise? They live in a period when the labor leaders they read about are a different breed of men, when the AFL-CIO Executive Council even refuses to endorse the August 28, 1963, March on Washington for Jobs and Freedom for Negroes! They live in a period when the once-militant Communist Party now urges its followers to "work within" the capitalist Democratic Party and support its millionaire President. They live in a period when the once-vibrant Socialist Party is today as opposed to the revolutionary overthrow of capitalism as its great leader, Eugene V. Debs, was for it, "The master class has always declared the war," said Debs, in his famous June, 1918, speech delivered at

Canton, Ohio, in opposition to the First World War, "the subject class has always fought the battles. The master class has had
all to gain and nothing to lose, while the subject class has nothing to gain and all to lose — especially their lives." Debs and
other Socialist Party leaders went to prison for their speeches
and articles in opposition to war, and for socialism; today's
Socialist Party is in opposition, not to the capitalist countries,
but to the socialist countries.

The capitalist tactic of splitting the working class by red-
baiting, so successful today, did not work with the Seattle
Central Labor Council in the era so pungently described in
these pages by Harvey O'Connor. The first general strike anywhere in the United States began in Seattle at ten o'clock in the
morning on February 6, 1919, and was called off on February
11. It had lasted five working days in which nothing moved in
the city except by special order of the General Strike Committee. Though the strike had been voted almost unanimously by
the 300-odd delegates from 100 local unions affiliated to the
Council, there were some who had had misgivings about the
wisdom of calling the strike. Nevertheless, in the ensuing hysterical outburst from the commercial press calling on "responsible"
union labor to purge the Council of the "gang of criminal, un-
American leaders" who had "misled" it, not one delegate lined
up with the enemy. The statement issued by the Central
Labor Council reflects the awareness of this body of workers
about their class relationship:

We hasten to assure the draft-slacking publisher of the *Star*, all
the employers who hate labor, and all those who love to lick their
boots, that we know exactly what they mean by "reds," and we know
exactly what they mean by "bolsheviki," exactly what they mean by
"cleaning house"; that organized labor in Seattle was never so proud
of itself, that it appreciates the reds more for the enemies they have
made, that it has no intention of cleaning house to please its opponents, and that the general strike is permanently in the arsenal of
labor's peaceful weapons.

What a difference then and now! Put alongside that declaration by the labor leaders of Seattle in 1919, this one by George

Meany to the convention of the National Association of Manufacturers in December, 1956:

> I never went on strike in my life, never ran a strike in my life, never ordered anyone else to run a strike in my life, never had anything to do with a picket line. . . .
> In the final analysis, there is not a great difference between the things I stand for and the things that NAM leaders stand for. I stand for the profit system; I believe in the profit system. I believe it's a wonderful incentive. I believe in the free enterprise system completely.

In the pages of this book, a consummate raconteur tells us fascinating and exhilarating stories of a bygone age; immediately there come to mind contrasts — sordid and depressing:

Item: In October, 1919, a trainload of 50 freight cars brought to the port of Seattle a shipment labeled "sewing machines," destination Vladivostok. A longshore crew, wondering why a country engaged in a civil war would be importing sewing machines, "accidently" dropped a crate on the dock. The clatter that ensued came not from bobbins, shuttles, and wheels, but from rifles. They were being sent, in a government-chartered ship, from Remington Arms to the counter-revolutionist Kolchak. The longshoremen's union refused to load the cargo and notified other ports of their action. The Central Labor Council backed up the longshoremen.

Contrast, 1963: Joseph Curran, President of the National Maritime Union, a labor organization with an outstanding record of militant struggle — in its earlier days — called upon the United States government to bring economic pressure on those countries whose ships carried cargoes to revolutionary Cuba. The AFL-CIO matched Curran in his efforts to smash the Cuban Revolution.

Item: In November, 1919, some employers, businessmen, and American Legionnaires plotted an attack on the I.W.W. hall in Centralia, Washington, during the Armistice Day parade to be held on November 11. The Wobblies were aware of the plan — it was generally known throughout the city — and about a dozen of them, advised by their lawyer that they were within their rights to defend the hall against attack, decided to defend it. "Prudent men," says O'Connor, "valuing their own skins, would have closed the hall in the face of the obvious threat. But prudence was not a Wobbly trait. Rather their shining glory stood out in audacity, courage, and stubbornness in defense of their rights, and for that they are remembered in history."

The parade was held, the mob attacked the hall, the Wobblies fired, and four men were killed. What followed is vividly told in the book and need not be recounted here. In the hysteria that ensued, fomented in great part by the Employers Association of Washington interested in destroying the organized labor movement, a paid advertisement by Edwin Selvin, editor of the *Business Chronicle,* appeared in the Seattle *Post-Intelligencer.* It was so full of falsehood and inflammatory material that Selvin was subsequently arrested for mailing unmailable matter.

Following the appearance of the ad in the early edition of the paper, the *P-I* printing trades workers held a meeting and presented a resolution to the management which said, in part:

In the page advertisement in the *Post-Intelligencer* of November 18, 1919, purporting to have been written and paid for by one Selvin, but which had as well have occupied the position in your paper usually taken up by your editorial page, your utter depravity as a newspaper, your shameless disregard of the laws of the land, your hatred of opposition, your reckless policy of appeal to the passions of citizenry, reached depths of malice and malignancy hitherto unbelievable. It is nothing less than excitation to violence, stark and naked invitation to anarchy.

With the resolution went notification to management that no union man working on the paper would touch type or run the press if the offending ad was carried in later editions. The ad did not appear.

Contrast, 1963: Though the press today is just as full of slander, misrepresentation, and dishonesty in its treatment of labor and radical groups, what printing trades union in the United States today would dare to reprimand a newspaper owner and take strike action, if necessary, against lies? None has.

Times have changed in Seattle as elsewhere in the United States, and the militant radical unionism of the earlier period was supplanted by the business unionism of the late 1920's. The corruption that became the characteristic of every aspect of American life pervaded the radical and union movements too. In place of men of the stamp of Hulet Wells, Sam Sadler, and Joe and Morris Pass, who believed in working class solidarity, and strikes, and socialism, came Dave Beck, head of the Teamsters Union, whose beliefs were epitomized in his Labor Day statement of September 7, 1953:

We call upon industry to join with labor in a new era of labor-management cooperation.

If labor and management could rid themselves of old-fashioned — actually Marxian notions — that they are forever locked in bitter opposition . . . then our country would soar to new heights of accomplishment.

The key to this magnificent future is not industrial peace, which implies a compact between warring factions but industrial fellowship, based on common understanding for a common goal.

The employing class hated Hulet Wells and Sam Sadler and the Pass brothers, and rejoiced when they were convicted, in 1918, on the charge of "seditious conspiracy" in connection with the distribution of a "No Conscription" leaflet. They were sentenced to two years in the penitentiary at McNeil Island.

The employing class liked Dave Beck. They could "do business with" a labor leader like him. And they did. The one-time laundry truck driver became a millionaire — and ended up in the same penitentiary at McNeil Island as Hulet Wells, Sam Sadler, and the Pass brothers. But there was a marked difference. Wells and his friends were principled, dedicated men who went to prison for their beliefs and for their activities in behalf of the working class. Dave Beck went to prison because he was a crook.

This is a timely book because it will give light and inspiration to an old struggle now entering a new, militant, potentially revolutionary phase — that of the Negro to attain rights which the radicals of Seattle fought for a long time ago. The "Freedom Now" movement frightens the business unionists of today but the Seattle militants of yesteryear would have given it their all-out enthusiastic support. They would have appreciated and applauded it because they, too, fought for the dignity of man.

Not least of the pleasures derived from *Revolution in Seattle* is the knowledge that this stirring account of great deeds by great men is narrated by one of them. O'Connor was there. He was part of the things he writes about. Characteristically, he buries that fact in two sentences in the long story of the launching, in July 1917, of that amazing radical paper, the *Seattle Daily Call:* "I gave a hand to the stereotyper in pouring lead for the molds, swept out the office, and wrote editorials while learning the knack of writing news stories. Eventually I had the distinction of seeing my name on the masthead as editor, a rather melancholy honor which others declined because it was the editor who took the rap when the cops asked for the person in charge."

The "cops" have been after Harvey O'Connor ever since. And always he has fought them with courage and honor — in the tradition of the old Wobblies whom he admires so much. He risked jail in his defiance of the McCarthy Committee in 1953, when he refused to answer their questions on the simple ground that "My political affiliations or lack of political affiliations are no legitimate concern of this committee."

In 1958 the "cops" were after him again. While addressing a public meeting called to protest the un-American activities of the House Un-American Activities Committee, he was handed a subpoena by the marshal for the Committee. He refused to take it. "The subpoena," he said later, "fluttered to the floor like a wounded bird." His trial for defiance of the Committee is now pending.

In a period so aptly characterized by Dalton Trumbo as "The Time of the Toad," it is refreshing to read this memoir, by so gallant a participant, of an era which could be appropriately called "The Time of the Lions."

LEO HUBERMAN

August, 1963

Preface

For many years I have been increasingly concerned lest one of the most dramatic chapters in the labor history of the United States go unrecorded. Already many of the men and women who helped to shape the radical movement in the Puget Sound country from 1900 to 1920 have died; very few remain who could write of the period from their own personal knowledge.

The inevitable distortions of history made by scholars who can rely only on the cold type of the newspapers of the period, the fugitive publications, the vague memories of old-timers, are too apparent in the honest efforts of aspiring candidates for masters' and doctors' degrees to record events even so recent as thirty to forty years ago. That period must indeed be almost incomprehensible now; stranger indeed than tales of the first American Revolution because, after all, the events recorded in this book are not remote in time, however remote they may appear when seen through the miasma of the Cold War.

I, too, have relied in large measure on the labor newspapers of the period. Unfortunately, exactly here the recorder of labor history suffers his gravest disability, for files of most of the radical papers of the early 1900's no longer exist. At the time, they were beneath the contempt of librarians and historians and if any have survived it is because old-time radicals with a feeling for history somehow preserved newspapers, pamphlets, and leaflets. Foremost among these is Marvin Sanford, union printer, amateur journalist, newspaper collector, and grandson of four members of the Socialist Party. For years he has diligently collected radical publications of western Washington and it is to his collection that I owe much of the information gleaned for this book. Part of the Sanford Collection fortunately is now sheltered in the University of Washington Library, whose curator of manuscripts diligently searches out the remnants of labor records. Unhappily, the search for many papers ends in frustration. No copies have been found, for instance, of two papers which I edited, the *International Weekly,* of Seattle, and the *Farmer-Labor Call,* of Centralia. Thus disappears much recorded history.

One of the main figures in the socialist movement of those times, Hulet M. Wells, has written his memoirs — "I Wanted To Work" — a manuscript which in other times would be deemed well worthy of publication in book form. His sharp memory, together with a scholarly mind which prompted him to save a wealth of clippings and fugitive material, have given flesh and blood to the dry bones of events in which he was a principal actor. His manuscript fortunately is lodged in the archives of the University of Washington Library.

It is regrettable that E. B. (Harry) Ault, whose name figures in most of the chapters of this book as an early socialist editor and agitator and later as editor of the *Seattle Daily Union Record,* was unable to complete his autobiography, "Thirty Years of Saving the World." His memoirs extend only to about 1912, but cover the period of Equality Colony of which his parents were members. Death — and perhaps a reluctance to continue writing of events in the dramatic war years, years in which he was so personally involved — have deprived us of what could have been the most authoritative account of the period covered by this book. His memoirs and papers also have been added to the University of Washington Library.

By all odds the most vivid account of the First World War years in Seattle has been written by Anna Louise Strong in her book, *I Change Worlds.* As staff writer for both the *Seattle Daily Call* and the *Union Record,* she was at the center of the wild currents of that time.

An intimate view of the period is afforded in the letters and papers of Mark Litchman, the doughty socialist lawyer who

defended many a workingman. His acute, inquiring mind recorded its drama in an informal way. His papers, too, are preserved in the University of Washington archives.

Friends of mine who lived through those years have read
the manuscript of this book and have furnished a wealth of
warm, personal sidelights, much of which is incorporated in the
various chapters. But for the flavor of those years, I have let
them speak for themselves in Appendix One. Because of Cold
War pressures, they have asked that their names not be used.
Deeply touched by the trial and tribulation of a fellow-pacifist,
my wife, Jessie Lloyd O'Connor, has written the story of this
forgotten anarchist, which appears as Appendix Two.

My own role, as a youngster, was minor in those years. After
graduating from Tacoma High School in 1914, I went to work
in the logging camps and of course joined Lumber Workers
Industrial Union 500 of the Industrial Workers of the World.
Occasionally between jobs I helped Walker C. Smith on the
Industrial Worker, and when the *Seattle Daily Call* was founded
in 1917, I became a member of the staff and later titular editor.
After a hitch in the U. S. Merchant Marine and work on
Armour's Sutter Basin irrigation project in California — neces-
sitated by my indictment for criminal anarchy after the Seattle
General Strike — I joined the staff of the newly established
Daily Union Record, became city editor and later labor editor.
For several months in 1919-1920, I edited the *Farmer-Labor
Call* in Centralia. As I left Seattle in 1924, my knowledge of
subsequent events is second hand. I am obliged to Terry Pettus,
former labor newspaperman, to Carl Brannin, John C. Kennedy,
and Hulet M. Wells for their insights into the later period.
Terry Pettus, Marvin Sanford, Hulet Wells, and James Weinstein have read portions of the manuscript, and to them I am
indebted for correcting many an error due to faulty memory and
for a wealth of fresh insights and information.

HARVEY O'CONNOR

Little Compton, R. I.
September 30, 1963

CONTENTS

1

The Rise of Radicalism

On the shores of Puget Sound, loveliest of inland seas, the Brotherhood of the Cooperative Commonwealth planned to create colonies from which the concept of socialism would spread throughout the state of Washington, converting it into the first of socialist commonwealths. Thereafter other states, stirred by this proof that poverty could be abolished, would follow suit. Such was a dream of Eugene V. Debs. If but a dream, nevertheless some 40 years later, in 1936, Postmaster General James A. Farley proposed a toast "to the American Union — 47 states and the Soviet of Washington."* From seeds sown in the 1890's grew some of the most daring and radical experiments ever seen on this continent.

The 1890's were hard times. Hunger in the cities, poverty on the farms. Workingmen revolted in great strikes as at Pullman. Thrown into jail, they had time to contemplate and they tried to plan a way of life outside the rule of gold and greed. Rebuffed on both the industrial and political fronts by the power of the new robber barons, these workers sought escape into a clean and wholesome society. Thus arose the Brotherhood of the Cooperative Commonwealth. There was much talk in the 1890's of the New Day, the New Era, the Dawn. Henry Demarest Lloyd, the sensitive prophet of the times, wrote of "our land filled with the voice not of one but of the multitudes crying in the

---

* The sources for direct quotations, and additional information about people and events, appear, by page and line number, in "Notes" beginning on page 263. Books and articles referred to are also listed and briefly discussed in that section. A list of radical papers published about 1900-1920 in the state of Washington begins on page 287.

wilderness — the wilderness of want, and . . . of that which is
worse than want, the sickness of heart of the people. . . ."

To many now the vehemence and passion with which the
early radicals held to their beliefs seem inexplicable. But in
those days workers were not shielded by welfare statism; the
built-in shock absorbers of the warfare state did not exist. Most
workers lived in an industrial jungle where neither justice nor
compassion tempered the harsh blows that fell upon the victims
of unending panics and depressions. Even "good times" offered
little respite, for waves of immigration passing through Ellis
Island bringing in 500,000 to 800,000 each year stymied any
effort to obtain lasting improvements in working conditions. In
nearly every basic industry efforts to establish unions met with
bloody repression. Unions existed for the most part only in the
skilled trades, and these stood like islands in a sea of industrial
despotism.

In those days there was no social security. The worker lived in
constant fear of unemployment, part-time employment, accidents, disease, old age, that might strike him down at any time
and leave his family helpless. In times of panic there were soup
lines to keep body and soul together; organized charity made
pallid attempts to assuage the worst evils. With monotonous
regularity the courts struck down laws aimed against child labor,
sweatshops, long hours, and wretched pay. In all that period
from the end of the Civil War until the First World War the
specter of insecurity — whether from joblessness, accident, disease, or old age — was the constant companion in working-class
homes, particularly in the larger industrial centers. Prosperity
was fleeting; the industrial system lurched forward by fits and
starts; the progress of the nation was built upon the broken lives
of millions. When the nation became fat and could afford the
luxuries of social security and continuous wars — hot and cold
— only then did the specter of insecurity lift itself in some
measure.

In Woodstock penitentiary after the Pullman strike of 1894,
Debs, leader of the American Railway Union, had time to read.

Laurence Gronlund's *The Cooperative Commonwealth* (1884) and Edward Bellamy's *Looking Backward* (1888) impressed him. After Bryan's defeat in 1896, ordinary reform politics appeared hopeless to Debs and he began to veer toward Marxist socialism.

Following the Populist convention of 1896, various socialists and idealists came together to form the Brotherhood of the Cooperative Commonwealth. Not Karl Marx but Edward Bellamy was godfather to this movement. Bellamy had followed up his famous book on Utopia with an article in the *Contemporary Review* in 1890, entitled "What Nationalism Means," and from this grew the Nationalist movement in the East, paralleling Populism in the agrarian West. Nationalists and Populists, with some socialists, joined in the Brotherhood, which aimed to educate the people in socialism, unite all socialists in one fraternal organization, and then form cooperative colonies and industries "and so far as possible to concentrate these colonies and industries in one state until that state is socialized."

The American Railway Union, broken by President Cleveland's troops, dissolved in 1897. Its remnants joined with various colonizing groups, socialist and union locals, and radical religious associations to form the Social Democracy, with Debs as chairman. "With a view to the immediate relief of the people," declared the new party, "all our efforts should be put forth to secure to the unemployed self-supporting employment. . . . For such purpose one of the states of the Union, to be hereafter determined, should be selected for the concentration of our supporters and the introduction of cooperative industry, and then gradually extending the sphere of our operations until the national cooperative commonwealth shall be established."

Socialists and radicals divided on the colony issue. None illustrated the doubts more clearly than Henry Demarest Lloyd who argued that if the colonists succeeded in winning one state for socialism, "the money power would force it into rebellion and then crush it with all the military power at its command." Nevertheless Lloyd's name was on the call for the Brotherhood convention, following that of Debs, and he was the nearly unani-

mous choice for president. Lloyd declined, preferring to work in
a wider field, but obviously he was pulled in two directions. He
compared the Brotherhood's colonies to abolish wage slavery
with those of the Free Soilers in settling Kansas to prevent the
spread of chattel slavery. But he feared that the colonists were
withdrawing from the main stream of the struggle for freedom,
and in danger of isolating themselves.

The Brotherhood gained 3,000 members and set up departments for teaching socialism, settling colonies, establishing industries, and propounding political action. On its letterhead
were the brave words:

TO USHER IN

A union of all	The Brotherhood of	Mutualism or the
Socialists in	The Cooperative	Kingdom of Heaven
the world	Commonwealth	Here and Now

In 1897 Debs was named national organizer, but strikes in the
mines of West Virginia and Colorado kept him from devoting
much time to the colony idea. Nevertheless he found time to
write one of the oddest letters ever penned by an avowed socialist to a capitalist. Debs wrote John D. Rockefeller, asking his
financial help for the Brotherhood.

The purpose of the organization, briefly speaking, is to establish
in place of the present cruel, immoral and decadent system, a cooperative commonwealth, where millionaires and beggars . . . will
completely disappear, and human brotherhood will be inaugurated
to bless and make the world more beautiful. . . . In this movement
there are no class distinctions: Rich and poor are equally welcome
to help dethrone Gold and elevate humanity. Then the strong will
help the weak, the weak will love the strong, and the Human
Brotherhood will transform the days to come into a virtual Para-
dise. . . . Believing that you will find yourself in accord with your
own feelings of social and patriotic obligations by your generous
contributions to a worthy cause for freedom, I remain sincerely
yours, Eugene V. Debs.

Rockefeller never bothered to answer the letter, and Debs came
to have a better understanding of why he didn't.

The Brotherhood chose Ed Pelton, a veteran woodsman, to

prospect the colony site. Louisiana he found objectionable because of race consciousness; onward he went to Puget Sound where he located 280 acres near Edison, on Padilla Bay, for $2,850. At that time the Puget Sound country was still virtually a primeval forest from the crests of the Cascades and Olympics to tidewater. In the sea were fish, along the shores rich flatland suitable for vegetable and forage crops, and everywhere timber awaiting axe and saw.

Asked to name the new colony, Bellamy christened it Equality. Colonists streamed in from the East, some 300 by early 1898. Families paid $160 for membership and this, with the rather meager financial help of the Brotherhood, provided the start for Equality. Mainly the colonists came in tourist sleepers — poor men's Pullmans with kitchens at one end whose stoves glowed all day and far into the night as families cooked their meals on the long journey West.

As befitted a socialist colony, the first buildings were large communal structures with a sleeping room for each family. The colonists served according to their ability and drew according to their need from the slender resources of the commissary. There was neither church, nor jail, nor saloon, nor police. After the sawmill, the next enterprise of Equality was a printing press from which rolled *Industrial Freedom,* its first issue dated May 7, 1898. David Burgess, who had been editor of a farm weekly in Arkansas, was an early editor. George E. Boomer, who wrote under the pen name Uncle Sam, came to set up the press. As there was no electricity, he got a gasoline engine to run the press. William McDevitt, a veteran *Appeal to Reason* booster, also gave a hand; in the shop young E. B. (Harry) Ault, later to be publisher of the country's first labor union daily, the *Seattle Union Record,* learned to set type.

Ault's father was typical of Equality's colonists. A metal polisher by trade in Cincinnati, he had joined the Populists in 1893 and his wife helped to feed the straggling cohorts of Coxey's Army when they streamed through Cincinnati a year later. The imprisonment of Debs in Woodstock turned Ault —

like so many others — from Populism to socialism; when the Brotherhood was organized in 1896 it found in him a fervent disciple. He cashed in his insurance policy, paid his membership fee, and spent the rest for tourist-sleeper fare to the Coast for his family. Death came to him in 1902, at the early age of 44. As a rationalist, he had asked to be cremated on a 50-foot pile of slashings from the sawmill, but the colony decided that this was too spectacular a defiance of the godly neighbors who looked somewhat askance at the socialist colony. It was too soon after the assassination of President McKinley, and feeling was running high against "anarchists" — the term then applied to society's dissidents.

It was unfortunate in a way that the refugees from money panics, industrial depression, and poverty in the East chose the year 1898 to establish Equality; for along came the Spanish-American War to give a shot in the arm to the stagnant economy, culminating in the burst of corporation mergers which riveted monopoly's hold on the basic industries. Also, gold had been discovered in the Klondike in 1897 and the fever drove thousands to seek their fortune in the gold rush. To many colonists, Equality seemed increasingly a backwater in a surging era; the lack of leadership and discipline discouraged others. The stream of incoming colonists dribbled away. More and more members began seeking work outside the colony to earn cash for necessities not available within Equality. Eventually the Brotherhood of the Cooperative Commonwealth and its colony vanished. In 1907 the land was sold.

Other refugees from railroad blacklists, wheat famines, and mine shutdowns were the core of colonists who in about 1898 established on Whidby Island in Puget Sound the community of Freeland. One and all they were Rochdalers, followers of the English cooperative idea, although most were also socialists. They established the Free Land Association, in which the land held by each family was to be practically free of cash cost through rebates earned on farm and industrial products. As true socialists, the Freelanders early set up their printing press to publish the *Whidby Islander,* edited by DeForest Sanford and his wife, Ethel Brooke Sanford. Among its contributors were Ella Wheeler Wilcox, Charlotte Perkins Gilman, Kate Richards O'Hare, Debs, and other socialist publicists. This seemingly obscure provincial paper acquired a national circulation, along with Equality's *Industrial Freedom.* A third colony, also called Freeland or Hertzka, was set up in 1905 near the defunct Equality, and persisted with varying fortunes until the First World War.

A colony had been set up near Tacoma in 1897, in the same year as Equality. This was Home Colony, established "to assist members in obtaining and building homes for themselves and to aid in establishing better social and moral conditions." By 1901 there were about a hundred members, among them many anarchists whose main tenet was liberty. The anarchists did better than the socialists in establishing a permanent colony; by 1915 there were nearly 300 at Home, with three cooperative stores, a school, and quite a reputation for unconventional living.

Home of course had its paper. At first it was *Discontent,* whose staff later were arrested for sending "obscene" matter through the mails — mainly, it seemed, discussions on marriage. At that time "free love" was in the air, and the lack of a marriage license was viewed by the more solid or hysterical members of society as an outrage against decency. The assassination of McKinley spurred an outcry against the anarchists at Home, and a boat was chartered in Tacoma to take a mob over to the colony to burn it down. Fortunately the crowd was dispersed before it could leave. In 1913 Jay Fox, editor of the *Agitator,* another Home Colony paper, went to jail for two months for publishing an editorial on the theme of Nudes and Prudes, in defense of swimming in the nude, an innocent custom which Russian and Swedish colonists had introduced from their homelands.

From New Harmony, Robert Owen's colony in Indiana in 1825, through the various Fourierite and religious-humanitarian

colonies down to Equality and Home, failure was written on
efforts which aimed to withdraw workers into ideal communities; certainly Debs soon realized that the Brotherhood of the
Cooperative Commonwealth was no answer to advancing monopoly and he abandoned his dream of a socialist commonwealth. For great-hearted Lloyd, though, the truth about all
these colonies was otherwise: "Only within these communities,"
he wrote, "has there been seen, in the wide borders of the
United States, a social life where hunger and cold, prostitution,
intemperance, poverty, slavery, crime, premature old age, and
unnecessary mortality, panic and industrial terror, have been
abolished. If they had done this only for a year, they would de-
serve to be called the only successful 'society' on this continent,
and some of them are generations old. All this has not been done
by saints in heaven, but on earth by average men and women."

Whatever the fate of these colonies, their voices reached out
far and wide; many a rebellious working man, fed up with
factory slavery in the East, headed West as a result, not always,
perhaps, to join a colony, but to be in a section of the land where
the voice of dissent could be heard.

There had, of course, been radicals in Washington long before
Equality. But the Socialist Labor Party, the main force in propagating socialist ideas before 1900, had little strength on Puget
Sound. Its membership comprised many Germans fleeing the
Kaiser's autocracy and Jews fleeing the Czar's. Few of these pene-
trated to the Pacific Coast, whose migration came mostly along
the railroad routes from Minnesota and included many venture-
some Swedes and Finns. These hardy people knew little of and
cared much less for the factory life of the East, with its industrial
slavery, ever-menacing unemployment, and slum warrens. The
major industry was lumbering, then mostly operated by small
enterprisers. The major corporations, as the Westerners knew
them, were the railroads, and Westerners had little to do with
their construction across prairies, deserts, and mountains. From
the 1860's, in California, to the 1880's in Washington, the railroads turned to distant China for their labor force. So to West-

ern workingmen the image of capitalism focused on two aspects — the soulless railroad corporations and the hapless Chinese laborers, working long hours for wages which were a fraction of what any American workingman would accept, and under living conditions which were an affront to the American standard.

At one time the Northern Pacific employed as many as 15,000 Chinese; when the Canadian Pacific was completed in 1885, thousands more were dumped unceremoniously on the crowded labor market. These flocked to the hop fields, mines, fish canneries, and sawmills, and into the cities where they inched their way into niches in the economy in their new role as launderers, cooks, domestic servants, and whatever other jobs they could get through their willingness, in a strange land far from home, to work any hours for any wage that would stave off hunger.

There was little disagreement on the Coast that the Chinese must go. But the federal government, which had financed railroad construction through enormous land grants, shirked responsibility, and the railroads washed their hands of their former employees. When no progress was made in dispatching the Chinese, radicals urged direct action. "Every socialist and anarchist who could walk or steal a ride to Seattle was a self-elected but none the less welcome delegate" to the anti-Chinese congress held September 28, 1885, according to one Seattle historian. In November, 1885, the Chinese were rounded up in Tacoma and put on a train for Portland, and their hovels burned. In February of 1886 the Chinese in Seattle were marched to "The Queen of the Pacific," about to depart for San Francisco. Troops were called out, the deporters dispersed, and those Chinese unable to get passage on the crowded Queen were permitted to straggle back to their wretched dwellings, to await another ship. Little physical violence was suffered by the non-resisting Chinese but a logger was killed in a fight between the Home Guards and the workers. The issue of Asiatic labor remained, though, to plague the union and socialist movements for three decades. The internationalists in the Socialist Party denounced racial prejudice, but the majority, while deploring prejudice, pleaded that "we must face the facts." Asiatic labor commandeered by corporations to break down American standards must be excluded.

Disgusted with double-crossing by the "dog-salmon aristocracy" who had called out the troops, Seattle workers, led by the Knights of Labor, formed the People's Anti-Chinese and Labor Party in 1886, in opposition to the businessmen's Loyal League, and swept the city and county elections. Across the country were flaming the eight-hour day movement, the upsurge of unionism, and the Henry George agitation for the single tax. The Seattle party contended that "our sad experience has proved that the old parties do not represent the people nor legislate in their interests, but vie with each other in their subserviency to the behests of capital and corporate monopolies." Their fiery spokesman was Mrs. Mary Kenworthy, a pioneer who had crossed the plains in a covered wagon. She bridged the gap between the intellectual community of the pioneer city and the workers in the sawmills, docks, and canneries. From suffragism she advanced to a kind of populist socialism. A tall woman with graying hair, dressed in somber black, she was famed for stirring speeches in which she accused the business elements of being insensitive to the needs of workingmen. Her home became the center for visiting Knights of Labor organizers, suffragists, populists, and other radicals, while she advanced toward a conviction that the conflict between labor and capital was irrepressible.

Spokesman for the young labor movement was the *Seattle Daily Call*, precursor of a socialist paper of the same name in a subsequent generation. The *Call*, like its New York counterpart, the daily *Leader*, agitated for the great labor issue of the times, the eight-hour day. On May Day, 1886, the banner headline was

EIGHT HOURS A DAY
The Movement Assuming
Wonderful Proportions
SUCCESS IN MANY INSTANCES

The *Call* was succeeded by the weekly *Puget Sound Cooperator,* which in turn gave way to the daily *Voice of the People.* This paper, of which no copies are known to exist, ceased publication in 1887.

All three papers were concerned with the possibility of establishing cooperative colonies as a refuge from unemployment. George Venable Smith, an attorney disbarred for defending workers in the anti-Chinese movement, was a main organizer for the Puget Sound Cooperative Colony, incorporated in 1887. A site was selected on the Strait of Juan de Fuca sheltered by the long curve of Ediz Hook. Behind lay the virgin rain forests of the Olympics. Here, at what is now Port Angeles, the cooperative built sawmills, docks, stores, hotels, office buildings, and homes, laying the economic foundation for a city. Their paper, the *Model Commonwealth,* extolled the virtues of cooperation, denounced the vices of capitalism, espoused the eight-hour day, and mourned on November 18, 1887, the executed anarchists of Haymarket. The colony went into receivership in 1895, but as late as 1900 there is recorded the publication of the *New Light,* a small four-page newspaper which may have been the first socialist daily published in English in the United States. Of this paper, too, no copies are known to exist.

In 1888 the Western Central Labor Union was formed in Seattle by Otto F. Wegener, a socialist. Into the WCLU — precursor of the Central Labor Council — went locals of the loosely-organized Knights of Labor, the more closely-knit crafts of the new American Federation of Labor, and the coal miners' unions in camps up on the slopes of the Cascades, nuclei of industrial unionism. In 1894 the American Industrial Brotherhood was organized for activity on the political front, its membership confined to bona fide workingmen vouched for by sponsors. In the same year, a time of intense unemployment after the panic of 1893, "General" Jumbo Cantwell demanded free transportation for his hosts to join Coxey's Army in the East. More than 2,000 unemployed seized a new hotel in Puyallup, near Tacoma, as headquarters and many rode the rods to

Chicago to join the march on Washington. Others were intercepted and derailed at North Yakima and Wenatchee.

The panic of 1893 culminated in the election in 1896 of John R. Rogers, a Populist, as governor, with the help of free-silver Democrats and Republicans, backed by a Populist majority in the legislature. He campaigned for free school books, state aid to education, reduced utilities rates, and woman suffrage. But the women had to wait until 1910 for suffrage, and in that year also the initiative, referendum, and recall were enacted to assure a more effective democracy. In 1907 Washington pioneered in the nation-wide agitation for direct election of U.S. Senators, through an advisory vote which was binding on the legislature.

The growth of socialism as an organized political force in the state dates from 1900 when Dr. Hermon Franklin Titus began publishing the *Socialist.* He had asked the WCLU to help the striking telephone girls; denied assistance, he started the *Socialist* on August 13, "to organize the slaves of capitalism to vote for their own emancipation." The first issue was a campaign sheet for the first candidacy of Debs for the presidency.

With this campaign the Social Democratic Party, successor to the Social Democracy and soon to be renamed the Socialist Party, got under way in Washington. By summer, 18 locals had been established and by November this had grown to 28, many of them in small towns to which the light of socialism was being beamed by the *Socialist, Industrial Freedom* of Equality, and the *Whidby Islander.* The staff of the *Socialist* recruited subscribers by going out on speaking tours. These were red-letter events in the backwoods of Puget Sound, and a rousing meeting usually resulted in another Socialist local. Not only workers — sawmill men, railroaders, and miners — but farmers from the surrounding countryside joined, along with many small businessmen whose economic status was certainly no higher than that of a skilled workman. In 1900 Joseph Gilbert, one of the peripatetic agitators, organized many locals in eastern Washington, particularly in farm areas, and in 1902 established, with Albert Strout, the *New Time* in Spokane.

Most of the new socialists were innocent of any knowledge of Marx and Engels, but they were eager to build a society better than the brutal system they knew so well. Usually in a sizable local there were those — often of British or Scandinavian origin — who had read Marx in the old country. In the back room of a store owned by a member, or gathered around the stove in a home, these staunch old-timers disputed the meaning of *Das Kapital*'s more elusive passages, planned the program for the next local meeting, or arranged for a public gathering to listen to an itinerant apostle of socialism. In locals and in meetings, sales of the standard Marxist pamphlets were pushed; the socialist publishing house of Charles H. Kerr in Chicago reported that Washington ranked highest among all states in orders for such literature.

Within a few years the Socialist Party claimed a hundred locals and several thousand members in the state. Socialist ideas spread so widely among unionists that by 1909 the coal miners declared for public ownership and democratic management of the means of production, including the mines they worked in.

Dr. Titus, the chief evangel of socialism in Seattle, was 48 years old in 1900 when he started the *Socialist*. Born in Massachusetts, he had been graduated from the University of Wisconsin and then attended a theological seminary. After seven years as a pastor in a New York State Baptist church, he resigned when he concluded that the churches did not represent Christ or his teachings, and went to Harvard to study medicine, as a more useful way to minister to man's needs. Later he headed West, and while doing social work on the Seattle skid road where lumber workers congregated, he read *Das Kapital* in the original. Marx convinced him that palliatives, whether of the other world or of this, would never solve the problems he observed on the skid road, so he practiced medicine as much as needed to make ends meet and devoted his major attention to propagating the socialist message. His wife, Hattie, managed a small hotel which became a rendezvous where radicals met the great and near-great of the socialist movement as they swung around the national lecture circuit. Dr. Titus' *Socialist* was a first-rate propaganda paper. At campaign time it blossomed into special editions heavily illustrated, with daring typographic displays and even the use of color, an unusual feature in early radical papers. Its usual circulation was about 5,000 copies weekly.

In 1906 Dr. Titus figured in one of the earliest free-speech fights in the West — a tactic that the Industrial Workers of the World (I.W.W.) were to use later with great effectiveness. In that year he was arrested six times for insisting on his right to soapbox on the busiest corners of the city. On refusal to pay $120 in fines he was jailed for 40 days along with many other comrades, including Harry Ault, Mrs. Titus, Alfred Wagenknecht, and Hulet M. Wells. After refusing to work on the chain gang, the socialists were freed as too troublesome. So effective was the outcry against the jailings that the Board of Health closed the city jail as a menace to prisoners' health, and juries refused to convict free-speech fighters.

Hulet Wells as a post office clerk had seen copies of the *Appeal to Reason,* the national socialist weekly, passing through his hands. One day he decided to read a copy; soon after, in 1905, he visited the Socialist hall and met Dr. Titus, whom he described later as dogmatic and dictatorial but possessed of an incisive mind and real platform ability. Wells was studying law on the side and was able thereafter to put his legal training to advantage in the socialist movement. For daring to organize a union of postal clerks and to edit its paper he was fired from the postal service — the first of many adversities which were to hound him because of his convictions.

On the staff of the *Socialist* was Vincent Harper, who shocked Chief of Police Wappenstein with his pamphlet, *The Terrible Truth About Marriage,* which assailed "the essential immorality of marriage." Wappenstein, protector of the red-light district, banned the pamphlet from the newsstands. "All children conceived in the womb of love," Harper asserted, "would be welcomed into the Cooperative Commonwealth. No more 'disgrace' to terrify the quivering mother into destroying the fruit of her immeasurable and rapturous love. No more 'respectable' abor-

tions and legalized prostitution under the sanctifying cloak of
'holy' wedlock. No more race suicide brought about by the increased cost of living and the frightful exploitation of the wage
slave. No more wholesale annihilation of children through insufficient nourishment and exposure to hardship. Socialism will
rehabilitate the family by making it possible and desirable to
bring children into the world and to keep them alive and well
after they are here."

In 1909 the state Socialist Party was riven by one of its
periodic internal crises. It seemed ironic that the good Dr. Titus,
himself a former preacher and social worker, should complain
about the domination of the national party by intellectuals and
professionals. Nor did he care for the national party's "trim-
ming" on the issue of nationalizing all farms; this he denounced
as a bait to win "petit bourgeois" farmers to socialism. Dr. Titus
and his group were expelled. After flirting with the newly-
formed Labor Party of the Seattle Central Labor Council — its
virtue was its proletarian composition — he formed the United
Wage Workers of Washington. The *Socialist* vanished and was
replaced by the *Workingman's Paper* which complained that
" 'socialism' is being used by all manner of freaks and reformers." Aside from its leader, Dr. Titus' new party was composed
exclusively of proletarians, "as defined by the *Communist
Manifesto*." We need such a proletarian movement, he wrote,
"uncompromising, unpatriotic, class-conscious, militant, revolutionary." Labor should not fight the trusts, Dr. Titus urged,
but rather encourage them so that in the final conflict between
trusts and labor the issue would not be complicated by an intervening middle class.

Dr. Titus calculated that workers produce enough wealth to
maintain themselves by four hours' labor a day, and the rest of
their labor furnishes the surplus value upon which capitalism
battens. "The 4-hour day," he concluded, "draws the class line
mathematically." To this idea he converted young Harry Ault,
who had published Dr. Titus' *Socialist* in Caldwell, Idaho, and
in Toledo, Ohio.

An even earlier paper than Dr. Titus' was the *Young Socialist*, started at Equality in 1899 by Ault, then 18. This paper gained national circulation as perhaps the first youth paper in the English language. After leaving Equality, Ault continued publishing his paper for several years, using his vest pocket as an office and whatever job press was handy. In one issue appeared the apologetic note: "Various changes of residence and insecurity of employment have precluded the earlier issuance of the *Young Socialist.*"

Elected a delegate to the Socialist Party's convention in 1904, Ault worked in the national office awhile in Chicago and then managed the presidential campaign tour of Debs and Hanford. Back in Seattle in 1905, he edited an attractive magazine with the title of *Next,* an effort to get away from didactic socialist propaganda lines. In 1910 he collaborated with Dr. Titus in publishing *The Four-Hour Day,* propounding the Titus thesis of mathematical socialism. After a disagreement with the increasingly dogmatic doctor, Ault decided to go Titus one better by publishing *The Three-Hour Day for Wage Workers.* All the while, working as a printer, he dreamed some day of publishing a labor daily in Seattle. Elected secretary of the Central Labor Council in 1912, he became editor of the official paper, the *Union Record,* in 1915 and soon pushed its circulation up from 3,000 a week to 25,000.

Dr. Titus' the *Workingman's Paper* attracted a rising young syndicalist, William Foster. Ault tells the story that Foster was sent to Spokane to cover the dramatic I.W.W. free-speech fight there in 1909. Facetiously Ault suggested that the byline "William Foster" did not sound too impressive. "Let's insert a 'Z' in your name," he suggested. "Fine, Harry," said Foster, "if it will help the working class, it's all right with me." While in Spokane, Foster gave a hand to the *Industrial Worker,* the new I.W.W. paper there, served two months in jail in the free-speech fight and, in prison, joined the I.W.W.

After 1912 Dr. Titus toured the country for his four-hour day idea, meeting with only fragmentary success. During the war he asked workers to sign a pledge to stop work after four hours on May Day, 1920, provided that three fourths of the working class pledged themselves likewise. By then he was regarded as something of a crank. He practiced medicine in the summers in the Adirondacks and in winter could be seen in front of a swank New York apartment house accoutered resplendently as a doorman. He who had once been known as the father of socialism in Washington died almost forgotten around 1930. Mrs. Titus stayed in Seattle where, years later, known as "Mother Titus," she was given a house by Seattle unionists in grateful remembrance of her unwavering loyalty to the labor movement.

The typical socialist editor of those days, like Harry Ault, was also a printer who usually "wrote" his copy while composing it out of the case. Pre-eminent among these, in the early 1900's in Washington, was George E. Boomer. Slight and frail, he was the son of cotton mill workers in Lewiston, Maine. At the age of 12 he went to work in the mill, at 65 cents for a 12¼-hour day. As required by law, he attended school three months a year. He became a newsboy and then a printer in Providence, Rhode Island, where he joined the Socialist Labor Party, ran for governor in 1893, headed the Central Labor Union, and edited *Justice*, the socialist-union paper.

In 1897 Boomer was in Girard, Kansas, helping J. A. Wayland on the fast-growing *Appeal to Reason*, the most widely read and persuasive evangel for socialism the country had known. Hearing of the Brotherhood of the Cooperative Commonwealth's new colony at Equality, he headed for the Coast in 1898, bringing with him the circulation techniques of the *Appeal*, which had already led that paper into a running battle with the Post Office Department. Hustlers throughout the land bought *Appeal* subscription cards at a discount and sold them to friends and neighbors — then the favorite way for struggling socialist papers to reward their boosters. Boomer went on to Tacoma and founded late in 1898 what may be the first simon-pure socialist paper in Washington, the *Spirit of '76*. He joined the new Social Democratic Party and was editing the *Tacoma Sun,* also a so-

cialist paper, in 1902. The next year Boomer shifted east of the
Cascades to Prosser where he edited the *Prosser Record* until
1909 and wrote a column for Titus' *Socialist*. Candidate for
governor on the Socialist ticket in 1908, he was mobbed twice
while on speaking tours. In 1910 Boomer, in Seattle, edited at
least one number of the *Wage Worker,* "the only 3-color 'roughneck' revolutionary monthly on earth." In 1912 he crossed the
Sound to Bremerton to edit the *Kitsap County Leader.* The next
year he was the subject of a colorful report in the *Commonwealth,* the Everett socialist weekly. While soapboxing in Port
Townsend he was attacked by a soldier from the nearby fort.
The state Socialist organizer reported that an attempt was made
to get a warrant "for the arrest of this uniformed beast from
Judge Lockhart, who refused, saying that the socialists ought all
to be thrown in the bay and he would be pleased to help do so.
This poor brainless little grafting political tool, a pillar of the
Methodist church, by the way, is like the vilest of the red-light
pothouse politicians and it's up to the Socialist Party to teach
him a severe lesson. The mayor refused to preserve order, being
like the other little grafters, but a tool of the bawdy-house
keepers and the like. The town seems to exist from the ill-gotten
graft money wrung from the poor unfortunate girls of the
working class prostituting themselves to the drunken soldiers."

In 1913 Boomer was back in Seattle, helping to edit the
Barbarian, a satirical socialist paper that poked fun at the upper
class and belabored right-wing elements among the socialists.
In 1914 Boomer was editing the *Peninsula Free Press* in Port
Angeles, and he died in that year, a minor figure in socialist
journalism but one typical in his resourcefulness, honesty, and
devotion to his principles.

David Burgess of *Industrial Freedom* at Equality was typical,
too, of these socialist editors. He was widely read and perhaps
the best known of early Washington socialists for it was he
who went out on the road organizing locals up and down
western Washington, while Dr. Titus preferred to remain in
Seattle. After Equality days, he was associated with Dr. Titus'

Socialist and several succeeding papers. True to his own concept of fundamental socialist principles, following the collapse of the Socialist Party in 1919 he returned, after a lapse of 20 years, to the older Socialist Labor Party and was its main figure in Seattle in the 1920's.

In 1912 the Socialist Party reached the summit of its electoral success nationally when Debs polled 900,000 votes for president, of which 40,000 were cast in Washington. In Seattle, Hulet Wells got 11,000 votes for mayor against 14,500 for George F. Cotterill, the winner, and one Socialist candidate for a county office amassed 21,000 votes. Mayors were elected in several smaller communities as well as two state legislators. A different type of "mathematical socialism" than Dr. Titus' calculated the constantly rising socialist vote and ventured predictions that ultimate victory should come in the 1920's. Such was not to be the fate of the Socialist Party. Already, in 1912, the Seattle locals were torn in conflict between the "Reds" and the "Yellows," reflecting the conflict in the national convention which, by not too large a majority, had abjured the use of violence and sabotage. At that "Big Bill" Haywood withdrew and the I.W.W. became even more openly syndicalist. Both the Washington and Seattle Socialist Parties were "Red" by a wide margin, which caused choleric Colonel Blethen of the *Seattle Times* to describe them as "dynamic" socialists — by which he meant dynamite. The other socialists he termed "respectable," although the epithets "constructive" and "impossibilist" were also used. At that time the division in socialist ranks ranged over the emphasis to be given the "immediate demand" planks in the national platform (most of which became law in the 1930's), and the nature of the eventual socialist triumph, whether by the ballot or, as many declared, by the violent opposition of the capitalist class to change which would precipitate a revolution. The issues gave rise to vituperative dissension. The emotional appeal was all with the "Reds"; the cautious "Yellows" with their talk of the inevitably gradual rise of socialist administrations in cities and states and eventually in the nation failed to

raise the blood pressure of most of the rank and file. And yet
it would be wrong to conclude that the "Reds" were all ready
for revolution — in Seattle for the most part they were solid
burghers, with rose gardens around their homes and a stake in
the community.

Factional papers sprang up such as *Revolution* in 1912 and
the *Barbarian* a year later, edited by Boomer and Bruce Rogers,
a somewhat bohemian type of rebel. The *Barbarian* was allied
with the *Truth* of Tacoma, a paper "so red that it sizzles."
Millard Price maintained Red News Wagons which sold the
red-hot socialist and radical papers. The chronic hard times
became worse in 1913; a Hotel de Gink was opened by an
enterprising "hobo king" and the city provided some casual
work at 17½ cents an hour. The *Barbarian* insisted that "the
only real issue" in the 1913 municipal campaign was "the contest between the working class and the capitalist class for the
possession of the powers of government." Nevertheless Seattle
socialists adopted a platform with these immediate demands:
municipal ownership of street railways, power and telephone
companies, markets, department stores, newspapers, "and other
industries which are essentially social institutions"; relief for
the unemployed; a minimum wage of $3.50 daily; 15 days' an-
nual paid vacations; abolition of job sharks (private employment
agencies); a free city crematory; and a public auditorium dedicated to free speech.

If 1912 was a big year for Seattle socialists — what with a
presidential campaign and mass meetings for Debs, Congressman Victor Berger and former Mayor Emil Seidel of Milwaukee,
the great British leader Keir Hardie, and Clarence Darrow —
some of the credit was due to Colonel Alden J. Blethen, publisher of the *Seattle Times*. A colonel by courtesy of a Midwest
governor, he had come to Seattle in 1896 and bought the *Times*.
A stocky, powerful man whose big head was adorned by a sena-
torial bob, Blethen took his colonelship seriously. He wor-
shipped the flag and adored soldiers. The flag always floated
majestically by day over the *Times* building, and at all times on

the masthead of the paper. Blethen hated the "dynamic" socialists; they were of the same stripe as the dynamiters of the
Los Angeles Times, and when the socialists paraded 4,000 strong
to Dreamland Rink to protest the arrest of the McNamara
brothers for the Los Angeles bombing, Blethen exploded with
rage. On May Day in 1912 they paraded again; as their line
passed the *Times* building, a group dashed out of an alley and
seized the American flag the socialists were carrying and in the
melee it was torn. The *Times* apparently expected this, for a
photographer dashed out and took a picture of the soiled flag.
Although Wells was not in the parade and had nothing to do
with its planning, the *Times* boomed out in three lines across
the front page: DENOUNCING FLAG AS DIRTY RAG MAY COST WELLS
CITIZENSHIP. Hulet Wells had said nothing about the flag, and he
was a native of nearby Skagit county. Nettled by repeated references to the "dirty rag" statement in Blethen's paper, Wells in
desperation sued for $10,000 libel. The suit was stalled for two
years and finally was given up when it was revealed that Blethen
had re-incorporated his paper in Nevada to escape suit in
Seattle.

After Debs had left town September 1, 1912, on his presidential campaign tour, the *Times* celebrated the occasion with a
story that Joseph Jarvis, a socialist, had absconded with $1,000
proceeds of the meeting. He was described as a friend of Wells,
the flag-desecrator. The facts that Jarvis was not missing, nor
any money either, and that he had not even handled the money,
did not deter Blethen. This time Wells was able to get a grand
jury to indict Blethen for libel, whereupon the Colonel demanded that the jurors be sent to Steilacoom, the insane
asylum, "until they be cured of their desire to defend the
Socialistic dynamiter." In a trial before Judge John E.
Humphries, a crony of the Colonel, the suit was thrown out,
even though Blethen admitted that he had no evidence for his
accusations. The affair was so farcical that Wells made it into a
play, *The Colonel and His Friends,* a drama that was to receive
more advance publicity than any other in local theatrical his-

tory. Unsuccessful in getting the mayor to ban the play, Blethen
pressured the Moore Theater into canceling its contract. As it
turned out, no hall in Seattle could be found, nor in Everett or
Tacoma, either. But by this time the play had been published
and was on sale at the Red News Wagons.

The business element sponsored an annual "Potlatch" to
entice country people into town and to empty their pockets,
quite unlike the Indian potlatch which was an occasion for gifts
and a general redistribution of the tribe's wealth. Sailors came
from the Bremerton navy yard to Seattle for diversion and
usually found it on the skid road. A group of sailors and
soldiers, a bit the worse for liquor, found sport in heckling a
woman speaker on a soapbox at Occidental and Washington
Streets, the center of the skid road. In the free-for-all which
followed their grabbing her stand, loggers, sailors, and soldiers
mixed it up, and three soldiers went to the hospital. Colonel
Blethen, a man easily tempted into apoplexy, particularly when
"soldier boys" were involved, opened wide the front-page
columns of the *Times* to red headlines and purple invective, denouncing the "gang of red-flag worshippers and anarchists." He
had one of the soldiers dead, although he was out of the hospital
the next day, not much the worse for wear. "The participants in
last night's outrage ought to be rounded up and driven out of
town," the National Guard commander was quoted as saying,
while the head of the Spanish-American War Veterans was all
for leading a parade past the hall of the Industrial Workers of
the World. The next evening, July 18, 1913, about 75 sailors
and soldiers, led by *Times* men who knew the city, headed from
the skid road for the Socialist Party's headquarters uptown,
stopping to wreck Millard Price's Red News Wagon, with its
display of the Wells drama on *The Colonel and His Friends*.
The wagon was broken into matchwood and the papers and
books scattered along the gutters. As the streets were crowded
for the Potlatch, a huge crowd quickly gathered and followed
the uniformed hoodlums from the Socialist headquarters to
another Socialist hall, where furniture and contents were like-

wise dumped on the street. Exhilarated by their successes the
rioters returned to the skid road to take care of the I.W.W. hall,
sacked it, and then set fire to the debris in the street. Inspired by
this bravado, they then marched back to the Socialist halls and
built bonfires of the furniture and literature, while the police
and firemen watched. An I.W.W. office had been overlooked;
that too was sacked and the contents burned. By midnight the
mob, exhausted, dispersed.

"Anarchy," roared the Colonel the next day in the *Times*,

the grizzly hydra-headed serpent which Seattle has been forced
to nourish in its midst by a naturalized chief executive for 18
months, was plucked from the city and wiped out in a blaze of
patriotism last night. Hundreds of sailors and artillerymen, who
carefully planned the entire maneuver yesterday morning, led the
thousands of cheering civilians to the attack and successfully
wrecked the I.W.W. headquarters and the "direct-action" Socialist
headquarters in various parts of the business district.

The smashing of chairs and tables, the rending of yielding timbers,
the breaking and groaning of sundered walls, and above all the
crash of glass of the windows on the east side all blended together
in one grand Wagnerian cacophony, and all the while the crowd
outside just howled and cheered. It was almost more joy than they
could stand.

The sailors were entirely orderly last night with the exception of
their attack on the Reds. Every I.W.W. headquarters in the city was
raided and wrecked and every anarchist and I.W.W. who offered
resistance was roughly handled.

The drunken mob also wrecked a gospel mission by mistake.
While the *Times* estimated 20,000 in the mob, the more sober
Sun cut the number down to a thousand. A raider at the Socialist
hall got hold of the party membership book. Aghast, Kate
Sadler, the party's most prominent woman speaker, edged up to
him and jabbed him with a hatpin. He jumped and dropped the
precious book; Kate grabbed it and ran to the street to escape in
an automobile. The hoodlum was after her, but Kate's husband,
Sam, who had a reputation as a pugilist, stopped him and said:
"Now, friend, you wouldn't hit a woman, would you? You
wouldn't hit a woman!" By that time Kate had gotten away, and

Sam didn't care whether the mobster would hit a woman or not.

Mayor Cotterill charged that the *Times* had stage-managed the riot. He closed the saloons, suspended all meetings, and threw a police guard around the *Times* building to see that no more riot-inspiring copies were distributed. Colonel Blethen, beside himself with rage, called the mayor "an advocate of anarchy, the leader of the red-flag gang, a loathsome louse. . . . So, squatting in his little puddle of self-esteem, this froglike thing struck at the fundamental principle of American liberty — the freedom of the press." Cotterill responded: "If I could be blown down by a putrid blast from the *Seattle Times,* I have no right or desire to publicly serve." The low point of the controversy was reached when the Colonel, according to Mayor Cotterill, began showing faked photographs of an eminent local divine and the prosecuting attorney in acts of degeneracy.

Angered by Wells's mocking play, Colonel Blethen's crony, Judge Humphries, on August 22, 1913, enjoined Dr. Titus, Kate Sadler, and Millard Price from soapboxing on a downtown corner. The socialists retaliated with a big meeting at Dreamland where 99 signed a communication to the judge asking also to be held in contempt. This was delivered by registered letter to the jurist, whose temper was as short as the Colonel's, and he issued warrants for the arrest of all of them. The socialists threatened to invoke I.W.W. tactics by inviting volunteers in from all over the state to help break the injunction. "Resort will be made," they said, "to the methods used by a free people of all time to maintain the guarantee of our fundamental law."

The court's staff was hardly prepared for such mass resistance; the serving of 99 warrants was a lot of work. The socialists entered joyously into the spirit of the affair and invited the deputies to a socialist meeting where many of the 99 would be available. A path was made for the deputies in the crowded meeting hall, and they were introduced to their victims. "Fall in behind the deputies and follow them to the jail," the chairman ordered. Thereupon the entire meeting filed out and paraded, two abreast, down the street. At the jail doors the

deputies were still nonplused by the situation. "Come in all of
you that are coming in, and those of you that aren't stay outside," said the flustered chief deputy. Nine marched in while
the crowd sang the "Marseillaise." Two victims presented a
special problem — Mr. and Mrs. William McNally, each of
whom bore a small child in arms. The deputies protested that
there were no facilities in jail for families, and they were ordered
to depart. The next day another socialist asked to be included
in the list of 99 to make it "an even hundred," and Judge
Humphries accommodated him.

When the trials started on October 2, and Judge Humphries
was administering fines and jail sentences up to six months for
contempt, two spectators applauded Mrs. Hannah Anderson
when to the judge's question, "Have you any respect for the
courts?" she answered: "Not for this court." The two applauders
drew six months and $300. Mrs. Anderson, fined $100, went to
jail on refusal to pay. Hulet Wells and Glenn E. Hoover, attorneys for the defendants, were disbarred "forever."

A wraith from the past provided a sensation in court the next
day. The judge was denouncing the socialists as nothing but
anarchists, like those of Haymarket and especially Parsons, who
was hanged. "That is untrue," said a voice from the rear of the
courtroom. "I am Parsons' widow; he was an innocent man." It
was Lucy Parsons, a frail little old woman, standing on a chair
and defending the memory of her husband. "Widow or no
widow," bellowed Humphries, "you had better keep quiet or
you'll find yourself down in the county jail." On the same day
Humphries accommodated the McNallys by sending them to
jail with their children. The judge admonished the sheriff to
put all the prisoners to work grubbing stumps at $2 a day in
working out their fines. "There are too many here that are
pregnant with speech," declaimed Humphries. "In fact that's
what's the matter with you. . . . I didn't interfere with free
speech. Go out to the woods and holler to your heart's content."

By October 6 there were 37 in jail. Even the *Post-Intelligencer*
was scandalized: "The 37 are not tramps or millionaires; thugs

or saints, for they have not suffered in silence. They are decent, neighborly folks who have gone to jail for expressing their opinion of Judge Humphries." By this time Governor Ernest Lister, the acting mayor, the State Supreme Court, the other judges in Superior Court, and the three opposition papers — the *Post-Intelligencer,* the *Star,* and the *Sun* — were aghast at the travesty of justice; Wells's original play which caused the furore was seen to be in no sense an exaggeration. The prisoners were freed; the injunction was vacated, and peace returned for a time to Seattle.

Thwarted in this effort, Judge Humphries struck directly at Hulet Wells. He was charged with being author of a play contemptuous of the court. Doggedly, he sued Blethen again for libel. The woman on whose sole testimony rested the "dirty rag" accusation confessed that the Colonel had been paying her grocery bills and giving her money. This time Wells won his case, nine of the jurors agreeing on damages of $5,000 to $30,000; but three would not agree and he finally won $500 — probably, Wells said, the only such suit ever won by a socialist against a big daily paper.

By 1912, alongside and intertwined with the socialists, had arisen a new revolutionary force in the country — the Industrial Workers of the World. Founded in 1905 by Debs, Socialist Labor Party leader Daniel De Leon, William D. Haywood, and others in the Western Federation of Miners, the I.W.W. developed into a syndicalist organization which rejected political action. Not at the ballot box but by a general strike would the revolution be achieved.

The Industrial Workers of the World were first heard of in the Puget Sound country in 1907 when they struck the Tacoma copper smelter. In the same year they led Portland sawmill workers in a revolt against wages of $1.75 a day. During the strike the I.W.W. opened an employment office and a restaurant, tactics then novel in the Pacific Northwest. John Kenneth Turner described the strike as "a new and strange form of unionism. . . . The suddenness of the strike and the completeness of the tie-up are things quite unprecedented in this part of the country." The I.W.W. answered that it was easy to account for the success of the strike — it was conducted by an industrial union which paid no attention to craft lines. The strikers organized their own police force and as a result there was only one arrest during the walkout — that of a man for trespassing who thought he was in the middle of a public street. Strikers were identified by red ribbons, there were day and night shifts of organizers and pickets, and daily rallies to listen to speeches and exhortations. At the I.W.W. convention of 1907 particular heed was paid to the lessons of the Portland strike and it was urged that special attention be paid to the lumber workers "before they are rent into fragments by the American Federation of Labor."

In the spring of 1909 appeared the first issue of the *Industrial Worker*, destined to become one of the most famous of American labor papers. It was published in Spokane, center of the short-timber and mining country, but its influence spread quickly throughout the entire West, and especially along the Seattle skid road.

To left-wing socialists, the I.W.W.'s were blood-red kin. The issue of political action did not worry such socialists much, for they doubted that the capitalist class would ever permit a peaceable takeover of power through the ballot box. For the I.W.W.'s, as migratory workers, political action meant less than nothing; perforce they had little to do with the ballot box.

By 1915, thanks to years of persistent propagandizing by the socialists and I.W.W., many working people in the Puget Sound country — perhaps most of them — became aware of the basic causes of unemployment, insecurity, and war. In this Colonel Blethen and his *Times* had been invaluable assistants. Where radicals had reached the thousands with their four-page weeklies, Blethen reached tens of thousands daily with his intemperate portrayals of their movement. Recognized as the mouthpiece of the Chamber of Commerce, the waterfront interests, and ultra-conservative Republicanism, the *Times's* blasts

against radicals boomeranged. Radicals thrived in the limelight
of such attention and could boast that in 1915 the state of
Washington ranked second in the United States, in proportion
to population, in the number of members of the Socialist Party.
Oklahoma was first. In Seattle two substantial weeklies, the
World and the *Herald,* proclaimed the tenets of socialism from
left-wing and right-wing points of view.

By 1915 the influence of the European war was beginning to
be felt around Puget Sound. The stagnation of the past decade
melted as war orders came in from Britain and France, giving
an impulse to commerce and to the lumber industry. The
deadly efficacy of the U-boats spurred shipbuilding. The shipyards began expanding. The labor surplus waned and men
filtered into the area on the news that logging and shipbuilding
were booming. Seattle stood on the threshold of new and dramatic times, reminiscent of the Klondike gold rush days.

2

The Bloody Voyage of the "Verona"

Thirty miles north of Seattle lies Everett, on a bay of Puget Sound. When the Great Northern Railroad swooped down from the Cascades in the 1890's and struck the sea first at Everett there were high hopes that this would become the Queen City but fate decreed it should aspire to no higher title than the City of Smokestacks. These were the stacks of the lumber mills; by night the sky was reddened with the glow of a score of sawdust burners disposing of mill refuse. The timber came from the slopes of the Cascades in Snohomish County by rail, and from the northern Puget Sound country in great booms of logs hauled by little tugs. The cedar was mostly cut into squarish blocks and then turned into shingles — the city's leading product.

There was no premonition in 1915 that in this rather drab little city of some 30,000 people would develop one of the nation's most famous labor cases, that the crude brutality of its ruling class would fan the embers that would sweep across the Puget Sound country two years later in the first general strike in the lumber industry, in which loggers and sawmill workers alike would win the eight-hour day and elevation from the status of timber beast to that of lumber worker.

As far back as 1901 the shingle weavers — the men who saw and pack shingles — had organized. With varying luck in succeeding years they had tried to resist wage cuts or to get increases, all the while the ten-hour day hung around their necks like the albatross. Ranged against them were a score of mills run by tough-minded rugged individualists, some of them, like former Governor Clough of Minnesota, men who had come to

Everett with some money, others who had risen from the ranks
of workmen through superior cunning and aggressiveness, but
all of them bound by no common tie but single-minded devotion to as low wages and as high prices as the market would
afford. There was no other industry in the city and the mill
owners, as in the cotton mill towns of Massachusetts and the
mines of Pennsylvania, were the lords of their creation, attended
by a small middle class dependent on their favors. Certainly in
few other cities in the Pacific Northwest were class lines drawn
more sharply between owners and workers.

Shingle-weaving is a craft demanding high skill and manual
dexterity. *Sunset,* the *Atlantic Monthly* of the Pacific Coast,
gave a view into inferno: "The saw on his left sets the pace. If
the singing blade rips 50 rough shingles off the block every
minute, the sawyer must reach over to its teeth 50 times in 60
seconds; if the automatic carriage feeds the odorous wood 60
times into the hungry teeth, 60 times he must reach over, turn
the shingle, trim its edge on the gleaming saw in front of him,
cut the narrow strip containing the knot hole with two quick
movements of his right hand and toss the completed board down
the chute to the packers, meanwhile keeping eyes and ears open
for the sound that asks him to feed a new block into the untiring
teeth. Hour after hour the shingle weaver's hands and arms,
plain, unarmored flesh and blood, are staked against the screech-
ing steel that cares not what it severs. Hour after hour the steel
sings its crescendo note as it bites into the wood, the sawdust
cloud thickens, the wet sponge under the sawyer's nose fills with
fine particles. If 'cedar asthma,' the shingle weaver's occupa-
tional disease, does not get him, the steel will. Sooner or later
he reaches over a little too far, the whirling blade tosses drops
of deep red into the air, and a finger, a hand or part of an arm
comes sliding down the slick chute."

You knew the shingle weaver on the street — by his mutilated
hands and the deadly gray pallor of his cheeks.

In 1915 the shingle weavers struck against a wage cut, and as
was customary in Everett, faced injunctions, gunmen, and strikebreakers. Hunger drove the men back to work, the mill owners

promising somewhat vaguely to rescind the wage cut if and when
the price of shingles went up. With the hot breath of war stirring
across the land in 1916, the price did go up, but not the pay.
The union, which had strength in other sawmill towns, set May
1 as a strike date and most mills outside Everett and one in the
city raised wages. The strikes in the other mills dragged on
through June and July, with hunger helping the owners to
recruit strikebreakers. On August 19 there were but 18 men on
the picket line. They were frisked by police, who found no
weapons, and forced to cross a narrow trestle 30 feet above the
channel. On the other side were 70 armed men. With no avenue
of escape, the men crossed over — to be beaten unmercifully.
The news spread through Everett and at nightfall the pickets,
their numbers now swollen by fellow workers, returned to the
Jamison mill to exact revenge. This time the police, who had
looked on nonchalantly at the morning's melee, charged with
drawn revolvers. The uneven contest continued, with more arrests and beatings.

Meanwhile in Seattle an historic convocation of loggers had
been called by the Industrial Workers of the World for July 4,
during the annual holiday shutdown. Although the I.W.W.
could claim only 50 paid-up loggers at the time, some 500 men
showed up from scores of camps. National headquarters in
Chicago, asked for an organizer, sent out James Rowan. His
first assignment was to scout Everett. On July 31 he spoke at
Wetmore and Hewitt Avenues, in downtown Everett, confining
himself to an industrial unionist propaganda speech drawn
largely from the famous report of the federal Industrial Relations Commission. Sheriff Donald McRae observed the scene.
Walker C. Smith, who wrote the official I.W.W. book, *The
Everett Massacre,* had frequent occasion to refer to the sheriff
and always — except once — he added the laconic sentence:
"McRae was drunk." Rowan was thrown into jail and given a
"floater" the next morning — the choice between 30 days in jail
or leaving town. He left. Another Wobbly organizer came to
town, opened a union hall and arranged for James P. Thompson,
the I.W.W.'s most prominent speaker in the Northwest, to

lecture. No large hall could be obtained so the meeting was scheduled for the downtown spot where the Salvation Army and various political speakers held forth. When printed notices were posted, Sheriff McRae entered the I.W.W. hall, tore them down and ordered the organizer out of town. "McRae was drunk." He went to a nearby poolhall, frisked the players and deported all those not residents. The shingle weavers' picket line was also raided and several men deported. "Not a man in overalls is safe!" said the secretary of the A.F. of L. Building Trades Council.

Thompson and some 20 members of the I.W.W. came over from Seattle for the announced street meeting. One by one the speakers were dragged from the platform and hustled off to jail. While the crowd sang "The Red Flag," the arrests continued. More than a thousand marched to the jail to protest. Obviously they weren't all Wobblies.

The socialist movement had struck roots in Everett around 1900; by 1911 the *Commonwealth* had been established and this persevered under various titles until 1917. One of its editors was Maynard Shipley, who had been editor of the Oakland *World,* a socialist weekly, in 1908. A young man in Stockton helped Shipley with the platform and literature, just for a chance to get some training in public speaking. His name was Tom Mooney. Shipley began editing the *Commonwealth* in 1913 and also, for a time, the Everett A.F. of L. weekly at a time when a majority of delegates in the Everett Central Labor Council carried Socialist Party cards. After campaigning for the U.S. Senate in 1916, Shipley went east to help Debs with his campaign for Congress. Later he became famous as a lecturer and founder of the Science League of America, which battled on the issue of teaching evolution in the schools. In 1916, H. W. Watts, editor of the renamed *Northwest Worker,* carried on in the Shipley tradition and protested at the jail doors, and was tossed into a cell for his trouble.

The morning after the arrests the Wobblies were deported, some by the interurban trolley that ran to Seattle, and others by the boat that made regular daily runs between the two ports.

The deportees conferred with their fellow workers in Seattle in the big second-floor hall on Washington Street, the center of the skid road. Chicago headquarters and *Solidarity*, the national I.W.W. paper, were alerted. The Free Speech Battle in Everett was on!

The I.W.W. thrived on repression. Their answer to bans on public meetings and to arrests was to send out a call to the "foot-loose rebels" to mobilize. The cry would be heard in "jungles" all through the West where migratory workers gathered after a hard day's ride "on the rods" underneath freight cars or in more sumptuous quarters in box cars and gondolas. There in the jungle near the railroad tracks they cooked an evening mulligan of meat and vegetables in stray cans and discussed conditions of their lives — the class struggle, which in its rudimentary form meant to them the prospects of finding a job, of getting better pay and cutting down the hours, and of dealing with the arm of law and order which was always around the corner eager to jail or deport them. The cry would also be heard in all the ramshackle Wobbly halls — usually store fronts in the dilapidated part of town near the railroad tracks but, nevertheless, often boasting a battered piano and shelves filled with books and newspapers. There the "bindlestiff" — the workingman with all his possessions rolled up inside a tattered blanket, known as a bindle — could find a free flop in a corner on the floor, if he were broke. A big can of coffee was steaming on the stove, alongside a five-pound lard can of mulligan stew for the men en route to and from harvest fields, construction and logging camps, and the "slave market" — the sorry streets such as Madison in Chicago and Washington in Seattle where "job sharks," the employment agencies, specialized in the sale of migratory labor. In the jungles and halls, workers scanned the columns of *Solidarity* and of the *Industrial Worker*, organ of western branches of the I.W.W. The *Industrial Worker*, formerly published in Spokane, had shifted to Seattle April 1, 1916. In its columns appeared the cry for footloose rebels to rally to Everett.

It was in 1909 that the Wobblies made their debut as "mili-

tant jail and soapbox belligerents in the free-speech fight," as
Paul F. Brissenden, chronicler of the early I.W.W., put it. In
the fall of 1909 free-speech fights erupted in Missoula, Montana,
center of a wide logging and construction area, in New Castle,
Pennsylvania, the sheet-steel center, and in Spokane. Some 20
such battles broke out between 1909 and 1913, including the
famous conflict in San Diego, unparalleled up to that time for
the brutality inflicted by the authorities. An editorial in the *San
Diego Tribune* reflected the intensity of the feeling aroused:
"Hanging is none too good for them [the I.W.W.]; they would
be much better dead, for they are absolutely useless in the
human economy; they are the waste material of creation and
should be drained off into the sewer of oblivion there to rot in
cold obstruction like any other excrement."

The classic free-speech battle of the I.W.W. was fought in
Spokane in the fall and winter of 1909. There the job shark
situation was particularly atrocious in the winter of 1908-1909.
It was customary for the employment agencies, in collusion with
the head boss on the job, to promote a rapid turnover — "one
crew coming, one working, and one going." The more rapid the
turnover the more fees for the job shark, to be split with the
boss. Times were hard and always there was a score of men for
every job; if the job-seeker had no money, the fee was deducted
from his pay. The I.W.W. had been campaigning for direct
hiring and abolition of fees, but in the wretched condition of
the slave market it could make no headway. In Spokane alone
there were 31 sharks doing a thriving business in human flesh
and blood. The Spokane *Spokesman-Review* reported January
18, 1909, that a crowd of two to three thousand idle men had
hurled rocks and chunks of ice through the windows of one
agency and were about to wreck it when the I.W.W. organizer,
James H. Walsh, mounted a chair and "stemmed the rising tide
of riot and pacified the multitude." In the opinion of the police,
if it had not been for the intervention of Walsh, "a riot would
surely have followed." Walsh led the men to the I.W.W. hall
and warned them that "Pinkertons" — private industrial detec-

tives — in the crowd were trying to provoke trouble so "they would have some excuse for shooting you down or smashing your heads in."

During the summer of 1909 the job sharks retaliated against the I.W.W. by having the city council outlaw street meetings, except for the Salvation Army. After protesting in vain to the council against the unconstitutionality of the ordinance, the *Industrial Worker* on October 28 sent out a call: "Wanted — Men to Fill the Jails of Spokane." On November 2, appointed as Free Speech Day, the council had a rock pile ready while the Wobblies had hundreds of volunteers who had answered the call. On that day 103 men were arrested as fast as the police could drag them from the soapbox. The story is told of one young Wobbly who had never before spoken in public and became tongue-tied on the soapbox. Finally he blurted out, in desperation, "Where are the cops?" The cops, who had been busy elsewhere, obliged him by pulling him off his box. By the end of November 500 Wobblies were in jail, consigned to bread and water when they refused to work on the rock pile. The jail filled to bursting and then a school was used for the overflow, and when this filled up the Army obligingly placed an empty barracks at the city's command. Eight men in turn edited the *Industrial Worker,* as previous editors went to jail. Elizabeth Gurley Flynn chained herself to a lamppost, as the suffragists were doing in London. The arrival of Gurley Flynn, pre-eminent woman speaker in an organization necessarily almost entirely male in membership, sparked the fight. Stewart Holbrook in *Holy Old Mackinaw* describes her as "young, handsome — with a western hat turned up in front, and a flaming red tie around her pretty throat — and she was a hellion that breathed reddish flame; fairly sober reporters affirmed that a flash from the girl's blue-gray eyes would serve to light a Sweet Caporal. The Flynn promptly entered the fight." From jail Miss Flynn broadcast the information that the police were using the women's section as a brothel and were soliciting customers for it.

The *Industrial Worker* was obliged to move to Seattle to be out of the reach of the Spokane police. William Z. Foster, who had gone to Spokane to report for the Seattle *Workingman's Paper,* joined the I.W.W. and served his brief time as an editor of the *Industrial Worker* before being thrown into jail.

During the winter the national spotlight swung to Spokane as correspondents flocked to the city to witness this most dramatic of challenges for observance of the First Amendment. They saw men marched to court matted with blood from the beatings administered in jail, but one and all they refused to flinch. On their weekly march to public baths they were showered with sacks of Bull Durham tobacco and fruit by friendly citizens. On March 4 victory came when Spokane freed all the prisoners and quit enforcing the ban on free speech. The licenses of 19 of the more offensive job sharks were revoked and the practice of direct hiring grew. From this great battle the I.W.W. emerged with reputation enhanced, and its fame spread far and wide. City authorities were loath to enter into conflict with an army of workingmen whose ranks swelled with persecution and whose jail expenses threatened to bankrupt the treasuries of cities even as large as Spokane.

Roger Baldwin, a connoisseur of techniques in the battle for freedom, recalls that his first contact with the I.W.W. was during their free-speech fight in Kansas City in 1912. Their technique, he said, was "to demonstrate the powerlessness of all the forces of law and order in the face of men determined to fill the jails if necessary to win the right to talk. No power on earth can beat men with the courage to go to jail, willingly and cheerfully, for a principle, and if there are enough of them." In no case, he recounts, did the I.W.W. engage in violence, but "the violence used against them was colossal." He estimated that they lost ten men killed and 2,000 jailed in the free-speech fights. It was this unending battle, Baldwin concluded, that built the personality of the I.W.W. as "the unrivalled spokesman of native American militancy."

So when the I.W.W. decided to test the issue of free speech in Everett, they brought with them impressive experience.

Cheerfully, rather carelessly, but in dead earnest they entered a conflict which they knew would run the gamut of lawlessness by official law and order. An old-time police officer, writing years later in a Seattle police magazine, gave some flavor of those times:

> The Wobblies agitated incessantly, provoked occasional acts of sabotage. This drove the lumber magnates to the point of desperation and to eventual violence. It is not easy to understand today just how thoroughly these "lords of creation" controlled the whole lifeblood of the state. They made governors and broke them, and the whole administration of justice was in some way influenced by them. Violence was no stranger to them and on more than one occasion they have broken strikes through the organization of "Vigilantes" and "Special Deputies."

Of Everett he wrote:

> The infiltration of a number of I.W.W. organizers into the area and the resulting agitation in favor of the strikers which they created drove the timbermen into speechless rage. David M. Clough, a former governor of Minnesota, and spokesman for the lumber interests, said: "We propose to clean Everett of all members of the I.W.W. and to forcibly prevent the incursion of any more of their ilk."

The Wobblies came, first singly, then in teams, and then by the score. After the Thompson meeting had been broken up, an organizer came to town and reopened the hall. Sheriff McRae stormed in: "You God-damned son of a bitch, are you back here again? Get on your coat and get into that auto!" The organizer was deported. Herbert Mahler, Seattle I.W.W. secretary, came over to see the mayor. McRae immediately deported him. Several I.W.W.'s returned a few days later and reopened the hall; for a time there was no interference. A rather odd thing happened one night: one of the I.W.W. speakers began to advocate the use of violence. He was pulled from the platform by his own fellow workers. His name was George Reese, of whom more was to be heard.

During this lull in the battle, caused by the presence in the city of a federal labor official trying to mediate the shingle weavers' strike, Secretary Mahler tried to intercede with Governor Ernest Lister and Mayor D. D. Merrill of Everett, but he

got no response to his appeal for law and order. Meanwhile, the
Commercial Club and Sheriff McRae laid their plans to take
over the city. On August 30 the leading mill owners and their
retainers met in the morning at the Commercial Club to prepare
strategy, and that night a public meeting was held there. To a
suggestion that it might be well to call in the federal mediator,
former Governor Clough retorted that there was nothing to be
mediated. The meeting then got down to business. By-passing
the chief of police, Clough asked Sheriff McRae if he could
handle the situation. McRae said he did not have enough
deputies. "Swear in the members of the Commercial Club,
then," said Clough. Some 200 volunteered. McRae swore in a
few and then, as Walker Smith remarks, he found swearing, for
the first time in his life, a little tedious, and he turned the job
over to the secretary of the Commercial Club. The deputies
were divided into special squads, one to watch incoming trains,
another the boats, and others for beating up and deporting
Wobblies. There were to be no mass jailings in Everett, à la
Spokane. Deportation was the weapon.

These developments tore Everett in two. Many merchants
resigned from the Commercial Club and posted notices in their
windows: "We Are Not Members of the Commercial Club."
The boycott committee took care of such recalcitrants, and also
those merchants who advertised in the socialist weekly, the
Northwest Worker. As it turned out later, on sworn evidence,
there was also a finance committee which paid for the accumula-
tion of an arsenal — blackjacks, leaded clubs, guns, and ammunition — and for the employment of special operatives. When
citizens complained to the chief of police about such activities,
that worthy shrugged his shoulders and said that the sheriff and
his "drunken deputies" had taken over law enforcement within
the city.

Then came the heat lightning before the storm. The federal
mediator, hopeless in his mission, had left town. On September
7 several speakers were thrown in jail; the following night, more.
An I.W.W. member sent to engage an attorney was beaten up

and deported. As trains and boats entering the city were being searched, the I.W.W. thought to circumvent the blockade by hiring a small boat at Mukilteo, a little sawmill town several miles south of Everett. The "Wanderer" could take only a dozen or so, and six men were towed behind in a dory. As the boat approached the harbor, the tug "Edison," known as the "scab tug" because there was a strike of tugboatmen and long-shoremen at the time, came out from shore with Sheriff McRae and about 60 deputies. At 200 feet, the sheriff began shooting. Captain Jack Mitten, a respected citizen of Mukilteo, shut down his engine and the "Edison" drew near. "You son of a bitch, you come over here," shouted McRae. "If you want me, you come over here," shouted back Mitten. The deputies boarded the "Wanderer" and ordered the Wobblies on to the tugboat. As Captain Mitten bent over to make fast a stern line, McRae hit him with the butt of his revolver and when Mitten remon-strated, hit him again, and then slugged him in the groin, causing a rupture. McRae then went after other men he recog-nized. At the dock they were herded into patrol wagons and carted off to jail — 21 in all, including the skipper and engineer of the "Wanderer." There many were beaten. After nine days without charges being preferred, they were offered liberty, ex-cept Captain Mitten. The 20 refused to leave the jail without him and so, reluctantly, the captain was released too.

During this time Organizer Rowan came to town, was greeted by three deputies at the train, and taken to jail. Later McRae came around. McRae was drunk. "We are going to start you off on the road to Seattle," he told Rowan. Several miles out of town near the interurban tracks he was released and told "to beat it." But some 50 yards on a group of deputies awaited him, their faces hidden by handkerchiefs. They threw a cloth over Rowan's head and proceeded to beat him unmercifully with gun butts. He was then put across a fallen tree and beaten across the back some 50 times or more with a sap — a leather thong loaded with lead at the end.

It would be repetitive to continue the tales of cruelty suffered by the I.W.W.'s as they continued to come in to Everett. By this time the deputies were beating up Everett citizens as well, some of them bystanders at Wetmore and Hewitt where the Wobblies doggedly continued to mount the box while the deputies pulled them down, jailed them for the night, and then deported them. Armed gangs of deputies roamed the environs, rounding up Wobblies coming from the harvest and bound for Seattle. "Sergeant" John J. Keenan, 65, related the story of his fellow workers. He had been working on a threshing crew near Great Falls, Montana, and after the harvest was in, joined up with a group of migratories coming from the Dakota fields. The Sergeant was bound for Seattle. "I winter in Seattle every year," he explained, "and work on the snow sheds." These were the sheds up in the mountain passes where the railroads come through the Cascades.

Many migratory workers "wintered" in Seattle. Some followed the crops up from California into the mountain states and then headed west for the milder climate of the Coast. The better-heeled might settle in one of the working-class hotels near the skid road run by enterprising Japanese. These hotels were reasonably clean and, although cell-like in their rooms, had large lobbies where guests could relax. But along Washington, Occidental, First and Second Avenues South, and other streets of the skid road there were flophouses where a "room" could be had for prices ranging from a dime to two bits. These were in old office buildings south of Yesler Way, long since abandoned for business as the center of town turned northward. The lofts were partitioned off into cells, large enough for a cot and some hooks for clothing. In the corridors dim yellow bulbs glimmered in the gloom, but denizens took candles to their cells. The partitions ran up six or seven feet and were surmounted by wire netting to the ceiling, to afford privacy and ventilation. The mattresses usually were filthy — bedbugs ran rampant and along the sides crawled vermin of many hues. But to the migratory this was a fact of life, to be met with in bunkhouses in logging and construction camps everywhere, and to be tolerated as one of those penalties fate inflicted on migratory workers.

Chinese restaurants supplied migratories with breakfast for a dime — a "stack of wheats" and coffee. Dinner was 25 cents — stew or beans with potatoes. The more affluent among the migratories, early in the winter, might splurge by going to Chauncey Wright's, located right off the skid road, where a dollar bought a good meal — a well-done Western style steak, or a juicy ham steak flanked by fried eggs. But to continue with the Sergeant's story:

We arrived in Snohomish [near Everett] on September 23 in the morning. I sent the food committee out with some money and they brought back $4.90 worth of food, including two frying pans, and when I was about cooking, a little boy, who was maybe about ten, he says, "Dad, are you an I.W.W.?" I says, "I am, son." "Well," he says, "there are a whole bunch of deputies coming out after you." I laughed at the boy, I thought he was joshing me.

About half an hour after the boy told me this the deputies appeared. In the first bunch were 42, and then Sheriff McRae came with more, making altogether, what I counted, 64. In the first bunch was a fat, stout fellow with two guns. He had a chief's badge on him. He was facing toward the fire and he says, "If you move a step, I will fill you full of lead!" I laughed at him; says I, "What does this outrage mean?" There was another old gentleman with a chin beard, fat, middling fat, probably my own age, and he picked up my coat which was lying alongside me and looked at my button [the red-and-gold three-star I.W.W. button]. He says, "Oh, undesirable citizen!" I says, "What do you mean?" He says, "Are you an I.W.W.?" I says, "I am, and I am more than proud of it!" "Well," he says, "we don't want you in this county." I says, "Well, I am not going to stay in this county, I am going to cook breakfast and go to Seattle." He says, "Do you know what this means?" I says, "No." He says, "The sheriff will be here in a few minutes and he will tell you what it means." I heard afterward that this man was the mayor of Snohomish.

I was sitting right opposite the fire with my coffee and bread and meat in my hand when Sheriff McRae came up and says, "Who is this bunch?" So a tall, dark-complected deputy says, "They are a bunch of harvest hands coming from North Dakota." McRae says, "Did you search these men?" And he says, "Yes, they had no shooting arms on them."

McRae then went over to the Sergeant, cursing and ordering

him and his fellow workers to walk down the railroad track
toward Seattle. They kept walking until late afternoon when
the Sergeant's feet gave way and they rested at a railroad station
to make coffee and wait for the evening freight into Seattle.
After the freight pulled in, four autos came along the road,
throwing their searchlights along the tracks.

I says, "Men, we have run up against a stone wall. Fellow-Worker
Love and I — he came off the machine with me in Great Falls —
we were first in line and Sheriff McRae and two other men with
white handkerchiefs around their necks came forward first and he
says, "You son of a bitch, I thought you were going to Seattle?" I
says, "Ain't I going to Seattle? I can't go till the train goes." I says,
"you've had me walking now till I have no foot under me. What do
you mean by this outrage? My father fought for this country and I
have a right here. I am on railroad property and have done nothing
to anybody." McRae then hit Fellow-Worker Love on the head and
I yelled, "Break and run, men, or they will kill you!" He turned
around then and he said to me, "You dirty old Irish bastard, now
I will make you so you can't run. I'll show you!" With that he let
drive and hit me, leaving this three-cornered mark here [indicating
place on head]. And when the others went up the track he says,
"Get now, God damn your old soul, or I will kill you!"

After wandering down the track in the dark, the Wobblies lay
down to sleep in the bushes. When the morning freight came
along, they boarded it. The trainman looked over at the Sergeant. "Do you carry a card?" he asked. "Yes," said the Sergeant.
"Produce!" he said. That was the trainman's way of asking to
see a man's Wobbly card, a credential to ride free. "You better
get back in the caboose, you are hurt," said the trainman, but
the Sergeant answered that "where the men are riding is good
enough for me." Eventually they got into Seattle and made a
report to the Seattle branches.

During October more than 300 men were deported from
Everett. By the end of the month it was obvious that a more concerted effort must be made; the deputies were able to pick off
the men who came in small groups. So 41 men, most of them
freshly in from the harvest fields, volunteered to go by boat to
Everett. Waiting for them at the dock Sheriff McRae ("McRae
was drunk") had mobilized some 200 deputies wearing white

handkerchiefs around their necks. They herded the Wobblies into trucks and autos. Those not quick enough were beaten with gun butts and saps. The cortege led out of town to a place called Beverly Park where the road crossed the interurban tracks. There the deputies formed two lines across the tracks and the I.W.W.'s were forced to run the gauntlet. From behind and in front they were slugged by waiting deputies in the cold, rainy night, illuminated by auto lights—until they reached the cattle-guard on the railroad tracks which was armed with sharp spikes. Here the men, many of them stunned and bleeding, stumbled into the mantrap and fell, painfully lacerating their feet and legs while the deputies swung hard and fast. So great was the outcry that people in a house a quarter mile away came running.

C. H. Rice, a harvest worker whose shoulder had been dislocated by the deputies, related:

Then the fellow who was on the dock, and had been drinking pretty heavily, because they would have to shove him back every once in a while, he shouted out, "Let's burn him!" About that time Sheriff McRae came over and got hold of my throat and said, "Now, damn you, I will tell you I can kill you right here and there never would be nothing known about it, and you know it." And some one said, "Let's hang him!" and this other fellow kept hollering, "Burn him! Burn him!" McRae kept hitting me, first on one side and then the other, smacking me that way, and then he turned me loose again and hit me with one of those slingshots, and finally he said, "Oh, let him go," and he started me along, following behind and hitting me until I got over the cattleguard.

I went down to the interurban track until I caught up with some of the boys. They tried to pull my shoulder back into place and then they took handkerchiefs and neckties, and one thing and another, and made a kind of sling to hold it up. We then went down to the first station and the boys took up a collection and the eight of us who were hurt the worst got on the train and went to Seattle. The others had to walk the 25 miles into Seattle. Most of us had to go to the hospital next day.

The next morning a delegation of Everett and Seattle clergymen, union leaders, and others examined the ground at Beverly Park. President E. P. Marsh of the State Federation of Labor reported that "the tale of that struggle was plainly written. The roadway was stained with blood. The blades of the cattleguard were so stained. . . . Early that morning workmen going into the city to work picked up three hats from the ground, still damp with blood. There can be no excuse for nor extenuation of such an inhuman method of punishment." The Beverly Park outrage was Everett's main theme of discussion the next day, and by nightfall it had been decided that there should be a mass meeting the following Sunday, November 5, at Hewitt and Wetmore in the center of town. The Reverend McGill of Seattle, who had taken the lead in marshaling support, consulted with Secretary Mahler of the I.W.W., who agreed to plans for the meeting. The newspapers were informed. The announcement was a signal for the Commercial Club to prepare for battle. Blackjacks and clubs were laid aside for a growing arsenal of revolvers and rifles, and additional deputies were sworn in. Sheriff McRae dropped into the little Wobbly hall on November 3. Looking around, he announced that "I won't have a lot of sons of bitches hanging around this place like in Seattle." The secretary remarked that there was a Constitution.

"To hell with the Constitution," broke in McRae. "We have a constitution here that we will enforce." The next day he raided the hall and seized all except the secretary. Turning to that man, he said: "I'll bet you a hundred dollars you bastards won't hold that meeting tomorrow!" McRae was drunk. The men were frisked for weapons, but none had been found on an I.W.W. member during the whole period; then the men were deported. That Saturday night there was a mobilization of deputies at the Commercial Club — a kind of pep rally. The blowing of the mill whistles Sunday would be the signal to meet at the dock where the Seattle boat comes in.

For Sunday, November 5, the I.W.W. chartered the "Verona," a vessel in the "mosquito fleet" that plied the waters of Puget Sound. Four by four, the Wobblies marched from their hall down to the Colman Dock in Seattle where steamers left for various ports of the Sound. The captain tallied them off as they boarded, and stopped them when the number reached 250, his legal safety limit. Among them were a few regular passengers.

Other passengers for Everett were told to take the "Calista," and 38 I.W.W.'s who could not get on the "Verona" boarded the other vessel. Most of the men were harvest workers but among them also were lumber workers, hard-rock miners, and other migratories. On this sparkling sun-lit day it seemed more like a holiday excursion as the lines were cast off and the "Verona" backed out into the waters of Elliott Bay. As the vessel headed northward, the Wobblies began singing the songs that had marked their rendezvous in many a hall, jungle, and street corner meeting, the words of which were contained in the Little Red Songbook, of which more copies have been printed across the century than of any other single collection. As the boat swung up to the City Dock in Everett the I.W.W.'s were singing the English transport workers' song:

We meet today in Freedom's cause,
And raise our voices high;
We'll join our hands in union strong,
To battle or to die.

Hold the fort for we are coming,
Union men be strong.
Side by side we battle onward,
Victory will come!

But the dock was strangely empty. Usually there was a crowd there, waiting to greet those coming, or to board the vessel. On this Sunday afternoon there were only a few men on the dock; the mill whistles had blown at one, and a rope had been placed along the end of the dock to hold back the Sunday crowd. On the hill behind the dock were thousands of Everett citizens waiting to greet the men on the "Verona" and to march with them to the meeting place. Young Hugo Gerlot climbed the flagstaff on the bow of the "Verona," waving greetings while singing "Hold the Fort." Men poured out of the cabin as a line went over to tie the bow of the vessel to the dock. Just then one of the three men on the dock, Sheriff McRae, hitched his holster to bring his gun directly across his middle. Then he raised his hand and hailed the boat:

"Who is your leader?"

Back came the usual Wobbly reply:

"We're all leaders!"

"You can't land here!"

"The hell we can't!" came the response from the ship as the men headed toward the gangplank which was being placed in position.

Then a shot rang out, followed by a volley. Hugo Gerlot's body slumped, then toppled to the deck. Shot through the head, both arms, hip, and leg, he tried to raise himself to continue the song. The volleys continued and there was a rush to gain the other side of the vessel to escape the hail of lead. The "Verona" listed sharply to starboard, submerging her lower deck, and many crashed through the railing into the cold waters of the bay. Already the deck was slippery with blood as the murderous enfilade poured from the dock, from the warehouse behind which some 200 deputies were hidden, from the opposite dock, and from the tug "Edison." Some of the Wobblies returned the fire but most of them were unarmed and quite helpless. The captain was hiding in the cabin behind a hasty barricade; one of the I.W.W.'s, realizing that the entire body of men might be massacred, ran down to the engine room, dragged the frightened engineer from his hiding place and forced him to start the engine. The "Verona" lurched at her lone bowline; it snapped and after ten murderous minutes at the dock, the vessel began backing erratically until the engineer got control of the rudder lines. The volleys from the dock continued until the "Verona" was out of range; the men struggling in the water then became the targets for the sharpshooters until they, too, disappeared.

The captain resumed command of the boat and approached the "Calista" to warn her back, while those Wobblies unscathed by the fire began caring for the wounded. Four men were beyond help; another died later. Shirts and ties were torn up to make bandages and slings for the 31 wounded men. Six more, it is believed, were drowned after being shot in the water. At any rate there were six unclaimed Wobbly cards at headquarters for men who had left on the "Verona," bringing the death roll up to 11. Back on City Dock two deputies lay dead — C. O.

Curtis, office manager of a lumber company, and Jefferson
Beard, a deputy who had taken part in the Beverly Park outrage.
Sixteen of the deputies were wounded. Most of them, it was
proved later, were shot down in the crossfire between the docks
and the "Edison." To the hoots and catcalls of the thousands on
the hillside, the deputies dispersed. An account of the feeling of
the crowd was given in the Seattle *Union Record*, the A.F. of L.
weekly edited by Harry Ault:

> Your correspondent was on the street at the time of the battle and
> at the dock ten minutes afterward. He mingled with the street
> crowds for hours afterward. The temper of the people is dangerous.
> Nothing but curses and execrations for the Commercial Club was
> heard. Men and women who are ordinarily law abiding, who in
> normal times mind their own business pretty well, pay their taxes,
> sending their children to church and school, pay their bills, in every
> way comport themselves as normal citizens, were heard using the
> most vitriolic language concerning the Commercial Club, loudly
> sympathizing with the I.W.W.'s. And therein lies the great harm
> that was done, more menacing to the city than the presence of any
> number of I.W.W.'s, viz., the transformation of decent, honest citi-
> zens into beings mad for vengeance and praying for something dire
> to happen. I heard gray-haired women, mothers and wives, gentle,
> kindly, I know, in their home circles, openly hoping that the
> I.W.W.'s would come back and "clean up."

President Marsh of the State Federation of Labor, himself an
Everett citizen, added his words:

> A dangerous situation existed in Everett after the battle of No-
> vember 5. Public feeling ran high and anything might have hap-
> pened. Half a thousand citizens were under arms enraged at the
> Industrial Workers of the World and deadly determined to stamp
> out their organization in Everett. It is no exaggeration to say that
> literally thousands of the working people of Everett were just as
> enraged toward members of the Commercial Club who participated
> in the gun battle.

As the "Verona" edged into Colman Dock, police and hospital
ambulances were waiting. All the uninjured were marched to
the city jail and the Wobblies on the "Calista" to the county jail.
To the morgue went the bodies of Hugo Gerlot, Gustav Johnson, John Looney, and Abraham Rabinowitz, and, within a few
days, that of Felix Baran.

In Seattle a fierce controversy was started by the *Times* and

the *Post-Intelligencer* which charged that Mayor Hiram Gill
was responsible for permitting the departure of the Wobblies on
the "Verona." Mayor Gill stood by his guns. "In the final analysis," he said, "it will be found that these cowards in Everett,
who, without right or justification, shot into the crowd on the
boat were the murderers and not the I.W.W.'s. The men who
met the I.W.W.'s at the boat were a bunch of cowards. They
outnumbered the I.W.W.'s five to one, and in spite of this they
stood there on the dock and fired into the boat, I.W.W.'s, innocent passengers, and all. McRae and his deputies had no legal
right to tell the I.W.W.'s or anyone else that they could not land
there. When the sheriff put his hand on the butt of his gun and
told them they could not land, he fired the first shot, in the eyes
of the law, and the I.W.W.'s can claim that they shot in self-
defense. . . . If I were one of the party of 40 I.W.W.'s who was
almost beaten to death by 300 citizens of Everett [at the Beverly
Park outrage] without being able to defend myself, I probably
would have armed myself if I intended to visit Everett again."
The mayor bought tobacco to be distributed among the prisoners and ordered them supplied with blankets. The Chamber of
Commerce thereupon tried to institute a recall campaign, but it
fell flat.

In the city jail, some 240 men were led, one by one, past a
darkened cell in which were hidden two Pinkertons who had
been on the "Verona." From time to time two fingers would be
pushed forward from the cell to indicate that the man who had
just passed should be held. One of the Pinkertons was George
Reese, the same who had been pulled from the platform at the
Everett I.W.W. street meeting when he began advocating violence. It was he, too, in the Seattle longshoremen's strike, who
urged the beating up of strikebreakers, who boasted that after
assaulting these men he also robbed them, who was active
mysteriously before many dock fires, and who had asked I.W.W.
members for help in buying various chemicals.

Seventy-four men were held and charged with the murder of
the two deputies. Most of them were native-born; four were

born in Sweden, three each in Canada and Ireland, and six others in various other countries. Their average age was 32 — a fair cross-section of the youthful membership of the I.W.W. None of the deputies, of course, was charged with the murder of the workers. Heavily handcuffed, the Wobblies were transferred to the Everett jail while I.W.W. headquarters in Chicago scoured the country for legal defense. The choice fell, after Frank P. Walsh, former chairman of the Industrial Relations Commission, and others had declined, on Fred H. Moore of Los Angeles, who had defended the Wobblies in the great free-speech fight in Spokane in 1909-1910 and later the San Diego free-speech fighters, and then had served as counsel for Joe Ettor and Arturo Giovannitti, framed on a murder charge in the I.W.W. textile strike in Lawrence, Massachusetts, in 1912.

The Seattle Central Labor Council, declaring that the I.W.W. free-speech fight in Everett had developed while assisting an A.F. of L. shingle weavers' strike, appointed an Everett defense committee consisting of Secretary James A. Duncan, C. W. Doyle, and Harry Ault, who proceeded to bail out the men of the "Calista," held on a weird "unlawful assembly" charge. They also helped the Seattle I.W.W. in persuading George F. Vanderveer, former county prosecuting attorney and a leading criminal lawyer, to assist Moore in the defense of the "Verona" defendants. Hard-hitting, resourceful, and aggressive, and thoroughly familiar with people and affairs in the Puget Sound country, Vanderveer had never before appeared as counsel in a labor case. Having fought his way up in the pioneer, rough-and-tumble jungle of Seattle law, he felt a contempt, barely concealed, for the Seattle upperworld. He knew only too well, having defended them, how they had accumulated their piles. He had declined to attach himself to a lucrative corporation retainer, in order to keep his independence. Intuitively, and not from any ideological persuasion, he felt far more at home with the underdogs of society whom he understood very well. A hard drinker and something of a pugilist, he had often found diversion after a hard-fought case by going down to the skid road and

challenging the soapbox orators. In the free-for-all that sometimes followed, he often retired bruised and elated. It was this
man who came to be called "counsel for the damned," and perhaps, after Clarence Darrow, he was the most famous legal
defender of the downtrodden in his time. Characteristically,
after taking the case, Vanderveer went to Everett where he sur-
veyed minutely the City Dock, measuring its angles, sketching
the scene, and talking endlessly with townspeople.

On November 18 the bodies of Baran, Gerlot, and Looney
were borne to Mount Pleasant cemetery in Seattle, with thousands marching in the cortege to the strains of "The Red Flag"
and the "Marseillaise." A chorus of 100 from singing societies
sang "Workers of the World, Awaken" by the graveside where
Charles Ashleigh, the young English poet who was handling
publicity for the I.W.W.; delivered the funeral oration. The
caskets were lowered as the throng sang "Hold The Fort" and
then showers of red roses and carnations filled the graves. The
next afternoon 5,000 met at Dreamland Rink where I.W.W.
and A.F. of L. spokesmen, clergy, and public officials joined in
commemoration of the dead and excoriation of the barbarism in
Everett. They demanded that President Wilson investigate the
massacre and the events leading up to it. The appeal was
ignored.

At Everett the 74 indicted men were held incommunicado for
two months, denied any reading materials, and subjected to the
mercies of Sheriff McRae and his deputies. Revolted by the vile
food, the prisoners went on a hunger strike, and won. Denied
blankets and mattresses and forced to sleep on the cold steel
floor in the chill November nights, the prisoners "built a battleship." With buckets and tins and such bits of metal as could be
wrenched loose, they beat upon the walls, ceilings, and floors of
the steel "tanks." Others linked themselves arm in arm and
jumped in unison, shaking the walls of the jail. All the while
they shouted at the top of their lungs. So great was the din that
townspeople gathered around the jail, thinking that the deputies perhaps were murdering the inmates. The prisoners won
their blankets.

On Thanksgiving Day a committee of Everett people, helped by members of the Cooks and Waiters Union, cooked a special dinner for the prisoners; Sheriff McRae turned them away and ordered a holiday feast of mush. At one time a different type of "battleship" was built to protest the bad food. The cell doors were pulled open by blankets tied to them. With small pieces of pipe the mechanism of the locking system above the doors was broken and then the entire system of locks demolished. Outside their cells the men had access to some 300 pounds of corned beef that had been piled in a corner. When the new sheriff arrived — McRae had gone out of office at the end of the year — he found the 74 men enjoying their first square meal in months. It cost $900 to repair the damage. After that the mere whisper of the word "battleship" produced results. In Virgil's words:

> If I cannot bend the powers above,
> I will rouse Hell.

On March 5, 1917, four months to the day after the massacre on the "Verona," the greatest labor trial up to that time in the history of the Pacific Northwest began. The charge had been changed from the murder of C. O. Curtis, the lumber manager, to that of Jefferson Beard, the deputy. The body of Curtis had been exhumed secretly and presumably it had been found that he was shot in the back by fellow deputies, for little mention of his death was made at the trial. The I.W.W. and Vanderveer had been able to change the venue from Everett to Seattle and Governor Lister had appointed Judge J. T. Ronald to hear the case. Because hundreds, sometimes thousands, sought admittance to the courtroom seating only a hundred, the judge asked the I.W.W. to appoint two "special police" to help patrol the corridors.

The first defendant, Thomas H. Tracy, was charged with murder in the first degree, "in having assisted, counselled, aided, abetted and encouraged some unknown person to kill Jefferson Beard . . ." The first, "or one of the first," shots fired was from the "Verona" and from a revolver held by Tracy, the prosecution asserted. Of the 140 deputies admitted by the State, about half were acknowledged to have been armed with revolvers, rifles, and clubs. The State brushed aside the Beverly Park outrage as not having "anything to do with this particular case." Then came the parade of State's witnesses. One, Owen Clay, a deputy, testified that he had been wounded in the right arm at the outset and had flung himself around the ticket office to be out of the range of fire. From that position he continued firing blindly with his left hand. On cross-examination Vanderveer had two questions:

"Who shot Jefferson Beard in the right breast?"

"I don't know," responded the witness.

"Did *you* do it?"

The deputy passed his hand across his eyes. "I don't know," he answered.

"Thank you. That's all," said Vanderveer.

Mayor Merrill testified that the I.W.W. had threatened to burn the city of Everett. Fire losses of $100,000 had been suffered during 1916. Thereupon Vanderveer introduced the annual report of the fire marshal showing that Everett had had fewer fire losses in 1916 than in any previous year. Sheriff McRae also testified. "McRae was sober," related Walker C. Smith. State witnesses described the scene on the dock as McRae hailed the men on the "Verona." One said that the sheriff raised his left hand, one said it was the right, another that it was both hands. The confusion on the dock could account for the diverging testimony. But one and all, the State's witnesses agreed that Tracy stood by an open window in the main cabin and fired from there. On this testimony there was no challenge from the defense; Vanderveer was well content to bide his time.

For the State's case the press table was overflowing — not only the local papers and wire services but special correspondents for Eastern newspapers and magazines. But on April 2 President Wilson appeared before Congress to ask for a declaration of war against Germany; suddenly the press table shrank by half and the defense case got short shrift in the commercial press. Fred Moore took over on direct presentation. Inasmuch as the State had introduced various I.W.W. publications and songs, James P. Thompson, a national spokesman, was put on the stand. For three days he expounded the principles of syndicalist industrial unionism over the heated objections of the prosecution. Judge Ronald observed drily that inasmuch as the State had introduced the documents, it was fair enough to have them explained. The defense presented dozens of witnesses — those on the "Verona," and citizens of Everett — to testify. One Everett citizen, Thomas O'Niel, was questioned about Wobbly street meetings. "It started in with rather small meetings," he said, "and then every time, as fast as they were molested by the police, the crowd kept growing until at last the meetings were between two and three thousand people." At first, he said, he had been shocked by the I.W.W. doctrines. Then how did he come to join the I.W.W., the State asked. "In this way, it was not the I.W.W. literature that convinced me so much as the actions of the side that was fighting them."

Perhaps the high point of the defense case came when the jury was taken to Everett to survey the dock scene. The "Verona" had been brought over from Seattle and lay at the dock in exactly the position she held during the massacre, with only a bow line to the deck, her stern swung out and away from the dock; the hour was selected so that the tide was the same as during the lethal ten minutes on November 5. Then Vanderveer placed a man of Tracy's height in the main cabin exactly where the State's witnesses had testified he stood while firing at the dock. The jurors were then placed in positions marked on the dock chart used during the trial to indicate where each witness stood who had testified he saw Tracy firing. The man standing by the window was invisible! It was a triumph for Vanderveer's patient examination of the scene in the many days he had spent in Everett.

One of the survivors of the Beverly Park and "Verona" expeditions was on the stand. The State was trying to get testimony from him that he had picked up shells from the deck of the "Verona." The State was nettled by his negative response.

"Did you pick *anything* up from the floor?" the State persisted.

"I picked up an eye, a man's eye," came the answer. From the blood-stained deck he had picked up a long splinter of wood on which was impaled a human eye.

On the crucial matter of the presence on the "Verona" of some armed men, James Francis Billings testified to the beating he had suffered at Beverly Park, which had left him with permanent injuries to back and hip.

"Why did you carry a gun on the fifth of November?" asked Vanderveer.

"I took it for my own personal benefit," replied Billings. "I didn't intend to let anybody beat me up like I was beaten on October 30th in the condition I was in. I was in bad condition at the time."

As the trial approached its end, the I.W.W., socialists, and radical unionists of Seattle held one of the biggest May Day parades in the city's history. Fifteen blocks long, the parade passed along the principal streets and to Mount Pleasant cemetery where three of the "Verona" victims lay buried. Minnie Rimer gave a moving description of the commemoration in a letter to Emma Goldman, published in *Mother Earth,* the anarchist magazine. On May Day, 1917, Miss Rimer related, the International Workers Defense League had sponsored a token 10-minute strike at 11:00 A.M. against the threatened hanging of Tom Mooney and Warren K. Billings in the Preparedness Day bomb frame-up in San Francisco. The Central Labor Council endorsed the strike and workers in the shipyards and elsewhere observed it — many even refusing to work on May Day at all. The parade assembled at the I.W.W. hall, then on Second Avenue South, and proceeded up Seattle's main business artery toward the cemetery. Miss Rimer reported:

The parade was the grandest spectacle I ever witnessed in Seattle. We were four abreast in the line of march which extended from the I.W.W. hall clear up to the Washington Hotel. Several thousand were in line; each member of the parade wore a red carnation. The American flag was carried at the head of the procession, and for this reason the Russian workers declined to march in the line but formed on the opposite side of the street and marched to the cemetery with us carrying the RED FLAG. All hail to the Russian rebels!

As the idea of the general strike grew, so grew this idea and by the time we were half way to the cemetery, someone had raised the red flag in our ranks. At the graves, speeches were delivered in Italian, Russian, Swedish, Hungarian and English. The "International" and many songs written by Joe Hill were sung. From the cemetery we went to the county jail where many of the Everett prisoners are incarcerated. We gathered around the jail and sang songs to those on the inside. The prisoners joined in the songs and let it be known that it was only their bodies that were in bondage, but surely not the minds and spirit of this courageous group.

On the hillside at the cemetery, in accordance with his last wishes, were scattered some of the ashes of Joe Hill, the I.W.W. song writer who had been shot to death in the Utah state penitentiary on November 19, 1915. At a meeting in the evening the final collection was taken for the Everett Prisoners Defense Fund and one half was voted to be sent to San Francisco for use in the liberation of Mooney and Billings. In all, some $38,000 had been raised across the country for the Everett defense.

On May 5, two months after the trial started, the jury returned its verdict, "Not guilty." All 74 men of the "Verona" were released and charges against the I.W.W. who had tried to go to Everett on the "Calista" were dropped. "It is the first victory of the kind ever achieved by labor on the Pacific Coast," claimed the *Union Record,* "previous trials without exception having been decided against the workers."

For the I.W.W. it was the greatest triumph of their history, too. The news flashed through a hundred Wobbly halls from Coast to Coast, setting off impromptu victory celebrations from Boston to San Diego. Far more important, to 50,000 loggers in hundreds of camps in the Pacific Northwest the news was astounding, something like a Declaration of Independence for workingmen from the barons of lumber. The refrain of the song "Solidarity," "For the union makes us strong," assumed for the first time reality to lumber workers. As for the men of the "Verona" and the "Calista," they reported to the Seattle I.W.W. hall for assignments as "job delegates," the organizers of industrial unionism, and began fanning out, with hundreds of others, through the logging and construction camps to carry the message. For them the moral of the Everett trial was aptly phrased by the famous Mr. Dooley when he said: "Do not ask for your rights; take 'em. There's something the matter with the right that is handed to you."

For George Vanderveer though, his legal triumph seemed to turn to ashes. Many of his associates, in the hatreds fanned by war, had turned their backs on him as a traitor not only to his class but to his country. He disappeared for two days after the trial and then showed up at home with haggard face, bloodshot eyes, a bruise on his jaw, and soiled clothes. He tried to enlist but was rejected as too old, although in the prime of life. But for Vanderveer the die had been cast. He was "counsel for the damned"; his lot irretrievably was to be with those of the lower depths.

In the lives of many outside the ranks of labor the Everett trial had been a decisive turning point. A handsome young apple-cheeked social worker, trained in philosophy at the University of Chicago, who had risen rapidly in Seattle to become a member of the school board with liberal-labor support, had taken time off to cover the trial for the New York *Evening Post* and the *Survey*. To Anna Louise Strong were revealed facts of life which had escaped her at the university and which were to give to "social work" an entirely new meaning.

For many another the Everett Massacre and trial proved turning points as well. The ranks of the I.W.W. suddenly began to swell. Before the massacre there had been but two paid officials at the Seattle hall, Secretary Mahler and Editor J. A. MacDonald of the *Industrial Worker*. By July 4, 1917, one year after the loggers' convention when there had been only 50 paid-up members in the lumber workers union branch, there were now 30 people under pay, working at top speed to take care of the constantly increasing membership. Locals of the A.F. of L. in the Puget Sound area also began to swell as shipyards expanded and new ones were built to meet the menace of the U-boats. Unions which had claimed members by the score began now to number them by the thousand.

EVERETT, NOVEMBER FIFTH

By Charles Ashleigh

[". . . and then the Fellow Worker died, singing 'Hold the
Fort' . . ." — From the report of a witness.]

Song on his lips, he came;
Song on his lips, he went; —
This be the token we bear of him, —
Soldier of Discontent!

Out of the dark they came; out of the night
Of poverty and injury and woe, —
With flaming hope, their vision thrilled to light, —
Song on their lips, and every heart aglow;

They came, that none should trample Labor's right
To speak, and voice her centuries of pain.
Bare hands against the master's armored might! —
A dream to match the tools of sordid gain!

And then the decks went red; and the gray sea
Was written crimsonly with ebbing life.
The barricade spewed shots and mockery
And curses, and the drunken lust of strife.

Yet, the mad chorus from that devil's host, —
Yea, all the tumult of that butcher throng, —
Compound of bullets, booze and coward boast, —
Could not out-shriek one dying worker's song!

Song on his lips, he came;
Song on his lips, he went; —
This be the token we bear of him, —
Soldier of Discontent!

3

From Timber Beast to Lumber Worker

From the crest of the Cascades to the sea, from British Columbia to the California line, the majestic Douglas fir was Nature's evergreen gift to the states of Washington and Oregon, the greatest natural wealth of this far northwestern region. David Douglas, the Scottish botanist, was the first scientist to view these forests, in 1823, as he scouted for botanical specimens for the Royal Horticultural Society, and this species of pine is named for him. The ordinary Douglas fir reaches a height of 180 to 190 feet, straight and tapering almost imperceptibly to its top where it is crested with small branches. Such trees measure three and one-half to six feet in diameter, but the giant Douglas fir can reach up to 300 feet, the largest tree in North America save for the sequoias of California. Such a tree can have a diameter of ten to twelve feet. Sunlight rarely filters down in these silent primeval forests so that the floor is carpeted only with brown pine needles and cones and with green ferns. Giant cedar and Sitka spruce are also abundant.

The first industry in Seattle, in 1853, was the tiny Yesler sawmill near where the 42-story L.C. Smith Building now stands. Other mills sprang up on Puget Sound to furnish lumber for building and for sailing ships and their spars, and soon schooners were hauling the lumber to California, Hawaii, and across the Pacific. The evergreen line receded gradually from the shores of Puget Sound; "stump-ranchers" laboriously tore out and burned up the stumps to clear fields. Homesteaders staked

58

out plots, a few logging their own property but most selling the uncut timber to companies, for the labor of logging such trees was beyond the strength of a single family. The lumber companies — in the early days mostly small operators — used horses and oxen to haul out the fallen trees and logs along a "skid road." This was composed of smaller logs placed in the fashion of railroad ties, and greased with a heavy fish oil. Along this skid road the logs were hauled to the nearest body of water or mill. Small donkey engines eventually supplanted animal power and by 1917 the high-line, high-lead, or "flying machine" had taken over the job of getting the logs from where they were felled to the tracks of the little logging railroad which connected with a mill or a regular railroad. A huge block was secured about 90 feet up the trunk of a guyed tree standing by the tracks. From this a cable was rigged to a similar tree in the stand of timber and a trolley line run along it. From this line, hooks were clamped around the log and it soared across the intervening space to the waiting flat car, where with other logs it was chained to the car. A miniature wood-burning locomotive hustled the train of flat cars down the uneven narrow-gauge railroad to the mill at the base of operations. A high-line unit was run by a crew of 20 men or so and in the larger operations there could be several high-lines operating in various parts of the forest and feeding into the railroad. Some of the logging railroads were by no means minor affairs. The Puget Sound Mill & Timber Company built the Port Angeles & Western, then the only means of transportation through the great rain forests on the slopes of the Olympics.

Even in 1917 the felling of the great Douglas firs was the job of fallers, usually two men to a double crosscut saw, called a Swedish fiddle. After the tree had been felled, buckers took over to trim it of branches and saw it into lengths — 20 to 40 feet — to suit the trucks of the flat cars. Felling and bucking were the key operations upon which all else depended; these workers were required to set the pace with the steady, laborious humming and whining of the big saws driven by nothing more than muscle and will power. It was the hardest of work and burned men out in a hurry.

All the operations, from the high-climber who topped the giant trees, to the lowly "whistle-punk" who signalled the operation of the high-line cable, were extremely dangerous. A tree might fall erratically, or the great log when lofted into the air on the high-line could plunge dizzily or fall from the grip of the hooks, or fall while being loaded on to the platform. On the logging railroad itself wrecks were common as logs slipped from their platforms, or the rails gave way, or flimsy trestles collapsed. The mayhem was enormous; in any sizable operation rarely a month passed that the little Heisler locomotive did not go down the line with one flatcar carrying only a solitary object — a body carelessly covered with a tarpaulin. On the highly dangerous high-line operation there was no outside inspection whatever; the "bull of the woods," the head bossman, was charged with speeding up work and was willing to take a chance with other people's lives to get out his quota each day. Many workers died of minor injuries for lack of medical attention. An injured man would be allowed to suffer until the cars were loaded and the bull of the woods gave the order for the train to pull out. Even then the nearest doctor or hospital might be far away from the end of the logging line. As late as 1939 in the big Weyerhaeuser operations in Willapa Harbor, there was no ambulance service nor any organized procedure for getting an injured worker out of the woods, although by that time highways had succeeded the logging railroads.

Such operations required great stretches of timberland. Fortunately for the bigger companies, the conservationists had set up a clamor early in the century against the shameful pillaging of the forests. Even then the green mountainsides were beginning to show great scars of wasteland — square miles of stumps, swept regularly by brush fires which burned any aspiring sapling and condemned the land to eternal sterility and erosion. The government began setting apart large tracts of land on the mountainsides and creating national forests, particularly along the slopes of the Cascades and the Olympics. Thus were assembled the large tracts whose timber rights were then sold to the bigger companies such as St. Paul & Tacoma, Puget Sound Mill & Timber, Weyerhaeuser, Bloedell-Donovan, Merrill & Ring, and Snohomish Logging. Weyerhaeuser bought from the Northern Pacific Railroad tracts of its government-granted land greater in area than some eastern states. Nowadays such companies run alluring advertisements extolling the virtues of forest husbandry — claims that bring a wry and cynical smile to Puget Sounders who see their mountainsides defaced, the evergreen draperies of the Cascades turned into bare rock, the watersheds ruined, and even the climate altered by this pillage of Nature.

Hundreds of logging camps dotted western Washington. These varied from small camps with a score of men to large ones with several hundred. The average camp operated with a hundred to two hundred workers. In the forest clearing, bunkhouses were often brought in on the flatcars and skidded into position around the central cook-shack. In the larger camps a power plant gave flickering illumination and furnished hot water for the kitchen, but usually kerosene lights were considered sufficient.

A bunkhouse sheltered 20 to 50 men. Two-high bunks lined three walls, with benches in front of them. A wood stove gave heat, a couple of kerosene lamps flickered dimly in the smoke and vapor. Ventilation was afforded by the door and guaranteed in any wind at all by the chinks in the walls. In some camps there were "muzzle-loading" bunks where men crept in at the foot of the bunk and inched forward. The system had the great virtue of packing more men, sardine-wise, into a small bunkhouse. Around the stoves the loggers dried their working clothes, for rainfall on the slopes of the Cascades exceeds 80 inches a year and on the western side of the Olympic rain forests, runs as high as 160 inches. For washing there were several basins on a bench and a bucket of water. The beds were usually straw mattresses on a wooden shelf and the logger furnished his own blankets,

which he packed on his back from job to job — the bindlestiff
and his bindle. Presiding over these bunkhouses was the bull-
cook, usually an elderly crippled logger no longer fit to work in
the woods. He lit the fires at five in the morning, furnished
water for the basins, swept out the bunkhouses, and fetched
wood.

The cook presided over a long range on whose flat surface the
morning flapjacks browned. Adroitly he tipped his pitcher of
dough to form long lines of cakes — staple of the logger's breakfast — then quickly flipped them, then returned the third time
to toss them onto plates for serving. In larger camps he had a
baker, for bread, pastries, and suchlike were the cheapest and
most filling fare. A dishwasher and several waiters, known as
flunkeys, completed the kitchen crew. Food in the camps had
been mostly beans and stew, but by 1917 the camps had begun
to feed in higher style. With wages much the same and a growing shortage of labor, the camps with the better food had an
edge in keeping a stable labor force. Quarters of beef and pork
began to supplement the barrels of pickled meats. In the better
camps food was abundant but there were, of course, no fresh
vegetables or fruits and a logger would hardly have known
what to make of a salad.

The quality of the fare varied a good bit with the cook;
"T-Bone" Walker could make any piece of beef tough and
black. Over this and the potatoes was poured a concoction of
burnt flour, lard, and water known as "monkey." In some camps
the cook, in charge of purchasing, could make a tidy rake-off in
collusion with the commissary company. Such "belly-robbers"
especially roused the ire of the Wobblies. It was bad enough to
work hard ten hours a day, often in inclement weather, but to
suffer bad food because the cook, himself a workingman, was in
cahoots with the commissary company was beyond all tolerance;
in some instances it was said that the men sat the cook down on
his own stove. There were even stories of some camps where the
tin plates were nailed to the tables and the cutlery made fast
with chains. Washing dishes was simple — the whole mess was

swooshed down with pails of water. Such cooks were not typical; usually the cook regarded himself as a workingman and acted accordingly, and the sanitary standards in most camps were probably a cut above that of the ordinary household.

Usual working hours in the camps were ten, from 7:00 A.M. to 6:00 P.M., although smaller operations in summer months might take advantage of as much daylight as possible. As the work was arduous, the employers felt no need to provide recreational amenities. After dinner the logger retired to his bunkhouse, took off the wet clothes and hung them hopefully by the stove to dry, and went to bed in a room reeking of sweaty drying clothes and tobacco smoke. It hardly occurred to the logger to demand the facilities of a recreation room for he was dead tired after a day's work. But a drying room for his clothes, a laundry room in which to wash them, a shower room in which to clean his body — these, too, ran beyond the expectations of a "timber beast." Everything he possessed, a blanket, an extra shirt, a razor, was wrapped up in his bindle, and when he went to town — usually Seattle — he went in his working clothes and his caulk shoes. The logger's clothing decreed his ostracism. In his bindle there was no room for a suit of "store clothes" or ordinary shoes. His trousers were known as "tin pants" because the incrustations of dirt and sweat enabled them to stand up by themselves. Cut off high above the ankles to avoid underbrush, they were also known as "high-water" pants. The caulk boots, needed for sure footing in the woods, barred him from any decent floor, for the points wore holes in the wood. On the Seattle-Tacoma boats a sign, "No Caulk Boots on the Upper Deck," confined the logger to the lower depths.

A man could stand this life — unending toil, no recreation, for only two or three months at the most. Then he quit and went to town. There, in a burst of release, he got drunk, whored, gambled, and spent his stake. Within a week he was down on the slave market looking for another job, another few months of work in a camp. Such was a logger's life. That the men who produced the fundamental wealth upon which the economy of the

region rested should be regarded as pariahs, condemned to body-
breaking toil and to animal-like existence whether on the job
or away, that in the city they should be consigned to a skid road
pale which existed only to rob and debase them — this was the
supreme confirmation to the I.W.W. and socialists of the fundamental truth of Marxist theory. It gave point to the line in the
"International," "We have been naught; we shall be all"; from
this arose the revolutionary determination to wipe out a system
that inverted values and condemned the most useful members of
society to the most repugnant existence.

In the dreary degradation of the skid road there was one
haven of hope — the Wobbly hall. This was a huge second-floor
hall near the center of the skid road. Apart from the small space
roped off for the office, most of the big hall was dedicated to the
needs of the migratory worker. Benches, chairs, a space in which
to check his bindle, the latest radical papers, books, but most of
all the confraternity of fellow workers from all parts of the West.
Every evening there was a program — first, the Wobbly songs,
then speakers on industrial unionism, first-hand reports from
hotspots of the class struggle, songs and sketches presented by
the foreign-language fraternal, choral, and literary societies, and
then more songs. These were his people, they spoke his language, their ideas reflected the hard facts of his life. He was at
home.

Confined to the skid road, the logger found entertainment
along the streets where itinerant vendors, missionaries, radical
orators, and the Salvation Army competed for attention. Each
evening near O'Hanrahan's news stand, which sold more copies
of the *Industrial Worker, Solidarity,* the *Masses,* the *International Socialist Review,* and the local socialist paper than of all
the local dailies, the I.W.W., socialists, and others brought out
platforms and started speaking. Will "Red" O'Hanrahan often
opened the radical soapboxing with his evening commentary on
the day's news in which he dissected, to the merriment of his
audience, the stories in the local dailies. To their satisfaction he

analyzed the oddities, barbarities, and ludicrosities of capitalism. O'Hanrahan's sardonic humor was a forerunner of the sophisticated monologues to be heard now in coffee houses and night spots in metropolitan centers. Younger apostles of industrial unionism and socialism then mounted the platform to warm up the audiences for the main speakers. Such could be James P. Thompson, the I.W.W.'s most fluent spokesman, J. T. "Red" Doran, Walker C. Smith, Bruce Rogers, Kate Sadler, and a dozen others, as ready in handling hecklers as in expounding their doctrines. Here, too, came the news, at first hand by participants, of the latest outrages against the working class in California, Arizona, Montana, or from wherever the itinerant radical hailed.

The penchant of the Wobblies for song arose, in some measure, from the activities of the Salvation Army across the street. A lively competition there, with the Army's brass band blaring out hymns to the beat of a big bass drum and the Salvation lassies in their bonnets screaming at the top of their voices, sometimes drowning out the best efforts of capable Wobbly speakers. Gradually, across the West, there grew the need for answering the Salvation Army noises with a countervailing force. Wobbly versifiers made up their own words for the favorite hymns and for the tunes of popular songs. These were collected, with classic songs of the labor movement, in the famous Little Red Songbook which has since run through some 30 editions. The early editions long since have become collectors' items. Through many of the songs ran the typical Wobbly humor — ironic, biting, reflecting the reality of life as seen by the migratory:

> Long-haired preachers come out every night,
> Try to tell you what's wrong and what's right;
> But when asked how 'bout something to eat
> They will answer with voices so sweet:

> You will eat, bye and bye,
> In that glorious land above the sky;
> Work and pray, live on hay,
> You'll get pie in the sky when you die.

Joe Hill, the Wobbly who was shot in Utah state penitentiary, wrote the words of that song, entitled "The Preacher and the Slave." To the camp-meeting tune of "There Is Power in the Blood," he wrote the refrain:

> There is pow'r, there is pow'r
> In a band of workingmen,
> When they stand hand in hand,
> That's a pow'r, that's a pow'r
> That must rule in every land —
> One Industrial Union Grand.

Perhaps the most famous of the I.W.W. songs was "Solidarity Forever," sung to the tune of "John Brown's Body," and to be the song of the CIO a generation later:

When the Union's inspiration through the workers' blood shall run,
There can be no power greater anywhere beneath the sun.
Yet what force on earth is weaker than the feeble strength of one?
But the Union makes us strong.

> Solidarity forever!
> Solidarity forever!
> Solidarity forever!
> For the Union makes us strong.

This song, written by Ralph Chaplin, paraphrased the philosophy of revolutionary industrial unionism so that the Wobbly who knew the words understood as well the basic ideas of his organization and its world outlook. Chaplin later wrote of "Solidarity Forever" that "nobody ever heard of it until 50,000 striking Puget Sound loggers bellered it out to a world that did not care a hoot about the problems of the voteless and cruelly exploited 'timber beasts.' " Much later, Chaplin, who became an ultra-rightist, wrote what was almost an apology for having written "Solidarity Forever," his most enduring claim to fame. The industrial unions of the CIO had adopted the song, and Chaplin as the now craft-conscious editor of the A.F. of L. Tacoma *Labor Advocate,* came to regard industrial unionism as a step toward the slave state and the crushing of individual liberty.

The devil-may-care humor that marked the Wobblies was

well expressed in verses written by T-Bone Slim, the laureate of the logging camps, ending with a sentimental strain that was also characteristic of these hard-bitten working stiffs:

> I'm as mild mannered man as can be
> And I've never done them harm as I can see.
> Still on me they put a ban and they threw me in the can,
> They go wild, simply wild over me.
>
> Oh the "bull" he went wild over me
> And he held his gun where everyone could see,
> He was breathing rather hard when he saw my union card —
> He went wild, simply wild over me.
>
> They go wild, simply wild over me,
> I'm referring to the bed-bug and the flea.
> They disturb my slumber deep and I murmur in my sleep
> They go wild, simply wild over me.
>
> Will the roses grow wild over me?
> When I'm gone to the land that is to be?
> When my soul and body part in the stillness of my heart —
> Will the roses grow wild over me?

The I.W.W. was accused of being anti-religious. What really irked them was their competitors on the skid roads, the "Starvation Army" and the hand-out missions which preached "pie in the sky." With characteristic verve, the I.W.W. pressed the assault on hypocritical Christianity with songs such as "Christians at War," by John F. Kendrick, which outraged the feelings not only of the orthodox but of the jingoistic "paytriots" who in 1916 were preaching war:

> Onward, Christian soldiers! Duty's way is plain;
> Slay your Christian neighbors, or by them be slain.
> Pulpiteers are spouting effervescent swill,
> God above is calling you to rob and rape and kill,
> All your acts are sanctified by the Lamb on high;
> If you love the Holy Ghost, go murder, pray and die.
>
> Onward, Christian soldiers, rip and tear and smite!
> Let the gentle Jesus bless your dynamite.
> Splinter skulls with shrapnel, fertilize the sod;
> Folks who do not speak your tongue deserve the curse of God.
> Smash the doors of every home, pretty maidens seize;
> Use your might and sacred right to treat them as you please.

Such songs "to fan the flames of discontent" also fanned the hostility of their enemies and were introduced in the Everett trial and in a dozen others to prove that the I.W.W. was anti-patriotic and irreligious, as well as a threat to the social system. But to the lumberjacks whether on the skid road, in the bunk-houses, or in the jungles, the words of their songs rang true and clear, and lustily they shouted them at the street corners to counter the Salvation Army hymns, and in their halls and meet-ings. These songs told of their lives, their ideas, and their hopes, and constituted for most Wobblies as much theoretical knowl-edge of the principles of the I.W.W. as they were likely to be able to express.

The Forest and Lumber Workers, in 1912, was the second national union, after the textile workers, to be formed by the I.W.W. Its main strength at first was in the Louisiana-Texas "piney woods" where in 1910 I.W.W. and socialists had formed the Brotherhood of Timber Workers. It was a "people's organi-zation"—lumber workers, preachers, merchants, doctors — united against the outside lumber interests. In its ranks were white workers and black, native-born including the Cajun French, and Mexicans and Italians. In 1911 the Brotherhood sent fraternal delegates to the national I.W.W. convention and a year later Secretary William D. (Big Bill) Haywood addressed the Timber Workers convention, which then affiliated with the I.W.W. This militant union struck often and encountered a rather unusual impediment to meetings held near the sawmills and camps. The managers would begin "tin-panning," beating upon circular saws, to drown out the union speakers. At such a meeting in Grabow, Louisiana, in 1912, shots rang out from the lumber office and three unionists fell dead. Fifty-eight timber workers were held in the "Black Hole of Calcasieu"; but the State was unable later to convict them. After the union had been broken up, many members drifted on to the oilfields of Oklahoma and helped to organize the I.W.W. Oilworkers Union around 1916.

In the squalid Grays Harbor, Washington, mill towns —

Aberdeen, Hoquiam, Raymond, and Cosmopolis — the I.W.W. shut down the mills in 1912 to get a 50-cent increase on wages of $2 a day. Vigilantes sprang up, there were mass deportations of foreign-born strikers, and 150 men were loaded into boxcars at Hoquiam to be sent away. Fortunately the mayor and the railroad workers stopped that, and the strike was compromised with a $2.25 scale. Strikes broke out sporadically from then on, a kind of guerrilla warfare conducted by an organization not strong enough to enforce a general shutdown. In this period the American Federation of Labor chartered the International Union of Timberworkers, with which the shingle weavers were affiliated. This union had some strength in the sawmill towns where other A.F. of L. unions could lend it support, such as in Ballard, a suburb of Seattle, in Tacoma, Everett, Bellingham, and Aberdeen. But it hardly ever succeeded in reaching out to the logging camps. Although an industrial union, its concept of collective bargaining, of contracts with the employers, and its membership of "home-guards," men living in towns, were worlds apart from the I.W.W., which scorned truces with the class enemy as embodied in contracts, and whose members for the most part were rootless.

In 1917 the I.W.W. union, which had become Lumber Workers Industrial Union 500, convened in Spokane on March 5. It was only a month before the declaration of war against Germany, and the growing shortage of labor was putting workingmen in a better bargaining position. The demands framed by the convention centered on the eight-hour day, six-day week, and abolition of bindles. These rather modest demands reflected the wretched conditions in the camps: the men wanted single beds with springs, clean mattresses and bedding, good lighting, not more than 12 to a bunkhouse, and, of course, no double-tier bunks. In the kitchens they asked for porcelain instead of enamel dishes. A drying room for wet clothes, a laundry room, showers, free hospital service, hiring on the job or from the union hall, free transportation to the job — these, with a minimum wage of $60 a month with board completed the union pro-

gram. The union soon claimed 6,000 members, organized in
three autonomous districts "left free to tackle the boss when-
ever they feel so inclined." The Duluth, Minnesota, division
had three branches, those in Spokane and Seattle, seven each.

In the short-log country — eastern Washington, Idaho, and
western Montana, so called because the trees are small — the job
delegates fanned out and by April a strike wave was eliminating
the 12-hour day prevalent there in springtime, and boosting
wages from $3.50 to $5 a day in the "river drives" when the
logs cut in fall and winter were floated downstream in the spring
freshets. Strikes spread throughout the Inland Empire and to
the Pacific slope. For once the I.W.W. seemed unprepared for
such a spontaneous uprising; perhaps it is more exact to say
perplexed, for war had been declared. The war was a major
threat to a revolutionary organization which had been frankly
anti-militarist. The I.W.W. convention in 1916 had adopted a
statement of policy that "we openly declare ourselves the determined opponents of all nationalistic sectionalism, or patriotism,
and the militarism preached and supported by our one enemy,
the capitalist class. We condemn all wars." The declaration
urged anti-militarist propaganda in peacetime and "in time of
war, the general strike, in all industries."

A favorite Wobbly propaganda weapon was the little "Red"
sticker; these were printed by the million and adorned every
boxcar, water tank, flophouse, bunkhouse, and jail cell frequented by Wobblies. The letters "I.W.W." were prominent on
these stickers, with admonitions in red and black to join the
union. Some featured a black cat — reference to the virtues of
sabotage; others reflected Wobbly aversion to war. Just before
war was declared Ralph Chaplin had designed a little sticker
with the phrase "Why Be A Soldier?" Red blood dripped from
the word "Soldier." It was stopped on the press, over the vehement objections of a minority on the General Executive Board
led by Frank Little. He was for blasting "the son of a bitch of a
war," but Bill Haywood reproved him for using the expression
"son of a bitch" so much. Bill's favorite cuss word was Gee Fuzz.

The G.E.B. decided to sidestep the war issue by calling for an intensified war on the master class while letting individual members decide for themselves whether to register in compliance with the conscription law. But it was far too late to recall millions of the red and black stickers or to erase the organization's militant opposition to war as expressed in a dozen Wobbly songs sung wherever they met.

Employers and the press fanned the idea that wartime strikes helped the Kaiser and that back of these demands for a better life was "Prussian gold." The Wobbly saw himself caught in an age-old trap; in peacetime the never-ending depressions and panics prevented him from attaining union strength; now in the one time when labor power was at a premium he was to be prevented from striking to abolish the ten-hour day and the bindle. *Industrial Worker* and *Solidarity* every week published the facts about the war-swollen profits of the employers; the contrast between his own plight and those who profited from the European bloodbath maddened him.

By the middle of July, 1917, a spontaneous strike wave was sweeping the long-log country west of the Cascades. The A.F. of L. Timberworkers had called a general strike and the I.W.W. could hardly do less, despite their exposed position. For one thing, the I.W.W. hesitated because in mid-July the loggers had been back on the job for only a week or so after the usual July 4 shutdown of the camps, and had not accumulated a stake to tide them over a strike. Already police persecution had broken out, particularly in the Spokane region where Wobbly halls were being raided and closed and loggers thrown into open stockades to force them back to work. In the Puget Sound country, camp after camp was shutting down as the strike wave rolled along; only in Seattle was it possible to keep the I.W.W. hall open.

Stockades were erected in nearly every county seat east of the Cascades as the merciless search went on for Wobblies. These "bull pens" existed in North Yakima, Ellensburg, Cle Elum, Pasco, Wenatchee, and elsewhere, to relieve the pressure on jails and to relieve the authorities of the need to provide sleeping facilities and in many instances even the barest minimum of food. Martial law was declared in Spokane on August 19, the I.W.W. hall was closed, and James Rowan and 26 other I.W.W. were arrested. The arrests brought a protest from the Spokane Central Labor Council against "Prussianism" and the activities of the hostile State Council of Defense. The labor council went on record for "a general strike of all industry until such time as may be necessary to insure observance of the law and the Constitution by officials sworn to uphold both." Authorities in Pasco neatly sidestepped the constitutional issue by declaring the state of Washington "in a state of insurrection." The Agricultural Workers of the I.W.W. joined the Spokane A.F. of L. in threatening a general strike if the terror were not ended. Such terror was ineffective west of the Cascades as the men, avoiding the smaller county seats, congregated on the Seattle skid road where mere numbers was protection.

As usual in such crises, the Wobblies had a song for it, to the tune of Portland County Jail:

> Fifty thousand lumberjacks, fifty thousand packs,
> Fifty thousand dirty rolls of blankets on their backs,
> Fifty thousand minds made up to strike and strike like men;
> For fifty years they've "packed" a bed, but never will again.

The lumber interests promptly organized the Lumbermen's Protective Association, raised a war fund of $500,000, and threatened to fine any company $500 a day for working their men less than ten hours a day. Under its aegis, so-called Patriotic Leagues arose throughout the state with the mission of raiding I.W.W. halls and terrorizing the loggers into submission. For its part, the Seattle labor movement responded by expressing its solidarity with the striking loggers; its influence was notable in restraining the city authorities from closing the I.W.W. hall and harassing the strikers. Said President J. G. Brown of the Shingle Weavers:

> The matter is so serious that all members of organized labor are affected. The great outstanding obstacle to all organization in this

state has been the lumber trust. The longshoremen feel it on the waterfront, the teamsters feel it at the sawmills and eventually in their work every organization comes in contact with it at some point or other and is temporarily balked. The lumber barons place themselves in opposition to the federal and state governments. Now labor must join battle in full force against them. If the federal and the state government and the unions combined cannot lick them, let's move off the earth and make room for the slaves they demand.

A mine explosion in Butte helped to precipitate the federal government's effort to exterminate the I.W.W. On June 8, 1917, the Speculator mine was swept by a blast which killed 190 miners as they beat upon iron manholes separating the mine levels in order to escape. The manholes, to save money, had been cemented! An independent metal mine union was formed to demand enforcement of safety laws, to abolish the rustling card which miners had to carry in order to work and which of course placed them at the mercy of the mine owners' blacklist, and to obtain wage increases to match the sharply climbing cost of living. On June 18 the A.F. of L. electrical workers struck and were followed by other A.F. of L. crafts, and soon "The Hill" was shut down tight. The news spread to Arizona; by June 26, Bisbee, Jerome, Miami, and Swansea were shut down, in support of the Butte miners, and for demands of their own. At Bisbee, on July 12, a mine owners' posse rounded up 1,164 miners — killing three in the process — packed them in cattle cars and shipped them into the desert; later they were put in a detention camp at Columbus, New Mexico. That broke the Arizona strikes and left Butte standing alone. Frank Little, the intransigent member of the I.W.W. General Executive Board, left Chicago to give a hand in Butte. Little was half-Indian, blind in one eye like Bill Haywood, and at the time had a broken leg in a cast. On August 1 a band of six men took him in the early morning hours from his hotel room, tied his body to the back of an auto and dragged him to the Milwaukee railroad trestle where they hanged him; whether he was alive when hanged is not known. His funeral was the largest Butte had ever seen, even the A.F. of L. union members joining in the great procession. Legend has it that not one of his six lynchers lived to see the first anniversary of Frank Little's death.

While members of the I.W.W. were active in the copper strikes, they had neither called them nor led them; in the lumber strike the I.W.W. had followed the A.F. of L. Nevertheless the full wrath of the federal government fell upon the I.W.W. They were said to be "pro-German," the favorite word of abuse in the First World War; in addition they were accused of being unpatriotic, opposed to conscription, and enemies of any war but the class war. So on September 5 federal authorities raided I.W.W. headquarters in Chicago and every hall from Coast to Coast. Five tons of records were seized in an effort to find evidence of German connections and of Prussian gold, but none ever turned up.

The incessant federal, state, and local raids provoked an ironic notice in the *Industrial Worker:*

To Our Patrons: Notice — Parties desiring to raid any of the various offices of the I.W.W. please book your dates well in advance, as this form of amusement is very popular with officialdom, and it is difficult to provide open dates for all applicants unless they apply early.

Even before the federal raids, the *Industrial Worker* on August 15 had advised transferring the strike "to the job." There, in the logging camps, the men would be safe from the federal and local police, and they could proceed to enforce their demands. On August 31, the situation being even more threatening, the Seattle district sent out a call for a meeting to be held September 7 so that activists could determine whether the strike should be transferred to the job and to plan tactics to be used — all with the understanding that no returning logger would work more than eight hours a day. The September 5 raids ended all doubts. Loggers returned to the camps, many taking whistles with them which were blown at the end of the eighth hour when the men downed tools. If fired, they went "down the line" to be replaced by another crew which did identically the same. Others soldiered on the job so that not more than eight hours' production could be obtained in ten. Senator Borah, the Idaho solon, complained: "The I.W.W. is about as elusive a proposition as you ever ran up against . . . it is intangible . . . you can't reach it. . . . It is simply an understanding between men."

Among tactics used by the Wobblies in striking on the job was that of "hoosiering up," playing dumb when orders were given. Men who had spent their lives working in the woods all the way from Finland and Sweden to New Brunswick, Maine, and Minnesota, suddenly became unfamiliar with the simplest elements of logging. Fired for incompetence, they went to the next camp and repeated their simple-minded stratagem. Another device was to wait for orders from the bull of the woods. Which tree to fell, which log to hoist next on the flatcar — a hundred minor operations that every man knew thoroughly well were postponed until the order was given. Production fell alarmingly. A variation was to carry out orders literally. The rule was to bring in all tools each day — saws, axes, peavies, etc. So one enterprising crew dismantled all the cables on the high-lead and fetched them into camp. The bull of the woods was fit to be tied. Such crews of course were fired on the spot, but they drifted on to the next job and repeated, and the crew that replaced them thought up other stratagems. One bossman who acceded to the eight-hour day was obliged to admit: "You know those crazy Wobs have an idea! It's not so bad to have all your work all over in eight hours."

The *Industrial Worker* summed up the effects of the new tactic:

The transfer of the strike to the job is a new one for the lumber bosses. They are willing to pit their full money bags against the empty bellies of the lumber jacks, but the idea of the workers drawing pay while in a state of insurrection does not appeal to them at all. Gone is the lash of hunger, gone is the court injunction, gone is the use of force against the picket line that extends to every individual worker who watches to see that he does not scab on himself by working ten hours a day.

From Aberdeen came the report that "the strike on the job is disgusting the bosses and their feelings are expressed by their meowing in the capitalist press. The men in the camps report that they have slowed down until it seems like drawing money for nothing. The cry of Timber!, so dear to the heart of the boss, is heard with less frequency than ever before."

From a Snohomish Logging Company camp, news was relayed that "the company got started with two sides running but on Thursday the steam went crazy and blew the whistle at 4 p.m. Sixty men rolled up and came out, leaving eight on the job waiting for the next shipment so the new crew could be instructed as to how the Wobblies get paid for striking. This is the second time this stunt has been pulled at the camp and soon it will be eight hours for ours."

Danaher's Camp 2 near Darrington was one of the most famous of Wobbly camps. There a distaste for strikebreaking spread even into feline ranks. As a job delegate observed:

The red card, red blooded, 100 per cent organized workers were recently surprised to see a coal-black cat with a kitten walk proudly into camp, deposit her burden, and walk out again. Curious to learn where the cat was going, some of the lumberjacks followed her a mile through the snow to the Sound Timber Company's camp, an infamous Weyerhaeuser outfit with gunmen and scabs. With evident disgust at her former surroundings and associates, the black cat picked up her second kitten and returned to the I.W.W. camp, where the three dumb animals are now the petted mascots of the men who are fighting for Industrial Freedom.

The Wobblies jeered at the government's meatless days. Declaring that lumber can't be produced on mush, the Wobblies struck camps that tried to introduce the system. The men wouldn't stand for "lithograph pictures of meatless days and wheatless days and leftover days, so they quit," the *Industrial Worker* reported. In revulsion against the Everett Massacre, workers in some camps banned canned and packaged foods sold under the Everett Best brand; at the Great Northern Lumber Company camp near Leavenworth the entire camp walked out rather than eat the stuff.

One small camp near Renton, worked by "scissorbills" — men deficient in their understanding of class-consciousness — went on working full blast. A young I.W.W. kitchen worker, annoyed by his failure to "shut 'er down," went to nearby Seattle and provided himself with the sinews of one phase of the class war. The next morning a liberal dose of croton oil in the big pot of coffee and cow-itch distributed in the bunks were enough. Production ceased.

Such sabotage was infrequent. Tales of damaged equipment, burned forests, and malicious destruction stemmed mainly from the inflamed minds of those who wanted to believe such tales, reinforced by the remarks of more gifted "spielers" on the soapbox who often concocted yarns about something far away to amuse their audiences. For one thing, the I.W.W. realized that there was no point in harming the property from which they hoped to make a living. Their beef was against the boss, not the machine. There were of course the pamphlets on sabotage written by Walker C. Smith and Elizabeth Gurley Flynn, and widely quoted in many trials. Neither was an official publication of the I.W.W., although advertised in their press. The more lurid aspects of French syndicalist sabotage never caught hold in the United States; to the Americans, sabotage was mainly slowing down on the job, "conscious withdrawal of efficiency," working to the exact rule.

One of the most serious charges made against the I.W.W. was that they drove long spikes into logs. When these went to the sawmill, they were supposed to splinter the big saw, hurtling lethal metal splinters in all directions, maiming and killing sawyers. After the First World War the late George Fishburne, a Tacoma lawyer and later postmaster in that city, was assigned as an assistant federal district attorney to make an investigation of these reports for the Department of Justice. He declared he was never able to find one authentic case of a spiked log. Such logs, he said, were always at some other mill, but he could never find the mill. The Department of Justice, anxious to find any evidence of sabotage against the I.W.W., never publicized Fishburne's findings. At the Seattle convention of the A.F. of L. in 1913, so the story goes, President Samuel Gompers was asked to comment on the I.W.W. and sabotage. His curt reply was said to be: "They only talk about it; we do it."

So successful was the I.W.W. tactic of strike on the job that Secretary James A. Duncan of the Seattle Central Labor Coun-

cil, reporting to the 1917 convention of the A.F. of L. in Buffalo,
urged an A.F. of L. campaign in the lumber industry. Warning
of I.W.W. progress, Duncan said:

Controlling the lumber production, they will be able to control
ship-building operations to a great extent. Already they have applied so successfully the sabotage known as "the strike on the job"
that a crew of 200 men, who formerly got out 20 cars of logs a day,
brought its production as low as three cars, until the employers gave
them clean beds and good food and higher wages they asked for.
It is this desperate, silent, elusive, yet terribly effective force, which
takes the name of I.W.W. but is largely made up of men who consider regular trade unionism "too slow." This is the threat to the
prestige of trade unionism on the Coast.

Production of spruce, needed for war planes because the
wood resisted splintering on impact, was dwindling toward
zero. President Wilson in desperation named Carleton H.
Parker, a University of Washington economist, as a peace
envoy. Parker recommended that the eight-hour day be instituted, wages raised, and better accommodations furnished in the
camps. In this he was joined by Secretary of War Newton D.
Baker and by Governor Ernest Lister. In December, 1917, the
Western Pine Manufacturers Association, centered in Spokane,
agreed "in principle" to the eight-hour day; in this they had
little choice as the I.W.W. had enforced the shorter workday in
most of the camps of the Inland Empire. But the operators
along the Cascades, Olympics, and the Grays Harbor country
were hard-nosed; they would agree to nothing and forced the
Inland Empire companies to renege on their pledge to the
government.

The mighty U.S. government was in a dilemma. It could not
treat with the I.W.W., whose leaders it had indicted and jailed
as seditionists. The A.F. of L. Timberworkers were ready to
bargain but had little strength in the woods. The operators
refused all collective bargaining, negotiation, or even discussion
with their workers. As a last hope Colonel Brice P. Disque, assigned by the War Department to get out the spruce at all costs,
organized a labor union all by himself. It was the Loyal Legion
of Loggers and Lumbermen, started in November, 1917. A

hundred Army officers fanned out into the camps, administering
loyalty oaths which were about the only semblance of membership in the Four L's. Under duress, the workers took the oath
but the production of spruce remained negligible. Colonel
Disque then sent 10,000 soldiers into the camps and mills, but
their contribution to the war effort, too, was negligible. Most
of them resented being used as strikebreakers and readily joined
in the spirit of the I.W.W. general strike — while the Wobblies
"hoosiered" on the job, the soldiers "soldiered." A few of the
Army officers, disenchanted with their role in the war to make
the world safe for democracy, publicly repudiated their dis-
agreeable task.

By mid-December of 1917 the Wobblies were claiming victory
for the eight-hour day as more and more camps swung over.
Carleton Parker's mediation board in recommending adoption
of the shorter workday was merely bowing to an accomplished
fact. Board members quizzed loggers of Lumber Workers Industrial Union 500. What do you think of this country, was a
favorite question. One logger answered: "I'd be more than loyal
if given the eight-hour day, wages, camp sanitation, and food
enough to make life worth living." Invited to the Wobbly hall
on Second Avenue South, board members enjoyed an evening
given over to an entertainment to raise money for the Butte
miners. The Wobbly assigned to escort the federal men explained during the collection talk: "The Kaiser is not attending
regularly to our remittances so we take this way of floating our
Liberty Bonds."

Colonel Disque on March 1, 1918, threw in the sponge and
dictated the shorter workday in all camps. The operators, faced
with cancellation of juicy contracts, grudgingly gave in. The
Four L's — or Four Hells as the I.W.W. called them — maintained a precarious existence, mostly in sawmill towns where the
forces of law and order were at the command of the Army.
President William Short of the State Federation of Labor attended their "convention" in December, 1918, and reported
that there were only 15 or 20 bona fide workers' delegates in
the meeting attended mainly by company men, Army officers,

and stooges. Those who voted in the negative were disfranchised and two A.F. of L. representatives in the gallery were
ejected by Colonel Disque. "Their autocracy was complete,"
reported President Short. After the war a Reed College professor was induced to head the company union, and it lingered
on as a phantom organization until the 1930's when Section 7a
of the National Industrial Recovery Act and later a similar
provision in the National Labor Relations Act outlawed such
organizations.

Lumber Workers 500 boasted 1,300 new members in December, 1917. New objectives were outlined:

> Booze, gambling and contract work are three evils [noted the
> *Industrial Worker*] that the I.W.W. is out to clean up along with
> bad camp conditions. The three evils are deliberately fostered by
> the lumber barons who know that they are the means of keeping the
> workers enslaved. While the I.W.W. has no desire to do police work,
> still there is the idea that the woods belong to the workers, and as
> more power is gained the workers must control the industry to a
> greater extent. The woods must be made safe for the One Big Union
> and this cannot be done where booze is plentiful. The bootlegger
> is the best friend the boss has — run him out of camp!

Spurred by their victory of the eight-hour day, the I.W.W.
took a referendum on their next objective, the abolition of the
bindle and the supply of blankets by the companies. This
carried by 976 votes to 58 and later was made unanimous. Some
extremists among the Wobblies even went so far as to demand
bed linen but this was considered rather radical by many of the
fellow workers. May First was fixed as the deadline and on that
day in many camps great bonfires were made of lousy old
blankets and of double-tiered bunks as the companies hastened
to install decent sleeping accommodations.

By 1919 the timber beast had become a lumber worker. Gone
was the old bindle, gone the ten-hour day. With better pay he
could now afford a suitcase with store clothes and a pair of
shoes for city wear. It was the greatest victory the I.W.W. was
ever to win on the industrial field.

4

The Radicals and the War

In 1914 the war was "over there." For a country which had been pretty much minding its own business — aside from forays into its Caribbean backyard — the struggle between the German and British Empires caused only thankfulness that the United States was well out of it. By 1915 when J.P. Morgan & Company decided to help finance the British, for a price, and Charley Schwab's Bethlehem Steel became interested in building ships for the British merchant marine, socialists and radicals began to see the handwriting on the wall. The war cloud was creeping over America, as well.

The Socialist local in Everett well expressed the feeling of most socialists in the state when it adopted a resolution in March of 1915 stating: "Whereas, the socialists of Europe at this moment are busily engaged in murdering one another for the benefit of their capitalist masters, with no possibility of gain for themselves . . . we, the Socialists of the United States do hereby agree: That we shall allow the said capitalists to patriotically do all the fighting and dying for THEIR country; and we do hereby offer this pledge to them and to one another, as socialists, that we will under no circumstances take up arms in defense of THEIR country."

The anti-war sentiment was by no means the exclusive possession of socialists, the I.W.W., and other radicals. The day after the European conflict broke out, the Seattle Central Labor Council of the A.F. of L. declared:

Whereas, the appalling loss of life which will inevitably result, the inexpressible suffering from the systematic mangling and crippling of human bodies on a vaster scale than has ever before been possible, the laying waste of lands and the destruction of homes, the ensuing industrial depression, the agony of bereaved women, and the brutalizing of those who kill their kind — all these hideous results and more — will fall with crushing force on the working class alone, while the kings, capitalists and aristocrats remain in safety, and

Whereas, no possible outcome of such an international war can benefit to any extent whatever the workers, whose enemies are not the workers of other nations, but the exploiting class of every nation, and

Whereas, all the nations now preparing to do wholesale murder are nominally Christian, and a majority of those who do the killing are affiliated with the various churches of the Christian religion,

Therefore, as representatives of the organized working class, we declare the European war to be an international crime and a horror for which there is no parallel in savagery, and we denounce the church, which claims to be founded on the principle of peace and good will, for having failed to interpose its opposition to this orgy of blood;

We further declare that one reason for the suspicious eagerness with which the rulers of all these nations have entered into hostility is because of the universal industrial unrest and the growing spirit of working class solidarity which, if unchecked, threatens the present ruling class.

To all those workers of Europe who have resisted the war craze we extend our sympathy and respect, and we pledge our efforts against any attempt to draw our own country into a foreign war.

The resolution was introduced by Hulet M. Wells, the socialist whose fidelity to his views was to result in his spending nearly two years in the penitentiary. In 1915 he was elected president of the Central Labor Council.

In Seattle there were two ways of looking at the approach of war. The deadly equations that were to dominate American thinking for the next two generations assumed form in this period: War (or defense) equals jobs and prosperity; peace equals unemployment and depression. To the business interests war meant boom in the shipyards, boom in lumber, in shipping. While to the labor movement war meant jobs, there was still a realistic appraisal of war as death, brutality, and an end to the democratic hope. After the boom had taken up the slack in employment, reserve labor began flowing into Seattle, Tacoma, and other Puget Sound centers from eastward, and as it eventually turned out, the majority of these new workers were men who accepted the shipyards as a "better 'ole" than the trenches, for such employment meant exemption from the draft.

Anna Louise Strong, a member of the school board, led in forming a local branch of the American Union Against Militarism, to which flocked people from the churches, liberal organizations, the Central Labor Council, and the socialists, to agitate against involvement in the European bloodbath. They conducted street polls which indicated that 90 percent of the people were opposed to war. Many of them were encouraged when Wilson won re-election because "he kept us out of war."

To soften up the country for what was coming, a preparedness campaign was launched in 1916, to culminate in a Preparedness Day parade. Behind the campaign was Colonel Blethen and his *Seattle Times* and those who stood to profit from preparedness. On May 28, 1916, a short time before the scheduled parade, 3,500 met at Dreamland Rink to express their opposition. W. G. Beach of the University of Washington was prophetic in his remarks: "If the cry of larger armaments is answered, there will be more war, and worse war, if that is possible. In this preparedness program we are subjecting all our hope of better things to the domination of the warlike spirit." Mrs. C. E. Bogardus of the Mothers Congress declared that "you don't have to go out and shoot a man's head off to be courageous. We must teach our boys to have the courage to stay in the minority when a great moral issue is at stake." President Robert Bridges of the Port Commission announced that the commission's employees would not be dragooned into marching in the parade. "Too many Scotchmen," he said, "are dying in the trenches. I left Scotland with my eyes open, and nobody will ever shoulder a soldier on my back. What, I ask you, will the young man get by going in for militarism?" "A wooden leg," came the answer from an old man in the front row. Miss Strong said there was an effort to stampede the country into war. A minister in a New England munitions town, she related, had termed the war "a godsend to this community." W. D. Lane of the city council denounced "armor plate patriotism" and also promised that city employees would not be forced into the parade. President Hulet Wells of the Central Labor Council argued that the preparedness propaganda was furthered by munitions interests.

But the propaganda machine, in control of the avenues of communication, rolled on inexorably toward the declaration of war. On the eve of the declaration, the Central Labor Council, then representing 25,000 workers, unanimously adopted a resolution pleading with Wilson and the state's Congressional delegation to avoid war. A counter-resolution to run up the United States flag on the Labor Temple met with such a storm of opposition that its proponents prudently withdrew it. The debate indicated not so much aversion to the flag, as to those who waved it, à la Colonel Blethen, to fan the flames of war.

Once war was declared, it became impolitic to oppose it. For the first time since the lapsing of the alien and sedition laws in 1801, Congress passed a sedition law, bearing the misnomer of an espionage act. Under this law few spies were sent to jail, but hundreds of socialists, I.W.W.'s and other radicals were to feel the fury of the persecution. Up until 1917 there had been no federal legislation restricting freedom of expression except for a law which denied entry of anarchists — enacted after the assassination of President McKinley.

The Seattle branch of the American Union Against Militarism (whose civil liberties bureau, under young Roger Baldwin, was to become the forerunner of the American Civil Liberties Union) converted itself into the No-Conscription League as the battle line shifted from outright opposition to the war to a fight on the compulsory draft bill. Its weekly cafeteria luncheon meetings dwindled in attendance to a few dozen hardier souls who braved the daily blasts of the *Times*, the *P-I* and the *Star*. With the coming of war, the Scripps-McRae *Star*, which had been liberal and pro-labor, veered sharply to the right and out-Blethened the Colonel in its denunciations of the "traitors" within the gates who saw something less than perfection in a nation joining in the European slaughter at the very time when both sides, exhausted, were sending out feelers for peace. General Hugh S. Johnson, put in charge of the campaign to enact and administer the draft law, admitted years later that "in most states, except in the East, there was only aloof and skeptical if not sullen acquiescence. By the persuasive power of the eloquence and idealism of Woodrow Wilson, by some arts we used of blatant ballyhoo and hokum national high-pressure selling, that was changed in a few weeks to a war-psychosis which approached hysteria."

It was in this strident period that the faithful of the No-Conscription League held a fateful meeting to consider the publication of a leaflet calling for opposition to the pending legislation. Drafting of the appeal was assigned to Bruce Rogers, a socialist, a wounded Spanish-American war veteran, and somewhat of a literary bohemian, who had been editing the *Red Feather*, in opposition to the right-wing *Herald*. "The *Red Feather*," he proclaimed, "is neither a newspaper nor an educator; rather it is a corrective iconoclast, a sarcastic pragmatist, a counter-irritant and scourge of frauds." It was his idea to hire one of the newfangled aeroplanes to scatter red feathers over Seattle to advertise his paper and show his contempt for those of a yellow feather. From the Cuban campaign he gained not only an ugly leg wound but friendship with an old German socialist in Havana who put him "on the road to socialism." In 1912 Rogers had received 40,000 votes for state attorney-general on the Socialist ticket. The draft of Rogers' leaflet read, in part:

Resist! Refuse! Don't yield the first step toward conscription. Better to be imprisoned than to renounce your freedom of conscience. Let the financiers do their own collecting. Seek out those who are subject to the first draft. Tell them that we are refusing to register or to be conscripted and to stand with us like men, and say to the masters: "Thou shalt not Prussianize America."
We are less concerned with the autocracy that is abroad and remote than that which is immediate, imminent and at home. If we

are to fight autocracy the place to begin is where we first encounter it. If we are to break anybody's chains we must first break our own in the forging. If we must fight and die, it is better that we do it upon soil that is dear to us against our masters, than for them where foreign shores will drink our blood. Better mutiny, defiance and the death of brave men with the light of morning upon our brows, than the ignominy of slaves and death with the mark of Cain and our hands spattered with the blood of those we have no reason to hate.

The leaflet was headed: "No Conscription! No Involuntary Servitude!" quoting from the Constitution, and ended with Daniel Webster's words:

Where is it written in the Constitution . . . that you may take the children from their parents . . . and compel them to fight the battles of any war in which the folly or the wickedness of the government may engage?

Whatever misgivings some might have had about Rogers' frank and lurid prose, the leaflet was approved. Miss Strong asked Hulet Wells if he would take it to a printer. Wells agreed, and in March, 1917, placed the script before George P. Listman, an old-time unionist in charge of the Trade Printery, who agreed to print 20,000 copies.

The appearance of this leaflet galvanized the Seattle dailies. Shouting "Treason," they called for the cops. The *Star* ran the single word "SEDITION" in red ink clear across the front page. The Department of Justice at the time operated a rather modest Bureau of Investigation, later to burgeon into the FBI. Its operatives went into action. Into their dragnet fell Hulet Wells, Sam Sadler, and several other socialists. Wells' offense was that he had taken the copy to the printer; as for the others, they had helped to distribute it at union halls, on the docks, and around the shipyards. They were charged with conspiracy to obstruct, hinder, and delay the government in its prosecution of the war.

The government was aptly discriminating in falling first upon the socialists. The liberals and pacifists of the No-Conscription League withdrew discreetly into the background after the arrests. As for the I.W.W., after the declaration of war they abandoned the field of anti-war propaganda, preferring to fight the boss directly. They took no part in the No-Conscription League, disdaining to appeal to a President and a Congress owned by "the class enemy." Registering for what was euphemistically known as "selective service," they left to the conscience of individual members. Nevertheless the I.W.W. was to suffer more savagely from repressive legislation than even the socialists.

Despite the war, the American socialists, unlike their European comrades, had refused to haul down the Red Flag. At the St. Louis convention of the Socialist Party, held on April 7-9, 1917, immediately after the declaration of war, it was declared that "the only struggle which would justify the workers in taking up arms is the great struggle of the working class of the world to free itself from economic exploitation and political oppression, and we particularly warn the workers against the snare and delusion of so-called defensive warfare." An even more drastic statement than this, advanced by Louis B. Boudin of New York, won the support of Kate Sadler, representing Washington State socialists. To the sour satisfaction of proletarian elements in the party, many of the intellectual luminaries of socialism deserted; the apostasy of the "clerks" proved to them, as they had contended all along, that the destinies of a socialist party must be in the hands of the workers themselves.

Wells, Sadler, a former president of the longshoremen's local, and Aaron Fislerman and R. E. Rice, active socialists, were arrested May 28, 1917. Bruce Rogers was dissuaded from surrendering only by the insistence of legal counsel. Wells was suspended from his job at the City Light plant, just as he had been discharged years before from the post office for his union activities. Dr. Sydney Strong, pastor of the Queen Anne Congregational Church and father of Anna Louise Strong, and Charles W. Doyle, business agent of the Central Labor Council, made the $5,000 bond for Wells. The labor council elected a committee of five to aid in the defense of the indicted men. J. D. Ross, the liberal superintendent of City Light, reinstated Wells, on the ground that he had not circulated copies of the leaflet since enactment of the draft law. The morning *P-I* edi-

torialized on its front page in shocked surprise, "For Very
Shame, No!" City Hall later yielded to pressure from the business press and Wells was discharged.

The grand jury which indicted the four socialists included
in the indictment the names of 12 men accused of failing to
register for the draft, bringing the total of pending prosecutions
for that crime to 30 in the federal district court. The arrests of
the "slackers," so soon after the enactment of the law which
Wilson said was "in no sense a conscription of the unwilling,"
reflected the widespread hostility to the draft. Throughout the
country 75 percent of the draftees claimed exemption on one
ground or another; in King County outside Seattle the per-
centage ran up to 88 percent. The army had always been held
in rather low opinion by the public; to its ranks came recruits
from the poverty-stricken parts of the South, from those who
preferred life in army camps to working, and in no small
measure from some courts whose judges offered young delin-
quents a choice between jail and army. Even after the enactment of the "selective service" law, the Green Lake, Seattle,
painters' union moved in the Central Labor Council that it be
repealed, and this was voted after Wells, in supporting the
resolution, had been greeted, in the reluctant words of the *Star,*
with "deafening applause."

In the trial, held in September, 1917, the prosecution introduced the charge, oft-repeated and never proved, that there was
"German money" behind the No-Conscription League. Secretary James A. Duncan of the Central Labor Council and a
member of the League, hotly denied the charge. "The people
with whom we met were loyal Americans." But the objective of
the League and of enemy Germans was the same, pursued the
prosecutor. "They are not," retorted Duncan. "Our object is to
maintain whatever liberty and democracy we can."

George F. Vanderveer, who had won the acquittal of the 74
I.W.W.'s in the Everett case several months before, defended
the indicted socialists. Little above medium height, with a
strong, wiry build, close-cropped thinning hair, and a mind like

a steel trap, as Wells described him, Vanderveer prowled the courtroom with panther-like tread, hammering away on the main defense line that this was a free-speech case, that citizens have the right to oppose proposed legislation and to petition for its repeal when enacted. Vanderveer won judicial dismissal of two counts, those of conspiracy to use the mails for unlawful purposes and of conspiracy to obstruct the execution of the draft law — which was not enacted when the leaflet was first circulated. Charges against R. E. Rice were dismissed. Only the charge of conspiracy to obstruct by force the proclamation of war and the enactment of the national defense act remained for the jury. A wave of applause swept the courtroom when Wells closed the defense case, speaking on his own behalf. After 17 hours, the jury split, 7 to 5, for conviction, and was discharged. Fislerman was acquitted but the district attorney promptly announced that Wells and Sadler would be reindicted.

In the courtroom sat Anna Louise Strong, reporting the trial for the new Seattle daily, the *Call*. After the declaration of war she had fled to the slopes of Mount Rainier (she had been a pioneer in developing alpinism in the Cascades). "I left in truth," she wrote later, "because my courage and my heart were broken. Nothing in my whole life, not even my mother's death, so shook the foundations of my soul. The fight was lost, and forever! 'Our America' was dead! The profiteers, the militarists, the 'interests' had violated her and forced her to do their bidding. . . . I turned like a wounded beast to the hills for shelter." There during the summer she led parties on the glaciers, busy with problems of pack-trains, commissary, cooking, and hikes. It was the *Seattle Daily Call*, in its four pages, which said "what I wanted to say about the war. It said them in harsh words and poor English — the things that respectable folk had ceased to say. . . . The raw, red words of the *Seattle Daily Call* were balm on the wounds of my soul. The call for the workers of all lands to get together to end war gave me a reason for coming back from the mountains; it gave me a home again among men."

Certainly the *Call* was one of the most remarkable ventures in socialist journalism to appear in this country. It was created mainly in the imagination of an "amateur journalist," a wanderer who had only recently arrived in Seattle — Thorwald G. Mauritzen. True, the times were with Mauritzen. The acquittal of the Everett I.W.W. members had sent a thrill through the radical movement from Coast to Coast, and nowhere more so than in the Puget Sound country. Membership in the I.W.W. was shooting upward. Thousands of workers were flooding into Seattle to escape the draft by working in the shipyards, and among them were few admirers of Wilson and his war. They flocked into the A.F. of L. shipyard unions. The regular Wednesday night meetings of the Central Labor Council drew 250 delegates or more from constituent unions; the gallery in the Labor Temple's auditorium where the Council met was filled with unionists and radicals, listening to the dramatic debates and to speeches by visiting luminaries. The suppression of ordinary rights of free speech added zest and exhilaration to the scene as people struggled, in guarded and Aesopian terms, to express the ideas that burned within them. Above and beyond all that, something had happened in the world which drew Seattle labor out of its provincial isolation — the overthrow of the Czar in Russia. In Petrograd the Council of Workers, Soldiers and Sailors Deputies — the Soviet — was in constant session, building unions and workers' parties, and eying with ill-concealed distrust the maneuverings of the various bourgeois ministries which struggled with the chaos left by war and autocracy in a ravaged land. The Seattle radical movement, which had been in-looking all its life, suddenly became world conscious.

To Mauritzen, the Seattle scene was a revelation — the fresher to him because he looked at it with a newcomer's eye. The amateur journalist within him kindled with a dream of his — to start a socialist daily here and now. He calculated costs: 10,000 copies sold at 2 cents each meant a gross of $200 a day, or $100 net after the newsboys were paid off. He consulted with Henry

C. Pigott, a liberal printer who himself had always had a notion that a fearless paper was what Seattle needed. Pigott himself was no socialist — perhaps something of an old-line populist. He estimated for Mauritzen that he could turn out a four-page daily for about $100 a day. But as an earnest of Mauritzen's seriousness, he demanded a cash down deposit of $500. The idea was of course fantastic — $500 with which to start a daily paper. Even then, people knew that it took a cool million to put a new paper on the streets. Mauritzen talked it over with the comrades at the Socialist hall. These veterans of the class struggle had seen a half dozen socialist weeklies bloom and then wither on the vine in Seattle in the past ten years; they regarded the newcomer as a visionary and his idea as highly commendable but impractical. Years later Hulet Wells recalled his own reaction: "For rushing in where angels fear to tread, for sheer, callow naïveté and foolhardiness, I can think of nothing to equal starting a daily paper on a thousand dollars of capital. . . . yet in 1917 some hopeful young socialists raised a thousand dollars and launched the *Seattle Daily Call*. When the promoter [Mauritzen] told me his plans it gave me something to laugh about at a time when jokes were scarce. With conservative management I thought they might last a week."

Mauritzen was a short, stocky fellow of Norwegian extraction, self-described as "a cowboy, hobo, rancher, soapboxer, editor and publisher and a rebel who wouldn't stay put." Back in 1898 he had started *Welcome News*, an amateur journal which he continued to publish intermittently for the rest of his life, the final copies being printed in Los Angeles in the late 1940's. He had homesteaded in Idaho, and failed, and promoted a dozen enterprises, all doomed to extinction. In Seattle he was selling insurance, with an income of $25 a week, which was more than enough for his spartan needs.

Mauritzen raised the $500 and the first issue of the *Call* appeared July 28, 1917, with a blistering front-page story on "Pawnbrokers' Patriotism: An Attack on the Employers' Association of Washington." He had rented a loft in a building

which reared itself up from the side of a cliff by the waterfront,
connected with the business district by a long boardwalk. In it
he had installed some rough board tables and benches, an
antique typewriter, and a Mr. Wheeler, aged 75, who was
charged with the responsibility of producing a daily paper all
by himself. Wheeler, who wrote under the piquant name of
Bertuccio Dantino, naturally had to busy himself with shears
and pastepot to keep the linotypers busy. Fortunately there were
the socialist press, the New York papers, and especially the *New
York Call*, the socialist daily, to clip. The Seattle paper was
named for its older brother in Manhattan for presumably no
one in the socialist movement had ever heard of the old *Daily
Call* of 1886-1887 which had been a spokesman for the Knights
of Labor and the Seattle Labor Party. A pony service from
United Press furnished 500 words of copy (but the telegrapher
usually slipped Mauritzen the entire daily report). The first
issue was 5,000 copies, and nearly all were sold. Within a few
weeks the skid road was good for several thousand copies, newsboys hawked other thousands on the streets, docks, and at the
shipyard gates. Soon orders for bundles began flooding in from
other towns and from the logging camps.

Perhaps no group was more surprised at the continued publication of the *Call* than the socialists themselves. The Socialist
local gave its official imprimatur to what was after all
Mauritzen's private venture, and circulation climbed to 10,000
and then to 15,000. Within a short time Bertuccio Dantino's
efforts were reinforced by local news stories, including those
signed "Gale," Miss Strong's pen name on the paper. After a
time there were others: Marguerite Remington Charter, an
English lady whose knowledge of French came in handy in
translating from *L'Humanité*, the great Parisian socialist daily;
Charles Ashleigh, the English poet (the "only Wobbly without
overalls" and who even sported a cane) in charge of publicity
for the Everett and the conscription cases; Joe Pass, active with
other intellectuals in the Young People's Socialist League; his
brother, Morris, an artist and the only competent cartoonist in

local labor ranks; Hays Jones, one of the few University of Washington students attracted to radical ranks; Art Shields, later of the *Daily Worker;* Lena Morrow Lewis, who prided herself on a knowledge of Marxism; Paul Bickel, a high school teacher who used the pen name of Mark Stone; and John McGivney, later the editor of the *Tacoma Labor Advocate,* the A.F. of L. weekly. Nearly all these worked in their spare time or between jobs in the camps, for the Mauritzen venture afforded little in the way of salaries. Ashleigh, the Wobbly publicist, came by his radicalism in London while working as a clerk in the Fabian Society, where he became acquainted with Shaw, Wells, and other luminaries of Fabianism. In 1907 he joined the hunger marchers from South Wales. After traveling through South America he landed in Portland, Oregon, and got into a Wobbly free-speech fight there. From then until 1917, when he was indicted under the espionage act, he worked up and down the coast, usually on the business press. In the 1930's he was on the staff of the *Moscow Daily News.*

Mauritzen, the publisher, got $12 a week, the top wage, for the onerous task of seeing that Pigott's bill was paid daily out of receipts from the previous day. The story goes that when he was behind on the printer's bill he would appeal to Sam Sadler, who had a way with the dice in crap games. After a few hours Sadler would return with enough to wipe out the day's deficit. I gave a hand to the stereotyper in pouring lead for the molds, swept out the office, and wrote editorials while learning the knack of writing news stories. Eventually I had the distinction of seeing my name on the masthead as editor, a rather melancholy honor which others declined because it was the editor who took the rap when the cops asked for the person in charge. McGivney, freshly back from Nome, Alaska, where he had edited the *Nome Industrial Worker,* the miners' daily, assumed responsibility for getting out the paper. He could be found occasionally out on the boardwalk staring sorrowfully and helplessly down at the waterfront below, wondering how soon the Department of Justice would show up to inquire into some of

the stronger statements of Miss Strong and Mrs. Lewis. Getting
out a socialist daily in wartime was a delicate adventure in tight-
rope walking. The *Call* never acquired second-class mailing
rights and was forced to pay commercial rates on the bundles
mailed out of town — part of the heavy financial burden borne
by Mauritzen. The government could hardly have been expected to look with favor on a paper which ran this kind of
editorial:

No labor organization, be it political or industrial, is worth pre-
serving or fighting for which does not aim at the overthrow of the
capitalist system and the substitution thereof the industrial democracy of the workers of the world. This is neither treasonable nor
seditious. The Constitution of the United States guarantees to
American citizens the right of Revolution — when they have the
might.

The *Industrial Worker*, the Seattle I.W.W. weekly, admiringly
reprinted the editorial.

The world was ablaze in 1917 with war and revolution, and
the *Call* did not lack for dramatic news. From Mexico came
dispatches about the world's first socialist revolution, which had
nailed the revolutionary ideology to the Querétaro Constitution;
from Petrograd, the manifestoes of the Russian socialist parties;
from the European countries, news of vast mutinies in the
armed forces and incipient rebellion against the continuing
senseless slaughter. As terror against the radical movement
mounted across the homeland, the *Call* reported the vigilante
hanging of the I.W.W. stalwart, Frank Little, from a Butte
trestle, the progress of the Wobbly strike in the logging camps,
the cruel repression of copper miners in Arizona and Montana,
the nation-wide raids on the I.W.W. halls, the efforts to throt-
tle the socialist press, the beginning of the "deportation delirium" against foreign-born radicals, the recall of Anna Louise
Strong from the school board, the arrest of the Pass brothers and
Louise Olivereau on anti-conscription charges, the outbreak of
the Soviet Revolution in November, 1917 (reported as a "social-
ist-anarchist uprising!"), the arrival of the first Soviet ship in
Seattle. The news was such as to make the *Call* a lively paper,
whatever the deficiencies of its staff!

To the business press the *Call* was "the red pamphlet," "the daily I.W.W. pamphlet" and there was a good bit of uncertainty as to how to deal with this strange paper that survived somehow with the meagerest advertising. For the most part the *Call* kept within the bounds of legality; its readers were sophisticated enough to know what the editors were talking about and there was no need to spell out ideas that would doom the existence of the paper. For that reason it became necessary to take extra-legal action. The Minute Men had been organized to spur flagging enthusiasm for the war effort; their main activity was to watch neighbors for signs of sedition. Perhaps the official denial of second-class mailing rights announced by the Post Office Department late in December, 1917, encouraged these elements. On a Saturday night, January 5, 1918, when the city ordinarily was crowded with sailors, a mob suddenly swooped down on the Pigott print shop, a short distance from the *Call* office. Armed with clubs and bars, they assaulted the printers working on the night shift and then proceeded to belabor the linotypes, presses, and office equipment. Ignorant of printing processes, none of the hoodlums knew how to start the machinery so that it could be ruined; the equipment was badly mauled but remained serviceable after superficial repairs; the *Call* was able to publish a Sunday "extra." More serious were the dumping of cases of movable type on the floor and the attack on office furniture and files. The damage was estimated at $15,000. The Navy suspended shore leave after the riot, the printing trades' unions denounced the assault on their members and on the free press, in which they were joined by the Central Labor Council, but it was not until January 12 that two of the mob's ringleaders were arrested. They turned out to be G. Merle Gordon and J. Fred Drake; promptly bailed out, they were given jobs with the government's Spruce Division which was warring with the I.W.W. in the logging camps. The Spruce Division asked that the cases be dropped because if the raid on the Pigott plant was a crime, at least it was "a patriotic crime." Brought up for trial, the pair pleaded a temporary "emotional insanity," despite an admission that they had been paid $1,000 by the

Chamber of Commerce to mobilize the sailors, and were let off
with an admonition to go and sin no more. Nevertheless Gordon
was arrested awhile later in Portland on charges of swindling.

Early in 1918 the hot breath of the draft board was being felt
down the necks of many of the young staff members of the *Call*.
Mauritzen, the financial genius, had to go to work in the shipyards to avoid the draft, and others went into the Merchant
Marine or sought other escape hatches.

Another amateur journalist, Harry Ault, editor of the A.F. of
L. weekly *Union Record,* regarded the *Call* with mixed emotion.
To him it proved that his long-held dream of a labor daily was
practical, for if a little socialist-I.W.W. daily could sustain itself,
certainly a paper backed officially by the union movement could
do even better. On the other hand the *Call's* continued existence
jeopardized his own plans. Fortunately there was a liaison between the *Call* and the *Union Record.* Sam Sadler, a stocky,
broad-shouldered pugnacious socialist who had been active in
the longshoremen's union, had a dual role. He was not only
close to members of the *Call's* board as a leading socialist, but as
a unionist he was on a committee of the Central Labor Council
appointed to promote a daily *Union Record.* The *Call* expired
April 22, 1918, having achieved the remarkable feat of publishing 228 issues under extraordinary circumstances. On April 24
the daily *Union Record,* the first labor union daily in America,
appeared on the streets. Instead of the *Call's* four pages and
15,000 circulation, the *Union Record* printed 12 to 24 pages,
had a circulation that climbed quickly from 25,000 to 50,000,
and carried a substantial volume of advertising.

By 1917 the throngs which came out to hear favored speakers,
to commemorate events such as May Day, or to protest the latest
atrocity had far outgrown the capacity of Seattle's largest halls.
In fair weather it became the custom to hold such rallies on
vacant lots near the business district which were being held idle
for realty appreciation. In mid-1917 national peace forces had
reorganized into the People's Council but a local meeting of
that organization to hear James H. Maurer, member of the

Pennsylvania legislature and president of the Pennsylvania Federation of Labor, was broken up. His theme, "Is Conscription Constitutional?" was considered too subversive to stand public discussion. On August 16 the People's Council held all-day sessions at the Labor Temple. Among the speakers were Mrs. Alice Parks of Palo Alto, California; Elizabeth Freeman, an Englishwoman; Mrs. Hannah Sheehy Skeffington, widow of the Easter Rebellion leader in Dublin; and Charles Erskine Scott Wood, the Portland, Oregon, writer and lawyer. To the mass meeting in the evening, held on an open lot, at least 4,000 poured out, according to the hostile press, and it is likely that the crowd was double that number. According to the *P-I*, Dr. Sydney Strong's "I.W.W. following" was out in full strength. While the I.W.W. contributed to the throng, it was pretty much a socialist rally. H. W. Watts of the *Northwest Worker*, the Everett socialist weekly, H. W. Pohlman, president of the iron molders' union and member of the *Call's* board, George N. Hanson and W. F. Johnson of the *Call*, Sam and Kate Sadler, Bruce Rogers, the anarchist Louise Olivereau, Herbert Mahler of the I.W.W. and Harry Ault of the *Union Record* were among the speakers and leaders.

While Kate Sadler was speaking, the police thought they heard her refer to Wilson as a "traitor." After her speech, they nabbed her and led her away from the platform. The astonished crowd, seeing what was happening to Seattle's best-beloved radical orator, closed in and rescued her. The police sought safety in flight and Kate returned to the rostrum in triumph. The next day the police showed up at her home where she found herself badly outnumbered and suffered another of her innumerable arrests.

Kate Sadler was the most extraordinary person in the Seattle radical movement. The best known nationally of any of the Seattle socialists, she never served the Socialist Party in any paid position, offering her oratorical and organizing services wherever required for the price of transportation, which she could not afford. Her husband, Sam, was a longshoreman whose chancy employment was their only income. Of her, Hulet Wells, a man not much given to emotional outbursts, wrote:

Brave, generous, tender, loyal, uncompromising Kate! The best of her life she gave to the workers. Wherever their cause led she followed. From Alaska to Oregon the toilers of our camps and mills knew her as their champion. Massed in thousands around her soapbox or platform, they hung upon the simple eloquence of her appeal for solidarity. She refused even such moderate compensation as her popularity brought her. All her life had been a struggle with poverty.

In the Pacific Northwest Kate was the peerless socialist orator and among women was rivalled nationally only by Kate Richards O'Hare and Elizabeth Gurley Flynn. Often she was the collection speaker at socialist rallies, but she disdained the tiresome eastern "Who will give?" gambit. Her talk, pitched on a class struggle theme, would rise gradually to its climax when she might lift her arms in a ringing appeal, such as "Oh, Labor, Labor, when will you know your strength?" The silver dollars would begin raining on the platform; the girls would pass the baskets through the audience. When the collection was finished, Kate finished, without having once mentioned the sordid subject of "funds."

A young socialist of the time remembers her in these words:

Kate was a mature, lovable human being. Mature in her thinking, mature in her work, and in her maturity she retained the dance of life. Kate was a happy person and because of her joy in living, her anger at injustice turned into thunder and lightning. When workers called for help, in strikes, jailings, free speech struggles, Kate came. Kate, the fearless one, the Joan of Arc! The police, of course, knew her, always hesitated to drag her off the soapbox, for the workers formed an iron ring, daring them to touch *our* Kate.

She was ingenious and loaded with common horse sense. In all serious situations she insisted on facts, facts, all angles, before acting. Then to work. I was told of a black period in the Puget Sound country when an anti-Japanese, anti-Chinese wave struck Seattle. Kate took to the streets to oppose it, from the skidroad up and down. Even Sam because of his union activities clammed up. Kate disagreed. Day and night, seven days a week, she swam against the tide, for the militant unions which should have been at her side were reactionary to the core on the Oriental issue. Wherever workers gathered, for lunch, for evening strolls, waterfront, boarding houses,

there you found Kate and her soapbox. Her technique was humor
and a first cousin to satire. That was always Kate in a dangerous
situation.

Kate was born in poverty in Scotland and learned socialism
at her father's knee. While working in Wanamaker's in Philadelphia she met Sam and they went West to Seattle about 1909.

Another woman, no orator or leader like Kate, was Louise
Olivereau, a quiet, heavy-set, dark-eyed, motherly kind of woman
in whose breast burned an utter loathing of war. Although an
anarchist of Tolstoian cast, she drew the devotion of many of
the young socialists of Seattle. The coming of war shattered her;
the enactment of the draft law drove her to desperation. At the
time she was working in the I.W.W. office, but every spare
moment and spare penny she devoted to drafting appeals to
young men not to register. These she sent through the mails;
many were distributed furtively at dawn by young socialists who
also painted Resist Conscription slogans on sidewalks and walls.
Miss Olivereau made little effort to conceal her own activities.
After the September, 1917, raids on I.W.W. halls during which
anti-draft leaflets were discovered by federal operatives in her
desk, she was arrested. Freely she admitted having sent out 2,000
circulars urging resistance. She was hustled over to Tacoma,
where most federal prisoners of the area were lodged in the
Pierce County jail (the King County jail in Seattle apparently
was too close to the Wobbly hall). On November 30 she was
tried. She refused legal counsel, pleaded guilty, and insisted only
on her right to explain her activities — an eloquent speech to
the jury. Miss Olivereau was sentenced to ten years, refused to
take an appeal, and was sent to Cañon City, Colorado, where
she served nearly three years. The perfect type of uncompromising anarchist, she flew to her fate like a moth to the candle.*

News of the arrest of Mooney and Billings in the San Francisco Preparedness Day bomb frameup reached Robert Minor, a
former cartoonist for the *New York World,* while he was cover-

*For a more detailed account of Louise Olivereau's life and her trial,
see Appendix Two.

ing the fruitless Pershing expedition which was trying to locate Pancho Villa in the mesquite and arroyos of northern Mexico. He tossed up the well-paying but distasteful assignment for a newspaper syndicate and got to San Francisco as fast as he could. Minor showed up in Seattle soon after as publicity representative for the Mooney-Billings committee and got a rapturous reception at the Central Labor Council. The editor of the *Star* was asked if he would run an interview with Minor. "Yes," he answered, "if Mr. Minor will draw a cartoon for me." Minor did, and the cartoon and Mooney interview were featured in the *Star,* which then claimed the largest circulation in Seattle.

About this time the "federals" began descending upon the foreign-born, raiding their halls and driving them into detention camps by the dozen and the score. An early victim was Ragnar Johansson, a silvery-voiced I.W.W. orator whose lilting Swedish so fascinated native-born radicals that it seemed they could understand his musical tongue. The Swedes and Finns constituted the main national minorities in the Pacific Northwest, and many of them continued in this region their old-country occupations as loggers and sawmill workers. Both groups guarded carefully their culture, expressed particularly in song and drama. The Swedes even had an I.W.W. Skandinavsk Sång Bok, containing the familiar Wobbly songs, international labor hymns, and songs from their native land. The Finns and Swedes prided themselves on their hall — invariably a well-built, well-kept building with a large auditorium and stage, many smaller rooms, always a library, and a spotless kitchen. A strong temperance vein ran through these national groups and not even beer was tolerated in many of the halls but an enormous business was done in their cafes in coffee and pastries. The Finns published their own socialist daily, *Toveri,* in Astoria, Oregon, a town dominated by Finns; even today a daily I.W.W. paper, *Industrialisti,* is published in Duluth, Minnesota. And to this day Finnish halls up and down the Pacific Coast remain often the only centers of free assembly.

On the raw frontier of the Pacific Northwest there was little enough of cultural life in the radical movement, aside from the foreign-language groups. Young Seattle radicals, inspired by the *Masses,* the brilliant New York monthly, organized a club which sponsored lectures on politics, literature, history, and art. Jay Fox, the Home colonist, spoke on syndicalism and anarchism; Morris Pass and a Japanese artist lectured on art; Joe Pass on Jack London, Frank Norris, Walt Whitman; Charles Ashleigh on the dance. News of this cultural club reached the University of Washington campus and several faculty members took a hand in discussion periods.

The Pass brothers persuaded Secretary Duncan of the Central Labor Council that the lobby of the Labor Temple might well be used for an art exhibit. Cartoons from the *Masses* by Art Young, Maurice Becker, John Sloan, Boardman Robinson, Bob Minor, and Glen Coleman were mounted, and a leaflet printed to describe the exhibit. Unionists enjoyed the show, guffawing over some of the more palpable hits on "the ruling class." The exhibit, in its way, revealed some of the essence of the Puget Sound country of those days — against the background of jailings, brutality, harsh working conditions, and even the massacre of dissidents, a belief in the true dignity of man, a militancy, the dream of a good world. The workingman faced reality, in his living conditions, in his relations with his employer and with his society, less clouded by far than now when truth is masked by the mass media.

Anna Louise Strong, who had started out as a kind of Christian humanitarian, developing into a militant pacifist before the declaration of war, and who had been given an insight into the inferno of working-class life by reporting the Everett trial for Eastern papers, became a main witness in the Wells-Sadler trial. Both Wells and Attorney Vanderveer warned her that involvement in the trial would be her end, politically, as a member of the school board and a respectable liberal adornment of the Seattle Establishment. Nevertheless she testified and was helpful in getting a hung jury. The respectables of the city turned against her and instituted proceedings to recall her from the

school board. But the campaign languished. A woman stopped
in front of recall headquarters to regard the placards. "What
are they recalling her for?" she asked. "She's against the war,"
came the answer. "My God, who isn't?" said the woman, and
passed on.

The campaign would have died a-borning had it not been for
Anna Louise's interest in the case of her fellow-pacifist, Louise
Olivereau. Louise asked her for moral comfort at her trial and
Miss Strong sat beside her. That was all that was needed. A
member of the school board befriending an anarchist who had
urged men to resist conscription! The recall campaign came
alive of a sudden, spurred on by the three business dailies. The
Federation of Women's Clubs, the Parent-Teachers Association,
the University Women's Club, the Municipal League, which
had urged her election, now turned against her. "Is anyone on
your side?" a friend asked Miss Strong. "Oh, yes," she answered,
"the boilermakers with 7,000 members, the blacksmiths, the
longshoremen, the machinists, the electricians, the Metal Trades
Council, even the conservative Building Trades Council" —
nobody who was anybody, just the working people of Seattle.
The three business dailies campaigned against her; only the *Call*
supported her. Nevertheless when the votes were counted, she
was recalled by a margin of only 2,000 votes out of 85,000. It
was a pyrrhic victory for the war forces; the Strong advocates
celebrated their "victorious defeat" at the Labor Temple. For
Miss Strong the campaign had been enlightening. Lena Morrow
Lewis, the didactic Marxist at the *Call*, had often corrected Miss
Strong's un-Marxist editorial deviations, but somehow the class
struggle was creeping through her naïveté. It rather emphasized
a point about "Marxism" in the Seattle radical movement.
Not too many in the socialist movement could be considered
students of Marxism. As Frans Bostrom, the secretary of the
Tacoma Socialist Party, observed after reading the *Call:* "It's
revolutionary alright, but it's not Marxist." Whatever Marxism
existed was emotional rather than intellectual; perhaps events
were whirling past too fast to permit a theoretical examination

of their meaning. To be sure, the Young People's Socialist League (Yipsels) insisted that all new members take courses in the classic Marxist pamphlets such as *Value, Price, and Profit* and *Wage Labor and Capital*. But the expounders were apt to know little more than their students about the profundities of Marxist theory, and talk easily drifted away into news of the latest strike, arrest, deportation, or atrocity, such as the assassination of Jean Jaurès. Action was the watchword, there was so much to be done, and theory could wait. It was a weakness, but preferable to the arid debates that went on in the musty little Socialist Labor Party hall in an old rookery down on Second Avenue. Far more interesting was it to discuss the latest details about the arrest of Bruce Rogers, who had gone to Nome to succeed John McGivney as editor of the Nome daily *Industrial Worker*, published by Local 240 of the Mine, Mill & Smelter Workers Union. He was charged with sedition for some remarks before a gold miners' meeting. Stories floated back from Nome on the first boat out in the spring that contact had been established between the Nome miners and the Bolsheviks from across the narrow strait — certainly an historic event if it ever took place. One story told of a Nome miner who had made his way over the ice to greet the Russians. On his return he was jailed. Another reported that the miners' union considered declaring a Soviet in Nome. Cooler heads argued that when the ice broke up the federals would come in and round up the entire camp.

But the Bolshevik revolution sailed right into Elliott Bay around Christmas of 1917, in the persons of 63 sailors on the good ship "Shilka." Its arrival was a nine-day wonder not only in Seattle but throughout the nation. The business press went to work on the "Shilka" — it carried $100,000 in gold for the I.W.W., its hold concealed munitions for starting a Bolshevik revolution in America, its crew hid bombs in their pockets. The prosaic fact was that the "Shilka" carried nothing more explosive than a cargo of licorice root, peas, and beans, its crew members were unarmed, and the captain, contrary to rumors that the crew had mutinied, was still in command. To be sure the

sailors after leaving Vladivostok had declared a "soviet" aboard
— a strange term which translated into nothing more menacing
than "council" — and had decreed a six-hour day, and the skipper, Captain Boris Budelov, whether willingly or not, had acceded to his new status as a "comrade" who took orders from the
ship's council on all matters aside from navigation. "All of us
are Bolsheviki," the mate explained to the *Industrial Worker,* in
a lengthy interview. Sailors had been divided into three grades;
now, he said, there were only first-class sailors aboard. The
federals surrounded the "Shilka" at her berth, arrested Captain
Budelov and held the crew incommunicado for several days until
the Central Labor Council was able to lift the iron curtain and
to express to the captain "fraternal greetings of organized labor
in Seattle for the organized workers of Russia in their struggle
for industrial and political democracy." Then the "Shilka's"
crew proudly paraded from the dock to the Wobbly hall where
they got a rousing reception upon announcing that they had
elected a committee of five to run the vessel's internal economy.
But when Seattle Russians pressed around the ship to greet their
fellow-countrymen, the federals arrested 27 of them, many of
whom were held for deportation. The "Shilka" left harbor on
January 8, 1918, with its band on the foredeck playing the
"Marseillaise," and hundreds of local well-wishers waving it
bon voyage. To many dock workers the presence of a band on a
tramp ship was also a wonder — who had ever heard of bands
on cargo boats?

The federals swept down on 58 Italian and Russian workingmen. The crime of the Italians was that they subscribed to a
presumably subversive paper, the anarchist *Cronaca Soversiva.*
The offense of the Russians, aside from their interest in the
"Shilka," was that they belonged to the Russian Workers Union,
whose main target had been the subversion of the Czar. This
mission achieved, they were jailed and held with the Italians for
deportation. Since many were workers in the coal fields lying in
the hills behind Seattle, the United Mine Workers furnished

bail and legal assistance. Charles Ashleigh was arrested in San
Francisco and found himself lodged in the same cell with Tom
Mooney. Ashleigh's deportation however was postponed to per-
mit him to serve part of a 20-year sentence in Leavenworth.
J. A. MacDonald, editor of the *Industrial Worker*, was deported
to Canada with many other Canadians.

The federals also descended on the state office of the Socialist
Party in Everett and arrested Secretary Emil Herman. At his
trial the government was triumphantly able to produce an anti-
war sticker, pasted on to an old bookcase, and copies of an
address to soldiers attributed falsely to Jack London. He was
sentenced to ten years on McNeil Island, the government's penitentiary which defaced an otherwise beautiful fir-clad island in
Puget Sound. About the same time H. W. Watts, editor of the
Northwest Worker, the official state socialist weekly published
in Everett and by far the best-edited and oldest-established
socialist paper in Washington, was seized and deported to
Canada as an undesirable alien. Socialists, I.W.W., and radicals,
among them Paul Haffer of Tacoma, who resisted conscription
received unusually harsh sentences ranging up to 25 years.

Before the war there had been in effect little of a border
between the United States and Canada and many workers
shifted back and forth between Washington and British Columbia in seasonal employment. The British Columbia labor movement was dominated by the Socialist Party of Canada, a far more
truly Marxist and sophisticated party than the American. The
B.C. Federationist, the A.F. of L. weekly in Vancouver, was the
best-edited of any labor paper on the West Coast, and on the
board of the B. C. Federation of Labor were many old-timers
from the Welsh mines, Lancashire mills, and the metal works of
the black Midlands — men who had forgotten more about Marx
and Engels than their counterparts in the rather raw socialist
movement in neighboring Washington ever knew.

The flow of radical workingmen across the Canadian border
was even more pronounced in the movement between Alaska
and Seattle, its point of contact with the rest of the country.

John McGivney, Lena Morrow Lewis, Bruce Rogers, Joe Pass,
Art Shields, and many others active in the Seattle labor movement had also worked in Alaska. McGivney, trained in a Jesuit
college in Ireland, served as editor of the *Nome Industrial
Worker.* To young radicals in Seattle, who knew him on the
daily *Call,* he was the ideal of a labor editor — well informed on
trade union strategy, labor history, economics, and socialism.
He could turn readily from a discussion of Marxist surplus value
to the novel, poetry, and drama, somewhat of a rarity in those
circles. He considered Daniel De Leon, the giant of the Socialist
Labor Party, as the best-informed man in the country.

Lena Morrow Lewis was assigned before the war to help bring
the message of socialism to the interior of Alaska. Daughter of a
Presbyterian minister, she had been graduated from Monmouth
College in 1892 and served the next six years as lecturer for the
Women's Christian Temperance Union which at that time had
an influential radical wing. After a fling in the woman suffrage
movement, she became the first woman member of the national
executive committee of the Socialist Party, from 1900 to 1911.
Unlike the stellar women orators of the movement, she was
more at home on the lecture platform than the soapbox. From
her experiences in Alaska, Mrs. Lewis veered from a somewhat
rightist position in socialist politics to centrist.

The Socialist local in Fairbanks met in the cabin of a Negro.
There it was decided to take over the local weekly, run by an
odd character out of the *Spoon River Anthology:* printer, editor,
publisher, advertising manager, newsboy — all rolled into one,
and also the town atheist. In return for good Alaska gold that
could be used in the saloons, he turned over the paper during
the long winter months to his socialist friends, and was salvaged
only at press time to get the press rolling — a feat only he could
achieve. Mrs. Lewis and her co-workers set the type and contributed the copy, which was avidly read by the miners, whose
Tanana Valley union had just been smashed. Arguments raged
during the long Alaskan winter nights — Lena quoting eter-
nally from Kautsky while the opposition countered with Debs'

Arise, Ye Slaves! and choice bits from Bill Haywood's writings. The miners turned out in droves for the socialist meetings and Mrs. Lewis became a prized possession in their lives: she was a friend, guide, and — it being Alaska in those days — one of the few women in town. In the congressional election, the Socialist candidate came in second, and close to the top.

5

The Unions Fight Back

The shipyards of Seattle turned out a fourth of all the tonnage built in the United States during the First World War. They also held the records for speedy launchings: 10,000-ton ships slipped down the ways 11 weeks after their keels were laid. The ships ranged from large steel cargo boats to scores of smaller wooden vessels, built because there wasn't enough steel to meet the deadly efficacy of the German U-boats which sank 2,000,000 tons of Allied shipping between February and April, 1917.

Manning the yards were 30,000 workers, most of whom had never seen a shipyard before. Around the core of several thousand skilled Seattle metal trades workers were added skilled newcomers from the interior and thousands of men unskilled in the crafts but quickly trained to do single operations.

The largest of the yards was Skinner & Eddy, where ten thousand men toiled around the clock in a 30-acre wilderness of roaring machines, whirling belts, and belching fires. Hulet Wells, who worked in that yard, gives this description:

The men worked wordlessly for one had to scream to be heard. Masts that had been tall trees moored the taut cables that swung great sheets of steel to clothe the ribs of the vessels. There were loftsmen, fitters, welders, winchmen, pattern makers, anglesmiths, riggers, riveters, bolters-up, cranemen, lathemen, furnacemen, press and machine operators, boilermakers, drillers, reamers, blacksmiths, machinists, electricians, molders, carpenters and painters. The huge skeletons stood on the ways near the water; back of the ways ceaseless traffic carried materials from the shops ranged against the street wall. In the shops were blast furnaces, giant shears, punch presses and table rolls. Boilers reverberated, planers screamed, long white-hot rods were shoved into bolt machines. On the angle-bending floor blackened men beat a tattoo with heavy sledges while steam hammers clattered and thumped. Ram presses straightened out the plates, bending rolls bent them to shape, press brakes flanged them and jogglers bevelled their edges. Lathes of all shapes and sizes were scattered about. High overhead rolled huge cranes with little houses on them where the cranemen sat peering down to catch the signals. Jib cranes and hand hoists did the lighter lifting. Outside, small trucks rushed about with clanging loads of metal, winches creaked, magnetic cranes let fall their jangling burdens, carborundum grinders whined and fizzed, and air hammers, chippers, drills and reamers swelled the raucous cacophony. It was Dante's *Inferno* and Chaplin's *Modern Times*, all in one.

The yards were organized, in accordance with a national agreement by which the unions gave up the right to strike during wartime in return for recognition. Largest of the shipyard unions was Local 104 of the Boilermakers and Iron Shipbuilders, whose membership at the peak ranged up to 20,000. Before the war it had had only a few hundred members. Next in size were Machinists Hope Lodge 79 and the Shipyard Laborers with about 4,000 each, and then a score of crafts, many with more than a thousand members each. These came together in the Metal Trades Council, which met weekly to consider major strategy and became by far the most progressive wing of the labor movement.

These locals and those from other branches of the movement were represented in the Central Labor Council, the main voice of Seattle unionism. The building trades, older and more traditional in their approach to union problems, had their own council. In addition there were sections for the maritime, service, and other trades. But there was no question that the Central Labor Council spoke for all unions and that the final decisions of labor were made on the floor of the Council in the Labor Temple in the weekly sessions on Wednesday evenings, meetings that opened at eight and often lasted far after midnight when especially crucial issues were at stake on which delegates disagreed.

For years the Central Labor Council had been known as a progressive labor body; in many a convention of the A.F. of L. the only vote cast against Samuel Gompers' inevitable re-election as president came from the Seattle body. To its enemies it was "radical," but most delegates would have denied that. What characterized the Seattle union movement in far greater measure than that of most cities was that its members saw their class relationship realistically and acted on their convictions with courage. The fate of Tom Mooney in San Francisco weighed heavily upon them because he was a union man, persecuted for his militant unionism — and no more was needed in the way of evidence when he was framed for the Preparedness Day bomb outrage. Had not Captain Dollar, the San Francisco shipping magnate, in the course of an open-shop drive there, threatened "to fill the ambulances with union men"? It was so, too, with Hulet Wells and Sam Sadler, both respected delegates to the Council. That they were also socialists was not the main concern of the Council; that they had devoted their lives to the advancement of unionism was the determining argument in the Council's staunch support of them when they were indicted for sedition. It was so when hoodlums raided the Pigott printing plant to stop the *Daily Call;* union men had been assaulted, the freedom of the press had been menaced, and the Council voted unanimous support. Conservative delegates from the building trades had little stomach for the *Call*'s radicalism or for the beliefs of socialists, but faced with a union issue, they added their voice to the unanimity.

In this cohesiveness and courage the Central Labor Council had invaluable allies in the business press of the city: the florid Toryism of Colonel Blethen and his evening *Times;* the cold, pitiless reactionism of the morning *P-I;* the demagogy of the Scripps *Star* which with the coming of war outdid its competitors in vilifying the labor movement. The voice of the business press was all too clearly the voice of the enemy and its tirades against radicals were properly evaluated. As Jay Fox, the old Home colonist serving then on the staff of the *Union Record,* observed: "The newspapers rule the minds of the majority. The government merely keeps the minority in check. Without the newspapers, the present order could not stand a month."

There had of course been a strong but never dominant socialist wing in the Council for years. Harry Ault had become secretary of the Council in 1912 and while he was no longer a member of the Socialist Party, socialist thought was strong in his mind. In 1915 when he became editor of the official weekly, the *Union Record*, he supported red-headed James A. Duncan for secretary. Duncan, a man of fiery speech and pronounced progressive tendencies, had come from Scotland soon after the turn of the century and had gone to work in a shipyard as a machinist. Although he won his papers as a ship's machinist mate, he abandoned the sea and in 1906 became a delegate from Hope Lodge 79 of the machinists to the Council. Duncan disclaimed adherence to socialist principles but with Ault helped to elect Hulet Wells president of the Council in 1915. To balance Duncan, the conservatives in the Council elected Charles W. Doyle of the painters as business agent, a position he held for a generation.

As far back as 1911 the Central Labor Council had endorsed the concept of industrial unionism, the main plank in the I.W.W. program, as the ideal form of organization. While at times it backed candidates of the Socialist Party when both old parties put up unacceptable candidates, the Council tended to work rather toward a concept of political action along the lines of the British Labour Party, but with the cooperation of farmers. In 1911 the council joined with the Washington Federation of Labor (the statewide A.F. of L. group), the Grange, and the Farmers Union in a campaign to defeat anti-labor legislation, and that cooperation continued through the years.

Solidarity with the Grange became even more pronounced under the progressive leadership of William Bouck, its master. This Sedro-Woolley, Washington, farmer was spokesman for thousands of poorer farmers, "stump-ranchers," families trying to make a living from meager holdings in the Puget Sound area, and in the dry-farming and irrigated areas east of the Cascades. The farmers were no more enamoured of the war than the workers and Master Bouck, a tough man of old American stock, was less inclined than city folk to have his mouth shut by the "pay-

trioteers." In 1918 when the Grange met in annual convention
in Walla Walla, vigilantes were able to prevent them from
meeting in any public hall; the Grange retired to a high school
auditorium where the vigilantes broke in and disrupted the convention, forcing the farmers to flee. Bouck soon after was arrested under the Espionage Act for declaring that it was a rich
man's war which should be paid for out of the rich man's war
profits rather than through the bellies of poor people. Bouck's
remarks were in line with the demand of the Central Labor
Council and the State Federation of Labor that the prices of
foodstuffs be fixed and that an income tax siphon off all war
profits. "Those who want war," observed the *Union Record,*
"should perforce pay for the war. They will not serve in the
trenches; let them serve with their fortunes." Bouck's arrest had
the desired effect of stopping in its tracks an initiative campaign
to establish state cooperative markets to reduce the high cost of
living.

The U.S. Supreme Court had just struck down the state law,
won through the initiative, to outlaw the collection of fees by
job sharks; and the State Supreme Court had followed up by
practically abolishing the right to picket, although a referendum
to this effect had just been defeated by popular vote. The U.S.
Supreme Court had also ruled that it was a punishable conspiracy for workers to organize and strike for the union shop.
"The decision," said the *Union Record,* "will but add fuel to
the flame of contempt for the courts that has been growing ever
stronger amongst the workers." The Central Labor Council
decided to withdraw from membership in the local fountain-
head of reaction, the Chamber of Commerce. Editorialized the
Union Record: ". . . the oft-repeated but sadly disregarded ax-
iom that the working class and the capitalist class have nothing
in common is the truest thing in the world. Utopia is coming
all right, but it is coming through the absorption into the working class of all classes and the final mastery of the world by the
workers of the world."

While the words reflected Editor Ault's opinion, he probably would not have expressed them so sharply. The words were those of Anna Louise Strong, who had become editor of the *Union Record*'s editorial page. The transformation of the paper from a weekly to a daily had been accomplished April 24, 1918, as the result of a whirlwind campaign among the shipyard unions. The Central Labor Council had agreed to Editor Ault's plan for a daily, conditional on obtaining 20,000 subscriptions at $1 apiece. When Local 104 of the Boilermakers, with more than 15,000 members, voted to pay the $1 per capita out of its treasury, the daily was assured. In those days Local 104 was rather overwhelmed by its riches. On payday, the money in dues came in so fast that bills and silver were literally swept into closets, to await sorting and counting when the staff could find time. As strikes were outlawed, there was no need to build up a strike fund, and Local 104's munificence became legendary.

Even so, $20,000 was little enough to start a daily, although considerably more than the $500 that Mauritzen had had for the *Call*. A press had to be bought, a building rented, a staff assembled. Devoted unionists in the printing trades took a chance on Editor Ault's ability to survive and moved into the new plant to get machinery ready. Miss Strong's pen name had disappeared from the *Call* for several weeks before the appearance of the daily *Union Record;* she was one of the first editorial workers. Several reporters on the business press, disgruntled by their reactionary policies, hopefully joined the staff. Gathering a network of newsboys to cover the city was perhaps the hardest job, for the *Record's* initial 20,000 subscribers were scattered across the wide territory of Seattle. For several weeks the circulation slid down to 15,000, hardly more than the *Call* had had. As the paper got on its feet and began to establish its personality, circulation climbed until it reached 50,000 by the end of 1918, establishing its rank as a major Seattle newspaper by any standard save that of advertising.

Harry Ault, a short, plump, bespectacled, dark-haired man of great nervous energy, found himself harried from the beginning by all the troubles of a publisher getting out America's first

labor union daily. Principally his troubles were financial, and
were so to remain for the life of the *Record*. The initial $20,000
had been absorbed in capital expenditures and left not a penny
of working capital. Many unions subscribed to *Record* stock and
enabled it to continue, but the big department stores confined
themselves to bargain basement advertising while the usual in-
stitutional advertising of the big companies was absent, and the
horde of small ads was costly to get. So Ault had little time to
spend at his desk in the small editor's cubbyhole at the *Record;*
Miss Strong wrote most of the editorials and selected the other
material for the editorial page. As an ex-*Call* reporter, she was
considerably more advanced than her publisher, which added to
his troubles with conservatives on the floor of the Central Labor
Council. Nevertheless, two months before the daily was established and Miss Strong had become its editorial director, the
weekly *Record* had called for "the return to the worker of the
full social value of the product of his labor," for "industrial
democracy, than which there can hardly be a broader term. . . .
A new political line-up is needed which will enable the workers
to choose principles rather than party names." The ideas had a
somewhat Marxist tinge.

In April and May of 1917 the laundry girls struck against
wages of $3 to $9 a week. The Central Labor Council set up
kitchens to feed the pickets and paid their medical expenses.
The girls won. In Tacoma the street car men went on strike, and
were followed by their Seattle fellow-unionists in July. The
street car company, allied with the private light and power interests and the Chamber of Commerce, retaliated by importing
strikebreakers all the way from Brooklyn, New York, and housing them in a fortified stockade. Police assigned to guard the
strikebreakers as they piloted street cars refused this distasteful
and dangerous business. That ended the usefulness of the strikebreakers and the company settled with the union. Crowed the
Union Record: "Policemen have gone on strike! Horrors! And
they struck because they set humanity above privileged property
and refused to protect the latter at the expense of the former. If

the policemen begin to think, it may follow that property will cease to be the Almighty God and the people will have a chance at supremacy." When the longshoremen threatened to strike on the private docks (the union was recognized at the public docks of the Port Commission) Naval Intelligence moved in, arranged a ten-day truce, and used the interval to weed out all known members of the I.W.W. That took the sting out of the long-shoremen's union for the time being, and hiring continued through the "fink hall" maintained by the Waterfront Employers Association, instead of through the union hall.

Disgruntled with the hung jury which had freed Hulet Wells and Sam Sadler, the socialists, on September 18, 1917, the government decided on another try at jailing them. Taking no chances again on the local federal district attorney, the Department of Justice sent in a special prosecutor, Clarence L. Reames, an assistant attorney-general. New indictments were obtained against Wells and Sadler and against Morris and Joe Pass as well.

The Pass brothers, eager young intellectuals of the socialist movement, had an ambition shared by many of Seattle's young radicals — to go to New York, a world center of the radical movement and seat of the much-admired *Masses-Liberator* and of other socialist enterprises. It was felt that Seattle was somewhat provincial and that one's horizons needed expansion. After surveying the Eastern scene, many a young radical decided that Seattle was indeed as exhilarating a center as any, and often they returned to Puget Sound. In those days the curious, ambitious, but penniless young man anxious to go ahead in the world knew of only two ways to do so. One was the hard way — to "ride the rods" on the freights — the equivalent of present-day hitchhiking although considerably more arduous. The other was to "ship out" on a job. In a time of labor shortage employers were willing to pay coach fare. One could, for instance, ship out to a dam job in Montana, then to the Chicago stockyards, then on to the Akron rubber factories, and thence to the Philadelphia shipyards. If the job turned out to be distasteful, there was no obligation to stay; as a matter of fact many dropped off the train at their own rather than the employer's destination.

In January, 1917, the Pass brothers made up their minds to make the pilgrimage to Mecca, Morris to study at the Art Students League and Joe to take some courses at Columbia. With $65 in their pockets they left Seattle in May. When the draft law went into effect June 5 they registered at Sand Point, Idaho. Sleeping in haystacks and barns, picking up odd jobs en route, they arrived in New York in September, richer by $400 and the experience gained.

Having been out of touch with Seattle, they knew nothing of the arrests, trials, or even their own indictment until after several weeks in New York, when they were arrested October 13 and lodged in the ancient Tombs, charged not only with seditious conspiracy in connection with the no-conscription leaflets but with failure to register for the draft, due to some misunderstanding with the Idaho draft board. Joe Pass had read *The Theoretical System of Karl Marx,* one of the few original contributions to Marxist thought in this country, written by Louis B. Boudin, and he sought the famous lawyer's help. Far beyond the call of duty, Boudin not only counseled the Pass brothers but visited them nearly every day. After three weeks they were sent to Seattle, Boudin's final advice being to keep in touch with Kate Sadler and follow her counsel.

Bail for the Pass brothers was set at $15,000, and as property was taken at only a fourth of its value, that meant a staggering sum in real estate. Joe was the first to be released. He was hailed on the street by a stranger: "Are you Joe Pass?" "Yes." "And your brother is still in?" "Yes." "I'll put up the rest of the bond." He did, but no one in the Seattle radical movement had ever heard of him. It was the kind of incident that could only have happened in the Seattle of 1917. While awaiting release from Pierce County jail, Morris Pass edited *The Prison Voice,* with Paul Haffer, also up on anti-draft charges, as assistant editor. This paper had sports and society editors as well as a circulation manager, whose job it was to have the single copy of the paper passed from cell to cell.

The cases of all four came to trial February 19, 1918. Unfortunately for the defendants, George Vanderveer was in Chicago fighting in the greatest trial in his life, that of the 174 I.W.W.'s arrested after the nation-wide raids of September, 1917. The defense was entrusted to a drunken old lawyer who had adorned the bench in his better days. This time the verdict of guilty was guaranteed. In state courts jury panels were chosen at random from the names of all property-holders and, as many skilled workers owned their homes, there was a chance of labor men being on the jury. But in federal court, officials hand-picked the jury panels. For the socialist trial, 12 good men and true, mostly real estate and insurance dealers, employers, and well-heeled ranchers, were empaneled. Not a single workingman was named. The judge awarded two years at McNeil Island to all four defendants. The verdict sent a wave of indignation through the ranks of organized labor. The machinists' union submitted a resolution to the next meeting of the Central Labor Council which read:

At the time war was declared, 90 per cent of the people of this city and probably of the nation (as far as could be ascertained) were opposed to it and the sentiment was overwhelmingly against conscription and everything resembling militarism. There is growing among the workers a distrust of the United States district attorney's office in this city and a thoroughly justified suspicion that the ends of justice are being defeated through the trickery and scheming of those sworn to uphold the law, which has resulted in railroading to the penitentiary our esteemed brother, Hulet M. Wells, and his co-defendants. We request the Central Labor Council to appoint a committee to act in conjunction with this local union in conducting a sweeping investigation into the methods of securing jurymen and setting the stage for federal trials, and particularly the Wells trial, in order to secure convictions.

The Council adopted the resolution unanimously.

The Council's action nettled Special Prosecutor Reames who termed it an attack on the very bulwark of the law and an affront to the blindfolded lady who holds the scales of justice in her outstretched hand. All four defendants were hustled off to jail, although Dr. Sydney Strong had posted property worth $20,000 and Wells's parents in Skagit County their farm valued at $18,000, to satisfy the government's demand for a $5,000 bond. Eventually bail was made for all four.

The appeal was an empty formality, the defendants knew, useful only to gain time. For Wells, the respite before going to jail was urgent, for he had been unemployed since being fired from City Light after his first indictment in 1917. He had been able to pick up only odd jobs to support his family. Unemployment and insecurity were the theme of his life and furnished the title for his unpublished autobiography, "I Wanted To Work." After his conviction, he thought of getting a job in the shipyards, but felt it was hopeless because of the screening process. To his surprise, an old friend of his was working in the employment office and passed him into the Skinner & Eddy yard. After a while the Metal Trades Council saw to it that he was upgraded to a better-paying job as an oiler, which he held until the penitentiary doors banged behind him.

The Central Labor Council, angered by the increasing number of political prosecutions, including that of Master Bouck of the State Grange, demanded the immediate freeing of all political prisoners and discontinuance of their prosecution. Wells, in a fiery address to the Council, related that "someone who thought he was a friend of mine recently stated that he would like to see me freed, but that he wanted to see the I.W.W.'s kept in jail. I don't want my liberty on any such terms as that." The delegates cheered him to the echo.

The black cloud of war lifted November 11, 1918, on a wild day of rejoicing in Seattle as everywhere. The hated draft was ended and "the boys" began returning home. In the collapse of the German and Austrian Empires, revolutionary forces were taking over. Seattle socialists celebrated the liberation of their fellow workers across the seas in a great meeting, and pointedly declared that the Armistice had liberated Americans as well. Hulet Wells came on the platform with a gag over his mouth and masked. Introduced, he tore off the mask and then the gag to symbolize the return of free speech.

Earlier in 1918 many radicals had been taking a new view of

the war. The Russian, and in particular the Bolshevik, Revolution, and the attack on it by the Prussian hordes, caused many to swing to a cautious support of the war. The *Union Record,* which had always insisted that it backed the war effort and aided the sales of Liberty Bonds and war savings stamps, on April 20, 1918, editorialized: "If there was a hesitancy in giving wholehearted support to war measures in the past, it has disappeared in the face of the very real menace the German autocracy has proven. This is the last fight between feudalism and capitalism and opens the way for the supremacy of the working class in all democratic countries. Let us not stint in our support of political democracy to the end that we may establish industrial democracy."

The *Union Record* was one of the few daily newspapers that was consistently pro-Soviet. Certainly it was the only daily to publish the speech of Premier Lenin of the Soviet Republic, made in April, 1918, to the Congress of Soviets on the next tasks of organizing power. The text was published by the socialist Rand School in New York in an edition annotated by Alexander Trachtenberg. This scholarly pamphlet was read eagerly by those concerned with the problems of the beleaguered infant Soviet Republic, then menaced by German armies. A copy reached Miss Strong in far-off Seattle, and she gained approval for its publication by the *Union Record.* Trachtenberg's notes and references to Mensheviks, Social Revolutionaries, and other idiosyncrasies of the Russian scene were removed as it was thought that this would be rather meaningless to Seattle workers and just clutter up Lenin's prose. Each paragraph was headed by a snappy catchline summary and Miss Strong contributed a foreword to "this description of the problems faced by a working class government on coming to power." Twenty thousand copies were published and avidly read by radicals up and down the Pacific Coast as well as in Seattle's shipyards. The extraordinary influence of this pamphlet was to be felt in subsequent events in Seattle as workers pondered the problems of "management" in a workers' state. There was of course an initial problem not considered in Lenin's speech — how to seize the power to create a workers' state in the first place. For Lenin's purposes that was not necessary — that problem had been solved in front of the Winter Palace on November 7, 1917. Not many Seattleites, fascinated by Lenin's practical approach to problems of management, had much of an answer to Lenin's initial problem of winning power.

As little or no authentic news from Russia was printed in the business press — the Soviet government was always on the point of teetering to its doom, women had been "nationalized," and already Riga was the main source of misinformation — the *Union Record* opened a Bureau of Russian Information which published from time to time such news as seeped through the Allied censorship.

After the Armistice the *Union Record* was bullish on the European situation, but rather bearish on the domestic: "Workers, your hour has struck! In Russia, in Austria and in Germany the producers are taking their heritage, long past due. In England, the toilers prepare to assume 'a place in the sun.' In America — aye, there's the rub."

What, for example, would be the role of the returning soldiers? Inured to the brutality of mass murder, indoctrinated against the "Reds," would they be used as a bludgeon against unions? Already the American Legion had been formed by far-sighted men who knew the danger of radicalism sweeping from Europe across the sea, and the usefulness of forming a quasi-military group which could take the law into its own hands if it felt that the authorities were too bound by legal formalities. The specter of Red Russia already tormented red-blooded patriots in their sleep. Cried Captain Bunn of Fort Lawton, the military establishment on the outskirts of Seattle, in a speech to the Harvard Club: "Gentlemen, it is not Germany that our government fears, neither is it Mexico or Japan. What it fears is internal industrial revolution which may be upon us within 48 hours, and you are the men to suppress such a revolution."

Two streams of thought met on the floor of the Central Labor

Council as delegates pondered the return of the veterans. Those who were pure and simple unionists foresaw the use of these men by employers as strikebreakers to lower union conditions; the men would be needing jobs and it would be hard to deny their right to even preferential treatment in employment. Those more radical had read of the Workers, Soldiers and Sailors Councils in Russia and believed that here was a perfect form of organization to weld unionists and veterans together. This appealed to all wings of the Council, and approval was voted for the organization of such a council in Seattle. Similar councils were being set up in Portland, Butte, and elsewhere, so the Seattle venture was by no means isolated. The purposes of the Workers, Soldiers and Sailors Council were spelled out: to help veterans readjust to civilian life, to see that they were integrated into the labor force as union men, and most of all to see that they did not become a reserve army of unemployed to be used against organized labor. The *Union Record* appealed: "The trade union is to the American workers what the Council of Workmen and Soldiers is to Russia, Austria and Germany. The labor council is the central soviet. . . . Whatever you and your beliefs represent, go to your union hall and register yourself as one member of America's council of workmen."

Across the country, in opposition to the American Legion, a new organization called the Private Soldiers and Sailors Legion was organized. In distinction to the American Legion, where officers played the predominant role, the Private Legion confined its membership to the rank and file of Army and Navy veterans. In Seattle a unit was formed under the leadership of Frank Pease — who said he lived on a pension from the Spanish-American War — was voted endorsement by the Central Labor Council and given an office in the Labor Temple.

As the postwar turbulence rose, terrified state legislatures began enacting little sedition acts, known as criminal syndicalism and criminal anarchy laws. The "syndicalism" was in tribute to the I.W.W. and the "anarchy" to the socialists. The Washington State legislature, by 85 to 6, voted such a law over

the veto of Governor Ernest Lister. It defined criminal syndicalism as "any doctrine which advocates criminal sabotage, violence or other unlawful methods of terrorism as a means of
accomplishing industrial or political reform." The dragnet was
spread with the words of the act that covered "anybody who
justifies these methods or who organizes or helps to organize or
becomes a member or voluntarily assembles with any society or
group formed to teach or advocate criminal syndicalism." Under
such laws hundreds, if not thousands, of radicals were to be
jailed the length and breadth of the land during the postwar
years of the "Red hysteria." In Seattle radicals knew they had
not long to wait to feel the effects of such laws.

Unionists and radicals alike were appalled by the life imprisonment decreed for Tom Mooney and Warren K. Billings
after world-wide protests had lifted the threat of execution. The
intervention of President Wilson, in response to the international clamor, had first delayed their execution, and then had
obtained a change in the penalty to life imprisonment. So much
accomplished, the labor movement had to press on to see that
the men were given a new trial, or freed forthwith. On this issue
the Seattle labor movement from left to right stood as one man:
Mooney and Billings must be freed. But while more conservative elements were for continued appeals to Wilson and to the
authorities in California, the radicals were counseling a general
strike throughout the United States to force action. So great was
the pressure that the Chicago Federation of Labor, then under
progressive leadership, issued a call for a national convention
of the Mooney forces. In Seattle the response was instantaneous.
The Central Labor Council named Secretary Duncan and Editor Ault as delegates, the Metal Trades Council named Frank
Turco of the blacksmiths, and some 40 delegates in all were
elected from the unions, many of whom also carried red cards
of the Socialist Party and the I.W.W. Among them was Kate
Sadler who at a great meeting in Seattle had said, almost despair-
ingly: "It lies within your power to get him [Mooney] out of

there, but to do so you must exercise a power that you do not realize you possess."

Kate Sadler was referring to the idea of the general strike. To most American unionists the concept was still strange. But to the I.W.W. it was the cardinal point of their doctrine — the key to workers' power. On the great day all the workers would down tools, industry would stop, and with it the profits of the capitalists. Then the workers would march back into the factories as their owners and operators. To many socialists the concept, while alluring, seemed to hide a certain defect: where would the police and the army be while all this was going on? The French syndicalist answer was that the army, made up of conscripts from the working class and the peasantry, would turn their guns if need be toward the rear where the officers were. But the experience in the United States with conscript armies was so recent that the French syndicalist answer seemed far-fetched. Nevertheless the I.W.W. ever since 1905 had been propagating the theory of the general strike not only for the final conflict but to get immediate demands. The 1916 convention had urged its use to stop war. By 1919 throughout the West, the general strike had become to most militant workers the answer to their problem.

The Mooney convention, the greatest gathering of progressive unionists ever to unite on a single issue, met in Chicago January 14-17, 1919, with Harry Ault of Seattle as secretary. The main issue before the convention was the same that was being argued in Seattle: when and how should labor call a general strike to free Mooney? The top officials of the A.F. of L., full of sympathy they said for Mooney, were adamant against the strike. At Chicago some were for a strike in the immediate future, some for setting the date as May Day, others for July 4 to allow time to organize a complete tie-up.

From Local 104 of the Seattle boilermakers, perhaps the largest local union in the country, Jim Lansbury argued: "I've had the pleasure of sticking two $1,000 bills through the bars of Tom Mooney's cell from the Boilermakers of Seattle. We voted 8 to 1 to go out December 9, and that vote holds. I tell you the

Pacific Coast would go out tomorrow. But the East is different. We've got to organize and it takes time to do it. I'm for July Fourth."

For Kate Sadler that was too long to wait. She cried:

What is holding us back when the case of Mooney has gone round the world. If we are ready for a general strike on December 9 to keep Mooney from hanging, why wait until July 4 to call a strike for his freedom? July 4 is too late. Demobilization will have taken place — the country will be full of unemployed — the employers will have months and months to prepare. And July 4 is the masters' day — it's the day your masters set you free to celebrate. Why start a strike on a day like that? Why stop work on the one day in the year when you're allowed to stop work? May 1 is the Independence Day of Labor — July 4 is the national day — May 1 is International Day. Why should we wait? This is the only civilized country in the world where the prison doors are still swinging in for political prisoners now that the war is ended!

The convention nevertheless settled for July 4, and its sponsors, over the clamors of a majority of delegates, hastily adjourned the sessions. They foresaw that once the main issue was decided, most of the delegates might proceed to discuss another issue that weighed heavily on them — the prospects for organizing a new American labor federation that would replace the A.F. of L., absorb the I.W.W., and reorganize unionism on industrial lines, the better to bring about emancipation. But that would have to wait another 15 years and the lessons of the Great Depression.

The day the convention adjourned, January 17, word flashed from Seattle that a general strike of quite a different order had been voted by the Metal Trades Council. That Council had ordered a general strike in the shipyards to start January 21, to enforce wage demands. As most of the Seattle delegates came from the shipyard unions, they boarded the next train home. They did not mean to be 2,000 miles away on that day.

6

The General Strike

On Armistice Day, 1918, the lid blew off the Seattle labor movement. Nearly two years of pent-up frustration were released in a storm of emotion. In that respect Seattle was no different from the rest of the world. Revolution was the order of the day in Central Europe; the Soviets were battling counter-revolutionaries and Allied intervention; France and Italy were convulsed; in Britain reconstruction of society was the concern of the Labour Party. In the United States great strikes broke out in steel, focus of industrial feudalism, and in the coal mines and on the railroads. The same pattern was to be repeated after the Second World War.

Foremost cause of the unrest which swept the country was the constantly soaring cost of living, up 50 percent in three years. Wages in the basic industries had been held under governmental control but there were few countervailing controls on prices. Huge shipments of food and supplies were being sent to starving Europe and the shortages resulting in this country led enterprisers to charge all that the traffic would bear. At the same time profits were soaring, too, and it was unbearable to thinking workers that the costs of the war should be piled on them while their employers never had it so good.

In Seattle the high cost of living was an especially exasperating prod. The Pacific Northwest had always been a high-price region, far off the beaten track of American commerce; costs of transport whether by ship or rail were padded by the extra profits extracted. Even more than in other sections, the Pacific Northwest regarded itself as in a colonial position, exploited by the Eastern captains of industry. The abnormal price situation was exaggerated by the influx of thousands of workers, straining the city's housing and public facilities to the breaking point. Landlords reaped a bonanza by heaping men and families into the scant housing available.

Seattle was exceptional also because of the advanced organization of labor — with a total population of 250,000, there were some 60,000 members in unions, flanked as in few other communities by radical wings of the socialists and I.W.W. If a speedy reaction to the release of wartime controls on the right to strike were to be found anywhere in the country, it would logically be in Seattle. And that was the fact, proudly reported by Anna Louise Strong just back from the Mooney convention in Chicago. In the *Union Record* she wrote that "Seattle is on the map . . . the place where big constructive ideas come from." She was proud that the Mooney meeting had had its genesis in Seattle.

The 30,000 shipyard workers in the city had been bound by the national A.F. of L. agreement with the War Labor Board which exchanged union recognition for the right to strike in wartime. While the Metal Trades Council held an overall agreement with the yards, neither that Council nor its 21 constituent unions had any final authority in wartime over the wage scales. That authority rested with the Shipbuilding Labor Adjustment Board, usually called the Macy Board, after its chairman, V. Everit Macy. This had been formed by agreement among the U.S. Emergency Fleet Corporation in charge of shipbuilding, the Navy Department, and the international presidents of the unions involved. The Seattle unions complained vehemently that the international unions, in violation of their own constitutions, had taken control over wages from the rank and file.

The Macy Board twice authorized wage increases in 1917. The unions better organized before the war won an average 60 cents a day rise; those representing mainly the unskilled and semi-skilled, much less. The increase for some of around 12½ percent contrasted with a rise in living costs during the period of

31 percent. The top wage for shipyard laborers was $4.16 a day, or a little under $100 a month. The Board's scales were said to be the minimum but in practice they became the maximum and employers were discouraged from paying more. The Board also tried to equalize wages nationally, which of course was detrimental to the Pacific Northwest, where both wages and prices were traditionally higher than on the East and Gulf coasts.

Immediately after the Armistice, the Metal Trades Council demanded a general wage readjustment. Its president, James A. Taylor, went to Washington to confer with Charles Piez, director of the Emergency Fleet Corporation, and with the Macy Board. When that Board's appeal committee split on the Seattle wage issue, Taylor returned to Seattle confident that he had permission to negotiate directly with the shipyards, provided that wage increases did not increase the price of shipping to the government. A strike vote, preliminary to negotiations, was authorized by the Metal Trades Council in November, 1918, and majorities were received in most unions. On January 16, 1919, negotiations opened on demands for an $8 scale for mechanics, $7 for specialists, $6 for helpers, and $5.50 for laborers. The Council calculated that its wage demands would leave a profit of $200,000 on each ship, as against the existing $286,000 profit, based on an 8,800-ton ship costing $1,350,000 and sold to the government for $1,636,000. The owners offered increases to the skilled trades but nothing for the unskilled. The skilled trades joined with the mass of the workers in rejecting the splitting tactic.

A Western Union messenger boy helped to precipitate the strike. He bore a telegram addressed to the Metal Trades Association, the employers' body; by mistake he took it to the Metal Trades Council. Its contents were explosive. Director Piez of the Emergency Fleet Corporation had cut through any hope of further negotiation by informing the employers that they would get no more steel if they agreed to any wage increases. Did Piez act on his own initiative, or was it a double-play between him and the companies? Were the unions up against the government as well as the companies? The Metal Trades Council promptly repudiated the agreement, signed illegally, it claimed, by the chiefs of the national unions without consultation or agreement by the local unions. On January 16, 1919, the Council authorized a strike, to begin January 21. On that day 30,000 men downed tools, augmented by 15,000 in nearby Tacoma. The yards made no effort to reopen; the unions banned demonstrations, parades, or gatherings, and an unearthly quiet enveloped the yards. To scotch rumors that many of the men were opposed to the strike, Local 104 of the Boilermakers, which comprised nearly half of all strikers, called a meeting to which 6,000 members responded. Dan McKillop, an official, denounced the shipowners who had taken the credit for the ships built by the workers. "If they think they can build ships, let them go ahead and build them." As for the threat to build ships only in the East, "Well," said McKillop, "let them try it. If they want to start a revolution, let 'em start it."

To bring pressure on the strikers, the Retail Grocers Association decreed that no credit would be extended. The Cooperative Food Products Association, a cooperative formed by unions and the Grange, answered that food would be available to any striker. Thereupon the "dry squad" raided the co-op on a liquor warrant. This was an excuse to go through the co-op's correspondence and business files, which were confiscated in an effort to put it out of business.

The stalemate was complete. The men were adamant; many of the yard bosses had gone to California for a vacation; the government, far from being eager for a settlement, was bombarding the yards with messages to stand firm and resist labor's demands.

The idea of a general strike swept the ranks of organized labor like a gale. If labor was prepared to strike for Tom Mooney, certainly it could strike in support of the shipyard workers. If the general strike was labor's ultimate weapon, certainly here and now was the time to use it, to break the impending coastwise assault on unionism. Possibly there had never been a more dramatic meeting of the Central Labor Council than that which convened January 22, the floor jammed with delegates from some 110 local unions, and the gallery filled with unionists. Every reference to the general strike was cheered to the echo; the cautions of the conservatives that such a strike was in violation of many international union rules and of contracts with employers were hooted down. It has been urged since that the absence of some 40 delegates returning from the Mooney convention gave the "radicals" dominance in the Council's deliberations. But most of the Mooney delegates were from the very same shipyard unions that were calling for a general strike; if they were willing to go to Chicago to plan a national strike for Mooney, they would hardly have been reluctant to counsel a general strike in Seattle in support of their own fellow workers. If anything, the conservative influence was stronger in the Council that night than usual because the delegates who went to Chicago represented the moderate and radical unions. The conservatives weren't so concerned about Mooney as to travel 2,000 miles to agitate a general strike for him.

The Council's vote that night to hold a referendum among all local unions on the issue of a general strike won the approval of all delegates but one. Scholars, writing a generation later, refer to the "mysterious snowball" of assent that was registered on the very next night in eight local union meetings, whose galleries if any were certainly not "packed" by Wobblies; "the unanimity of sentiment and the rapidity of assent were astonishing." Perhaps now it seems astonishing, but in post-Armistice Seattle it was natural and inevitable — this great emotional wave. By the weekend it was so obvious that the strike votes would carry in most of the locals that a special meeting was called for Monday, January 26. There it was agreed that if the votes continued overwhelmingly in favor, another special meeting of union representatives should be called for Sunday, February 2, to decide on action. The strike votes in the metal trades unions of course were favorable; most of their members were already on strike. The crucial votes were in the old-established locals of the building, teaming, printing, and service trades. But the painters and carpenters and teamsters and cooks also voted "Yes."

In this they had the unanimous if left-handed support of the business press, which was busy taunting the "radical" leaders of the Central Labor Council that the rank and file, being patriotic Americans, would not strike against the government. Editorialized the *Times:* "A general strike directed at WHAT? The Government of the United States? Bosh! Not 15 percent of Seattle laborites would consider such a proposition." But consider it they did, and with the greatest enthusiasm! Edwin Selvin's *Business Chronicle,* spokesman for the open-shop interests which included most of industry and commerce, helped too. Selvin began inserting lurid advertisements in the business dailies proposing that all radicals be arrested and deported or jailed, that "the most labor-tyrannized city in America" be converted pronto into a bastion of the open shop. "Here is Seattle's solution to its labor problem: As fast as men strike, replace them with returned soldiers." Even conservative unionists who doubted the wisdom of the general strike recoiled when confronted by such evidence from the implacable class enemy.

On February 2 the special meeting of union representatives, three from each union, voted to set the strike date for Thursday, February 6. This group constituted itself the General Strike Committee and took over from the Central Labor Council complete authority for the strike. This relieved the Council of direct responsibility for an action which was thoroughly disapproved of by its chartering body, the A.F. of L., and which could result possibly in the revocation of its charter. Already the international unions were sending in their officials to hold back local unions which had voted to strike. An executive committee of 15 was chosen by the general committee to plan the details of the strike.

On the same day an industrial relations committee of businessmen, clergy, and unionists negotiating with the shipyard owners got a promise to raise laborers to $5 a day minimum, but with no raise for the skilled trades. The Metal Trades Council spokesmen indicated that the offer could be discussed; but Piez was adamant. Not a ton of steel would be furnished the shipyards if the Macy award were altered.

Almost immediately the relevancy of Lenin's speech on management, which had aroused so much discussion among workers, became apparent. If the strike were to be completely effective, the life of a city of 300,000 would grind to a sudden halt, with catastrophic consequences. If essential services such as light and power, fire protection, hospitals, were to continue, it was up to the Committee of 15 to cope with the problem of civic "management." Thousands of single workers ate in restaurants; were they to starve during the strike? How about milk for babies? And how was the strike to be policed? Certainly the unionists had little faith in the impartiality of the custodians of law and order.

An even more crucial question came up at the Committee of 15 meeting on Tuesday, February 4. How long would the strike last? Was this a demonstration of sympathetic support for the shipyard unions, to be ended as soon as labor had shown where its heart was? Or should it continue until the shipyard owners and the government agreed to confer? The leaders of the Central Labor Council, including Secretary Duncan, Editor Ault, Robert B. Hesketh (a city councilman), and others urged that a time limit be fixed — whether of one day or one week was less important than fixing some terminal date. But such was the wave of emotion that the proposal was defeated; the General Strike Committee was not yet ready to talk about ending a strike that had not even begun.

As a matter of cold fact, just what were the aims of the strike? Most unionists saw it as a demonstration of sympathy, calculated to strengthen the arm of the shipyard unions. Others felt that the first general strike in America would be so conclusive in its show of strength that the walls of Jericho would come tumbling down — not the walls of capitalism, but the walls of pitiless hostility to the earnest demands of the shipyard workers. For the proposed strike slogan, "We have nothing to lose but our chains

and a world to gain," the Committee substituted, "Together
we win."

As if to answer the question about aims of the strike, the
Union Record on Tuesday, February 4, published the most
famous editorial of its entire history — excerpts of which were
read by millions across the country, who by now had their eyes
riveted on what some were already proclaiming to be a revolutionary situation. The editorial, written by Anna Louise Strong
and approved by Editor Ault and the Metal Trades Council,
read, in part:

ON THURSDAY AT 10 A.M.

There will be many cheering, and there will be some who fear.
Both these emotions are useful, but not too much of either.
We are undertaking the most tremendous move ever made by
LABOR in this country, a move which will lead — NO ONE KNOWS
WHERE.
We do not need hysteria.
We need the iron march of labor.

LABOR WILL FEED THE PEOPLE.
Twelve great kitchens have been offered, and from them food will
be distributed by the provision trades at low cost to all.
LABOR WILL CARE FOR THE BABIES AND THE SICK.
The milk-wagon drivers and the laundry drivers are arranging
plans for supplying milk to babies, invalids and hospitals, and taking
care of the cleaning of linen for hospitals.
LABOR WILL PRESERVE ORDER.
The strike committee is arranging for guards, and it is expected
that the stopping of the cars will keep people at home.

A few hot-headed enthusiasts have complained that strikers only
should be fed, and the general public left to endure severe discom-
fort. Aside from the inhumanitarian character of such suggestions,
let them get this straight —
NOT THE WITHDRAWAL OF LABOR POWER, BUT THE POWER OF THE
STRIKERS TO MANAGE WILL WIN THIS STRIKE. . . .
The closing down of Seattle's industries, as a MERE SHUTDOWN, will
not affect these eastern gentlemen much. They could let the whole
northwest go to pieces, as far as money alone is concerned.
BUT, the closing down of the capitalistically controlled industries
of Seattle, while the WORKERS ORGANIZE to feed the people, to care
for the babies and the sick, to preserve order — THIS will move them,
for this looks too much like the taking over of POWER by the workers.

Labor will not only SHUT DOWN the industries, but Labor will REOPEN, under the management of the appropriate trades, such activities as are needed to preserve public health and public peace. If the strike continues, Labor may feel led to avoid public suffering by reopening more and more activities,
UNDER ITS OWN MANAGEMENT.
And that is why we say that we are starting on a road that leads — NO ONE KNOWS WHERE.

It could be said that the editorial contained no clearcut answers to the questions about the purpose of the strike. Or rather it might be more correct to say that people could draw their own answers, to please their own interpretation. To most unionists the editorial stated plainly what was intended: that the city would be shut down but that essential services for life and security would continue. But others could read in ominous ideas that the workers, having shut down the industries, would reopen them on their own terms. Most of all the phrase that "we are starting on a road that leads — NO ONE KNOWS WHERE," created an alarm that Seattle labor was leading down the road to revolution. But the sentence meant exactly what it said — this was the first use of the general strike weapon anywhere in America, and who could foretell the outcome? Undoubtedly, in Miss Strong's mind, there were the undertones of Lenin's speech on worker management but such notions were hardly in the heads of leaders of the Central Labor Council. They were launched on a trade union trial of strength, and not a revolution.

But there were people who did see the shipyard and the general strikes in revolutionary terms. Since the death of the *Daily Call,* the socialists had been publishing the *International Weekly.* The editors of this paper felt that the situation called for drastic action by labor. They weighed not only Lenin's speech on worker management but Lenin's previous actions in the seizure of power. And so they called bluntly and sharply for a revolutionary solution — let the shipyard workers take over the yards and operate them for the benefit of the workers. This idea, expressed editorially in the *International Weekly,* was put into a leaflet. Morris Pass, the artist, drew a cartoon showing a huge figure of Labor pushing a fat little capitalist into a coffin. Over this appeared the caption RUSSIA DID IT, a take-off on the slogan in the current Victory Bond drive, THE YANKS DID IT. Underneath appeared the editorial appealing to the shipyard workers. While the leaflet's contents appealed to many strikers, no union endorsed its proposal. Nevertheless the little socialist handbill was reproduced far and wide across the nation subsequently to give substance to the notion that the general strike was revolutionary in intent. A resolution offered by socialist unionists in the Central Labor Council February 5 echoed the sentiments of the leaflet. If the strike is prolonged and the employers refuse to reach a settlement, the resolution advised, the strike committee should arrange to "take over the shipbuilding industry, eliminate the bosses, and operate it in the interests of the workers." The resolution was tabled.

As the fateful day of Thursday, February 6, neared, tension mounted. The more fearful among the upper classes departed for Portland and California to escape the rigors of revolution. Those of such persuasion who remained at home laid in stocks of food, kerosene, and candles against the dreadful nights ahead. Others cleaned their guns or acquired small arsenals the better to resist the hordes of Wobblies who presumably would roam the city, sacking, looting, and raping. The gun stores saw a windfall in prospect. Letters went out to selected lists such as this:

Dear Fellow Kiwanian: Are you prepared? Not only to assist, if necessary, in controlling the despicable human element which has sprung up in our midst, but to defend, if necessary, the sanctity of your home and aid in protecting the property and wealth of the community? Although there has been a considerable scarcity of all firearms during recent months, we are fortunate in having in stock, at the present time, a very good assortment of revolvers, automatic pistols, rifles, shotguns and ammunition.

Correspondents for Eastern newspapers and magazines began arriving to see for themselves how a revolution is conducted in the United States. The local business dailies became shrill.

UNDER WHICH FLAG? asked the *Star,* in an editorial spread across
the front page. In answer to the *Star,* the *Union Record* said:

Sane men there are, some, who believe that in the end all peaceful means to abolish the profit system will fail, and the age-long
struggle between the suppressors and the oppressed will close with
violence. But no sane man believes that time is now. The *Star* pre-
tends to believe that the unarmed and defenseless workers mean to
capture City Hall and run up the Red Flag in spite of the fact that
it knows that the workers know that there are thousands of soldiers
at Camp Lewis and Fort Lawton. . . . No revolution of violence will
be started during this strike, be the strike long or short.

Said Selvin of the *Business Chronicle* in editorials which he
ran as advertisements in the business dailies:

Seattle today is overrun by red-flag agitators in the guise of "labor
leaders." This is the attitude of the renegades the business men of
this city have coddled, hesitated to "irritate," and subsidized in
spreading their corroding propaganda by supporting with advertising the anarchistic *Daily Union Record,* without which the Bolsheviki would not now be in the saddle in Seattle. So now we have the
Seattle of today — once a proud city brought to the brink of industrial ruin; the Seattle that has come to be known throughout the
length and breadth of the land as a hotbed of sedition, branded by
the Department of Justice as one of two cities that constitute the
danger points of revolutionary Bolshevik propaganda.

At the Labor Temple the Committee of 15 worked from early
morning till midnight dealing with the problems of keeping the
city a going concern during the shutdown. A call went out to
returned veterans, members of organized labor, to enlist in the
Labor War Veterans Guard to maintain law and order during
the strike, and 300 responded. Exemptions were granted from
the strike as local unions brought in their problems involving the
health of the city. A sampling of the exemption requests and
the decisions of the Committee of 15:

King County commissioners ask for exemption of janitors to
care for the City-County Building. Not granted.
Janitors ask for the Labor Temple. Not granted.

Additional staff for the Cooperative Market to handle food for strike kitchens. Approved.

Port of Seattle asks to be allowed to load a government vessel, pointing out that no private profit is involved and an emergency exists. Granted.

Garbage wagon drivers ask instructions. May carry such garbage as tends to create an epidemic, but no ashes or papers. Wagons to carry large signs: Exempt by Strike Committee.

Retail drug clerks ask instructions. Told that drug stores must be closed except for prescription service.

To many citizens the most frightening aspect of the approaching tie-up was the threat by Leon Green, business agent of Electrical Workers Local 77, to shut down the City Light plant. This would plunge the city into darkness, cut off the water supply to many parts, and affect many essential services. As it turned out, the threat was an empty one; Local 77's membership was confined largely to linemen and did not include most of the operators within the light plant itself. But either this was not realized at the time, or else the threat was blown up out of all reason for political purposes by the mayor of Seattle, Ole Hanson. The spotlight shifted from the Labor Temple and the Committee of 15 to focus on the persons of Leon Green and Ole Hanson.

Green was a newcomer in Seattle. Handsome, dark-haired, voluble, dynamic, he was elected business agent because no other member cared to leave a steady job to take over that position. He shared with Mayor Hanson one attribute — a love of limelight. In an interview with the *P-I* he was quoted as saying: "We shall place the city in such a position [by shutting down City Light] that the strike will last but a few short days." Green's favorite phrase was, "We must use our Economic Power."

Mayor Hanson was feeling his way toward the best political posture. He was in and out of the Labor Temple, greeting officials there intimately as "Jimmy," "Harry," and "Jack," asking only, he said, that essential light and water service be assured. Meeting Hulet Wells, a member of the strike committee, in the corridor, to that socialist leader he expressed his admiration: "I don't care what they say about you — let the newspapers rave as they please — but no one can make me believe that you are not one of the finest of our citizens." A few months later he was saying that Wells should be kept in prison for the rest of his life.

The Committee of 15 overruled Leon Green and informed Hanson that City Light would operate. But by then Hanson had dropped his air of familiarity with the Labor Temple; he had seen the vision, bathed in a national spotlight, of himself as the hero who smashed the Seattle "Revolution." He swore in extra police and summoned Governor Lister to rush in the National Guard. President Henry Suzzallo of the University of Washington, chairman of the State Council of Defense, beat him to the punch and demanded that Secretary of War Baker send in federal troops. As was usual during strikes, students at the University, most of whom came from the middle and upper classes, were paid to act as guards in their ROTC uniforms "to help save the world from the Bolsheviki." Army trucks entered the city in the early morning hours of Thursday, February 6, from Camp Lewis, the Army's West Coast concentration center near Tacoma. Machine gun nests were mounted at strategic points. The United States Government was taking no chances with the Labor Temple.

At 10:00 A.M. that Thursday the general strike began. Street cars headed for the barns, trucks for the garages, transportation ceased. Second Avenue, then the main thoroughfare, was silent and empty from the Washington Hotel down to Yesler Way. At a few minutes before ten the pressmen at the *Times* and other papers began covering the presses with tarpaulins. Silence reigned over the city. Here and there small groups of unarmed men with armbands — the Labor Guards — patrolled the streets, with orders to disperse any gatherings of union men. But there were no gatherings of any kind to disperse — public transportation was at a standstill and in any event unionists had been advised to stay at home for the duration.

The peace that had descended was disturbed only by Mayor Ole Hanson. From City Hall he thundered a proclamation on Friday, the second day of the strike:

I hereby guarantee to all the people of Seattle absolute and complete protection. They should go about their daily work and business in perfect security. We have 1,500 policemen, 1,500 regular soldiers from Camp Lewis, and can and will secure, if necessary, every soldier in the Northwest to protect life, business and property.

The time has come for the people of Seattle to show their Americanism. Go about your daily duties without fear. We will see to it that you have food, transportation, water, light, gas and all necessities.

The anarchists in this community shall not rule its affairs.

All persons violating the laws will be dealt with summarily.

The proclamation was all huff and puff. People stayed home. The New York *Tribune's* correspondent, sent out at some expense to cover a revolution, reported that "there was absolutely no violence. The normal police docket of a hundred a day fell to about 30." Mayor Hanson had sworn in 600 extra police and deputized 2,400 more at a cost to the city of $50,000. But the commanding general of the U.S. troops brought into the city said he had never seen such a quiet and orderly city. The *Star* managed to get out a bobtailed edition with the few printers working, distributed free from trucks manned by police with machine guns. It was headed, in red ink, SEATTLE, UNITED STATES OF AMERICA, across the top of the page. It boasted that clubs, revolvers, rifles, carbines, automatics, and machine guns were being distributed among the fearful. It reported that trucks, sandbagged and with machine guns able to sweep the streets, were lumbering up and down the main avenues of the city. But there was nobody there to shoot down. Rumors spread fast. The strikers had dynamited the city's water supply dam, Ole Hanson had been assassinated, buildings were being blown up and troops were engaged in bloody battles with strikers on downtown streets. In all this Mayor Hanson was hardly a help. To eager newspaper correspondents he was already proclaiming that he had quelled, almost single-handed, an attempted Bolshevik revolution. Newspapers in the East greedily gulped down such news, as the nation gaped with bated breath for the outcome of this killer-diller thriller. Hanson telephoned Secretary Duncan to demand that the strike be ended forthwith. Although he refused "to treat with these revolutionists" in statements he gave the wire services, he invited the Committee of 15 to City Hall and promised if the strike were ended that he personally would go to Washington to plead the shipyard workers' case. If not, he would call out the army and declare martial law — a prerogative beyond his power.

The *P-I* in a front page editorial thundered: "The issue is no longer in doubt; the leaders of the revolt are openly proclaiming that the shipyard strike is only a pretext; that it is a camouflage. It is not a strike; it is a delirium-born rebellion." The *Star* chimed in: "A part of our community is, in fact, defying our government and is, in fact, contemplating changing that government, and not by *American Methods.* This small part of our city talks plainly of 'taking over things,' of 'resuming under our own management.' "

In the meantime the strike machinery was working a lot more efficiently than the most hopeful had expected. Thirty-five milk stations were functioning in the residential sections; 21 cafeterias were serving meals for 25 cents apiece to union men, for 35 cents to others; hospitals were getting their linen and fuel. A union card was the only credential for the 25-cent meal, and an I.W.W. card was as good as an A.F. of L. The Japanese Labor Association, comprising hotel and restaurant workers, struck in sympathy with the labor movement which had never recognized them nor even regarded them as a part of unionism. The I.W.W. saw to it that the ginmills on the skid road were shut down (Washington had had official prohibition since 1916) and that I.W.W. members kept off the streets.

The exhilaration from the marvellous display of solidarity experienced Thursday and Friday began by Saturday to give way to apprehension. The purpose of the strike was to help the shipyard workers get an honorable settlement of their wage demands. But nobody on the other side seemed inclined to negotiate anything. While Mayor Hanson's fulminations helped to keep up the backs of unionists, the ominous silence in Washington was dismaying. It had been assumed that the general strike would shock officialdom into action and negotiation. No one had questioned that the government would insist on a settlement of some kind. It was assumed that ships were needed, and the government would come to terms. But the war was over and while more shipping was needed to replace the tonnage sunk by German submarines, there was no longer any great urgency about it. The shipyards along the East and Gulf Coasts and in California continued operating. The truth was that Seattle was expendable, despite its record-breaking speed in delivering ships. For all Washington cared, the Seattle yards could remain closed; moreover it was desirable that the unions be taught a lesson. The *P-I* observed that "the big fact that stands out from the temporary confusion of business is that Seattle, given a brief time for readjustment, would be well off, if not better than before, if the whole of its striking population were suddenly withdrawn from the city."

That the shipyards were expendable was apparent enough to the Citizens Committee, headed by a distinguished divine and an eminent banker. The Committee of 15 was informed that because the strike was considered a revolutionary attempt, it would not bargain on surrender terms. Call off the strike, and then, perhaps. . . .

From the Citizens Committee Mayor Hanson got his cue. Friday evening he ordered the Committee of 15 to end the strike Saturday morning, or else. His "or else" was an empty threat but it had the effect of stiffening opposition among unionists to yielding to such pressure.

Far more effective were the threats of international union officials to revoke local union charters, particularly in the printing trades. Small editions of the dailies began to appear. On Saturday a few unions returned to work; that afternoon the

Committee of 15 voted 13 to 1 to end the strike at midnight. Although several more unions had voted the same day to return, the General Strike Committee, with final authority, voted to continue the strike by 76 to 45. In late afternoon it had seemed that the vote to end the strike was assured; but after a dinner recess several unions changed their position upon the urging of the metal trades and longshore unions.

The General Strike Committee met again Monday morning and then adopted the motion to end the strike. More unions had gone back to work, but others which had returned Saturday voted to resume the strike and bring it to an end with united ranks at noon Tuesday, February 11. The strike had lasted five working days.

For the majority of Seattle unions, there was no sense of defeat as the strike ended. They had demonstrated their solidarity with their brothers in the yards, and the memory of the great days when labor had shown its strength glowed in their minds. It was not until many years later, in a very different climate of opinion, that some of the leaders began apologizing for what could be excused as a momentary aberration by an otherwise solid body of citizenry. It became needful to rewrite history, to blame the general strike on "radicals" or "the I.W.W. element." Forgetful of the evident fact that the strike was voted by some 300 delegates chosen for the purpose from a hundred local unions, almost unanimously, and that none but these regular delegates and their Committee of 15 made the decisions, some have apologized for the great general strike of Seattle as merely an incident to be forgotten, glossed over, or explained away.

The Central Labor Council resumed its normal position in the movement on Wednesday, February 12, the day after the strike ended. Delegates reviewed the impressive achievements of the committees which had carried out the tasks assigned them in guarding against violence, in feeding the hungry, caring for the sick, and keeping essential services running. Chairman Ben F. Nauman of the strike committee summed up: "We did something in this strike which has never been done before by the A.F. of L. We pulled off a general strike with craft unions, with ironclad contracts which had to be broken, and with a constitution that had to be ignored." There had been two mistakes, he said: the failure to decide on the duration of the strike at the beginning, and the failure to call it off Saturday night when it became evident that the ranks were breaking.

Absent from the Council meeting was the business agent for the Electrical Workers union, Leon Green. He who had bluffed Mayor Ole Hanson on shutting down City Light and had provided most of the fireworks that spread the idea of a heartless attempt to crush the life out of a city, had left Seattle never to return. In 1923 a story in the *Union Record* reported that Green had been found guilty by the Chicago retail clerks' union, of which he was business agent, and by the United Hebrew Trades of accepting a $3,000 bribe from the Retail Merchants Association while negotiating a new contract. He was expelled. In Seattle radicals regarded Green as an agent provocateur; leaders of the Central Labor Council were content to describe him as a loud-mouthed seeker of the limelight.

From the general strike arose a Knight of Reaction in shining armor. Ole Hanson, often referred to as "Holy Ole," became the nine-day darling of the nation's open shoppers. Messages of congratulation showered upon him from New York, Washington, Chicago, and way points. He did nothing to dispel the myth that single-handed he had slain the dragon of anarchy. Overcome by the adulation and feeling Seattle to be too narrow an arena for a man of his talents, he resigned the mayor's chair in August, 1919, for a year-long lecture tour on the theme of Americanism vs. Bolshevism, which he elaborated into a book. Always a man with an eye on the main chance, he left a job paying $7,500 to lecture at $500 an audience, or $38,000 for the entire tour. He was even boomed for the presidency, but the "Massachusetts Ole Hanson," Calvin Coolidge, beat him to the draw by quelling the Boston police strike to become reaction's newest hero and Republican candidate for the vice-presidency.

By 1920 Ole's message had been drowned out in the national anti-red hysteria which he had helped to whip up. He returned to Seattle to dispose of his real estate interests and retire to southern California, the realtor's haven, pursued by ugly rumors about his part in the purchase by the city of the street car system from the Stone & Webster interests. To a former police official, writing years later in the Seattle police magazine, "Hanson was the type of man who so frequently appears in Seattle's chronicles as a mayor. He was energetic and picturesque, made rabble-rousing speeches, but did not say anything and accomplished even less. As a result of the way he conducted himself during the strike, he became a Chamber of Commerce hero everywhere but in Seattle."

Seattleites read with some astonishment the lurid accounts of the general strike which appeared in the nation's leading magazines. To the *Saturday Evening Post* it was evident that "bolshevism has put forth its supremest effort in America and has failed." There followed a curious tale, typical of that hysterical period. "The I.W.W. themselves," said the *Post*, "openly boast that the Russian revolution was planned in the office of a Seattle lawyer, counsel for the organization, during those three over-heated days wherein Lenine and Trotsky tarried in the city's midst, en route to Russia; and that an American revolution was planned or at least discussed at the same time." The *Post* referred to "an especially illuminating little treatise in booklet form entitled *Russia Did It,* by an ambitious young Bolshevik author who, alas, now languishes behind prison bars in lieu of $10,000 bail. Two and a half tons of this booklet alone were distributed. Equity [the socialist-I.W.W. print shop] ran its presses frantically day and night." Alas, too, for the truth: it wasn't a booklet but a rather small leaflet; the "Bolshevik author" far from languishing in jail was working to help Armour's construct a huge agricultural irrigation project in the Sutter Basin of California; the leaflet was issued in a modest quantity of 20,000 amounting only to several pounds weight in all; and Equity managed to get its work done in one eight-hour shift each day.

World's Work, then a leading national magazine, was not to be outdone by the *Post.* A full-page photo of Mayor Hanson was captioned:

A citizen of Norwegian ancestry who, by a quick display of intelligent energy, crushed in a few hours a Bolshevist outbreak in the city of Seattle, over which he rules as mayor. A conglomeration of aliens from Russia and Finland attempted to give American "Bolshevism" an example by establishing a Soviet in this Washington city, but Mayor Hanson, by the prompt announcement that the headquarters of the city government was the City Hall and that the first "reformer" to interfere with its operations would be shot, immediately dissolved the "revolution." The aliens who started the disturbance have been deported to their European homes.

Sunset, the Pacific Coast monthly, did not intend to lag behind its Eastern competitors: "Instead of crawling into the cyclone cellar, Seattle walked right up to the gate, a gun in either hand, to meet the Social Revolution. That in a nutshell is the reason why the Bolshevist upheaval did not take place according to schedule."

Closer to home, the *Post-Intelligencer* joined the chorus. Proclaiming February 11 that "The Revolution is Over," the *P-I* editorialized:

Whatever may have been the motives of the rank and file of the strikers, those who engineered the strike did so with the hallucination that the whole country would flame into revolution. In fact, the idea of revolution was the sole idea with any logical foundation for the whole undertaking. . . . The revolution is at an end. The serpent head of Bolshevism has been crushed under the heels of an onward-marching citizenry led by a fearless mayor.

To this the *Union Record* responded:

If by revolution is meant violence, the killing or maiming of men, surely no group of workers dreamed of such action. But if by revolution is meant that the Great Change is coming over the face of the world, which will transform our method of carrying on industry and will go deep into the very source of our lives, to bring joy and freedom in place of heaviness and fear — then we do believe in such a Great Change and that the General Strike was one of the definite steps toward it. . . . Some day when the workers have learned to manage, they will *Begin Managing.*

Truth was, a revolutionary spark did exist in Seattle in February, 1919. The strike leaders knew that as well as the government, and were mortally frightened. For that reason unionists were ordered to remain at home and avoid any gatherings; the *Union Record* was ordered not to publish; no incident was to be permitted that might flare into provocation of the Army and the thousands of armed vigilantes. By the third day of the strike they realized that the Seattle labor movement stood all alone; the strike wave did not even spread down the coast to California nor was there any move across a nation falling under the spell of the anti-Red hysteria to give aid and comfort, even verbally, to the labor movements of Seattle and Tacoma. Seattle, unfortunately, was all too unique in its militancy.

7

Postwar Turmoil

Ole Hanson faced a perplexing dilemma after the general strike. Single-handed he had, according to his own account, quelled a "revolution." And unsuccessful revolutions presumably are illegal. Yet no one was in jail, the "revolutionists" were walking the streets and even feeling cockier than ever after the amazing display of organized labor's strength. The real "revolutionists" of course were up in the Labor Temple. But what charges could be pressed against these men and women who had supervised the most non-violent revolution in history?

In such situations, the police had an easy and obvious way to obtain victims. Raid the Wobbly hall! Of course the I.W.W. had not ordered the general strike, and their only participation, aside from sympathetic support, occurred when I.W.W. members also held A.F. of L. cards. There may have been several thousand such "two-card" men, but it is doubtful if they accounted for more than five percent of Seattle's union membership. Nevertheless the police swooped down on the I.W.W. hall on Second Avenue South and arrested the more prominent members there. Plainclothesmen stationed themselves in the I.W.W. office in another building and arrested men as they came in to pay their dues. But aside from the satisfaction of being able to see glaring headlines in the business press about the wholesale arrests, the police could pick up no evidence connecting the men with the "revolution."

Fortunately for Ole Hanson, there was a slender thread which might tie some suspects in with his revolution. Had there not been that socialist leaflet before the general strike which urged the shipyard workers to take over the shipyards? The leaflet had nothing to do with the general strike and, oddly enough, never even urged its use. Nor was it authorized by any union connected with the general strike. Nevertheless it was known to have been written by the staff of the *International Weekly*, the socialist paper, and printed at the Equity printshop, owned by socialists, I.W.W., and various radical groups. The police, flanked by operatives of the Department of Justice, descended upon the Equity plant, arrested its manager, Walker C. Smith, who was also editor of the *Industrial Worker*, the I.W.W. weekly, and padlocked the shop. Warrants were issued for the arrest of various socialists and others presumed to have written and distributed the offending leaflet.

Attorney George F. Vanderveer called those being sought into his office for a conference. A sizable group assembled and it is noteworthy of their cohesiveness and integrity that this could be done. The FBI was yet to assemble its staff of informers; as for the police, they had not perfected the details of "red squad" operation. Their dragnets were large-meshed and their operations notoriously clumsy, so much so that the Wobblies referred to them as "town clowns" and the parody on their operations exhibited in Keystone Kop movie comedies excited the risibilities of the general public. Vanderveer was the kind of labor lawyer who liked to have as few clients as possible; he advised the group to seek safety in flight to other states. Then, casting an eye on the assembled radicals, he asked one, a newsboy, and a most unlikely inciter of revolutionary action, if he would be willing to surrender, bail being assured at the time of arrest. The newsboy eagerly agreed, the rest of the group packed their suitcases for Oregon, California, and other way points, to await there the outcome of the newsboy's trial.

The *International Weekly* met a dramatic end. The editors, pondering the significance of the general strike amid the world-wide conflagration of a dying system, concluded, rather too optimistically, that the end was near. In addition to the story on the general strike, the editors had assembled reports from Munich, Budapest, Paris, and elsewhere which indicated all too clearly that the social system, such as it was, faced a mortal crisis. Soviets were arising through central Europe and even staid old England was in turmoil. The editors searched the Equity print-shop for the biggest type available, known in printers' parlance as "boxcar type." With this was composed the headline stretch-ing across the front page: CAPITALISM TOTTERING! It was after this that the police and the Department of Justice closed in on the Equity printshop. It was the *International Weekly*, alas, that tottered. But within a few weeks a new editorial staff had been assembled and *Freedom* appeared as a socialist weekly. No copies are known to exist of either paper but fortunately editorial excerpts survived. The Senate Judiciary Committee had named a sub-committee to probe into the brewing industry and Bolshevik propaganda — the first forerunner of McCarthy-ism. This unlikely pair of targets was connected by what to the inquisitors was an obvious link: the American brewers bore mostly German names and it was well known that Bolshevik propaganda was financed by the Kaiser. To this inquiry we owe the existence of excerpts from editorials in the *International Weekly*.

In the December 20, 1918, issue that paper called for the release of all political prisoners and referred particularly to Emma Goldman and to the Seattle anarchist, Louise Olivereau.

There is nothing to gain [the editorial advised] by appealing to the government for the release of these, our prisoners. We must act! Agitate! Expose the system which prates of democracy and Chris-tianity and yet makes of the beautiful earth a living hell for workers. Open the eyes of the dullest workingman to the monstrosities being committed throughout the length and breadth of our land.

Organize! on the industrial and political field in effective organi-zation, so that when the time comes you can arise and throw off the shackles that bind you to slavery, and thus you will

Emancipate! not only thousands of our prisoners who are living in death in the prison camps of our masters, but yourselves as well.

The *International Weekly* proclaimed:

The Revolution is on! Within the next ten years the most monumental changes in all human history will take place and the fourth decade of the Twentieth Century will see the Workers supreme over the earth and the products thereof to which they give value.

In its Christmas issue of 1918, the paper sent greetings

to all those who have no Christmas. . . . And we hope that all you prostitutes feel grateful that you live in a country where every citizen has equal opportunity and where womanhood is sacred; and we hope that all you thousands of little children who toil in factory or mill realize the greatness and unselfishness of our Government and especially the Supreme Court which permitted you to stay at work; and we hope that all you political prisoners are happy because of living in the land of liberty.

The Seattle socialists, meeting in convention December 28, 1918, adopted a municipal program for a workers' city council "modelled very directly after the Russian method of municipal administration." They asked for the creation of a city government similar to the Soviet plan — "an industrial government of workers which will eliminate bourgeois control and disfranchise the useless members of society." The workers' city council was to sit alongside the bourgeois council until the workers took over. Its functions would be to expose the existing city government and to draw up legislation on subjects before the council, or ignored by it. "Thus it shall reveal to the workers the class nature of all bourgeois governments and the futility of the workers hoping for any material benefit from any bourgeois government, and prepare for the organization of their own government against the time when the workers shall seize power." The program called for immediate expropriation of privately-owned public utilities and their control directly by the workers. Absolute freedom of speech, press, and assembly was demanded. In deference to their I.W.W. fellow workers, the socialists said: "We advocate militant industrial unions as the only correct form of organization on the industrial field, and pledge ourselves to constant support thereof." This was prob-

ably the most advanced municipal program ever urged by a city
Socialist Party in the United States.

The release of political prisoners was becoming a key issue
among Seattle radicals and unionists, as elsewhere. The long
trial of the 166 I.W.W. in Chicago, defended by Vanderveer,
and the trials of 146 in Sacramento, 38 in Wichita, seven in
Tacoma, 27 in Omaha, and 28 in Spokane, had resulted in
imprisonment for virtually all the defendants. Embittered by
capitalist justice, the Sacramento Wobblies treated their trial as
a farce; they refused to retain lawyers, laughed at the prosecutors, ignored the judge, and sat with their backs to the bench
— as good a defense as any since it saved the I.W.W. the heavy
burden of providing defense funds. True to their rejection of
the leadership principle, the I.W.W. denied that their "leaders"
were in jail — the heart of the movement was still in the logging,
construction, mining, and harvest camps. But the proud organization was nevertheless badly maimed and mangled with its
most prominent spokesmen and organizers behind the bars.
The national executive committee of the Socialist Party and
many of its most active agitators were in prison or awaiting trial
for opposition to the war.

Eugene V. Debs could not stand the spectacle of his comrades
in the socialist and I.W.W. ranks going to jail while he was
outside looking in. Deliberately he accepted an invitation to
speak in Canton, Ohio, on June 16, 1918. "I may not be able
to say all I think," he told his audience, "but I am not going to
say anything I do not think. I would a thousand times rather be
a free soul in jail than a sycophant and coward in the streets. . . .
The master class has always declared the war; the subject class
has always fought the battles. The master class has had all to
gain and nothing to lose, while the subject class has nothing to
gain and all to lose — especially their lives." That was enough!
On September 14 Debs was condemned to ten years in Atlanta.
In his final speech before being sentenced, the Socialist said:
"Let the people take heart and hope everywhere, for the cross
is bending, the midnight is passing, and joy cometh in the

morning." Early in 1919 the Supreme Court rejected his appeal, declaring that the First Amendment had nothing to do with the case. "Great issues," replied Debs, "are not decided by courts but by the people. I have no concern with what the coterie of begowned corporation lawyers in Washington may decide in my case. The court of final appeal is the people, and that court will be heard from in due time. . . ." The Seattle Central Labor Council wired Debs its "heartfelt appreciation of your splendid efforts to secure for the American wage slave a life of comfort and beauty." On April 12, 1919, the weary old man, his head high, left for prison. The Great Red Scare had jailed its greatest victim.

In Seattle repeated raids on the I.W.W. hall, Socialist Party headquarters, and the Equity printshop had netted 39 victims by February 13, 1919. "This move," announced Prosecutor Fred C. Brown, "is for the purpose of arresting the ringleaders of anarchy, bolshevism and the I.W.W." The charge was criminal anarchy. This was defined as "the doctrine that organized government should be overthrown by force or violence or by assassination of the executive head or any of the executive officials of the government or by any unlawful means. The advocacy of such doctrine, either by word of mouth or writing, is a felony."

The *Union Record* scorned the flimsy pretext of indictment. The authorities, it said, "could go down Second Avenue and pick out business man after business man, yes, and charming ladies in the University district, who have been hoping and preaching that the streets should run red with blood of workingmen of this city. And boys who not only talked, but went out and got guns, remarking that they were going to have a chance to 'pot an I.W.W.' "

Prosecutor Brown was embarrassed. Among his suspects, he said, seven "were responsible for last week's attempted revolution in Seattle. By revolution, however, I wish it to be fully understood that I am not referring to the strike of organized labor last week. This office takes the position that this small

body of reds and radicals attempted to capture the strike machinery and turn it to their own revolutionary purposes. The
strike is one thing; the attempt by a few to convert it into a
revolution is quite another."

The prosecutor conceded that the leaflet *Russia Did It,* the
basis for prosecution, did not itself advocate violence, but
Morris Pass's cartoon did: "The cartoon was intended to
illustrate just how the thing was to be done; it meant that the
individual workers in the Seattle shipyards were to push the
individual owners of the shipyards into the coffin, and this
would constitute overthrow of the government." This absurdity
was denounced by the Central Labor Council — which understood all too well that the indicted men were being victimized
for the general strike — as "an invasion of fundamental rights,"
and a committee was instructed to lend all assistance to the
indicted men. The leaflet, the Council concluded, advocated not
anarchy but socialism. The Council was quite right, as the text
of the leaflet attested:

You and 30,000 of your fellow workmen are on strike. You have
decided that the increase in wages denied by the capitalist Macy is
long overdue. Millions and millions of dollars have been reaped
from the sweat of your labor for the past two years in the shipyards
of Seattle and have been pocketed by a few capitalist owners who
didn't do one iota of work in building the ships that helped to win
the last war. While your fellow workers were being killed outright
and maimed by the thousands in the shipyards, while you were living hand to mouth wondering where the next cent was coming from,
those of the Mighty Few were making millions from the mere reason
they OWNED the machines, the tools with which you worked.

Now when you ask for an increase of a few cents in your wages, you
are refused and told to go to hell. You who build the ships have
nothing to say about the conditions under which you build them
and to secure even a measly increase in wages to keep you from
going to the dogs, you have to go on strike.

Is this as it should be?

You constructed the shipyards. You built the ships. It was by your
sweat that hundreds of great boats now cross the ocean, and if it
had been left to Messrs. Skinner, Eddy, Ames, Duthie & Company,
not a ship would ever have slipped down the ways into the waters
of Elliott Bay.

You have built the ships for your boss. Why not build them for yourselves? Why not own and control, through your unions, YOUR jobs and YOUR shipyards? Why not dictate yourselves the number of hours you should work, the conditions under which you work, the pay you should receive for your labor?

The workers of Russia did it, why not you? They refused to be starved by the capitalist class and when the capitalists refused to meet their conditions, they took over themselves the industries, and operated and managed them in the interests not of the parasitical capitalists but of the workers.

The majority of the class conscious workers of America are with you. IT IS UP TO YOU.

THE WORLD FOR THE WORKERS.

Something of the same idea had occurred to the *Union Record,* although not along revolutionary lines. The *Record* asked:

Would it be such a calamity for our beautiful town if, for instance, the Metal Trades Council should lease the shipyards from Mr. Skinner, Mr. Ames, Mr. Duthie, paying them 6, 8 or 10 percent on their investment? Would it be such a calamity if the income of these gentlemen were definitely limited, instead of the income of the workers being limited? They need a higher inducement in order to do their best, you say? Ah, well, so do the workers!

The harassing raids continued and by March 15, 31 had been indicted and in mid-April 22 were still in jail for lack of bail funds. The trial opened May 21, with James Bruce the first defendant in the docket. The prosecution was confined pretty much to the generalities of the Everett trial — proving to its own satisfaction that the I.W.W. was indeed a revolutionary organization. Several witnesses were found to testify to acts of sabotage but all the evidence seemed to be wide of the mark in proving that the I.W.W. and socialists intended to or had any power to turn the general strike into a revolution. Paul F. Brissenden, the Columbia professor who had written what is still the standard work on the early I.W.W., testified for Bruce. Fortunately for him, the jury was chosen by lot from Seattle taxpayers, unlike the handpicked federal juries, and two members of the Central Labor Council and four women were on it. Bruce was acquitted June 5 and that ended, for a time, the

Great Red Scare in Seattle. The state, having gone through the needed motions to provide a victim for the general strike, gave it up as a bad job and dismissed the other cases. Gradually those who had left began returning to Seattle. Ole Hanson's nation-famed "revolution" had fizzled out.

A shameful piece of business had been perpetrated by the federal authorities during the red scare. The immigration officials had been rounding up Russian, Italian, and other immigrant workers, mostly from the coal mining camps back of Seattle, and herding them into the Seattle detention station. Fifty-four of these men, their hands knotted by hard labor, most of them possessing little or no command of English, penniless, were herded the morning of the general strike into two railroad cars, known as the "Red Special," and sent to Ellis Island in New York harbor. These were the men reported by national magazines to be the inspirers of the general strike, but mostly they were utterly unknown to the leaders of the Central Labor Council. At Ellis Island these workers joined hundreds of other unfortunates, huddled in squalor and despair, until word of their plight seeped out in the *New York Call,* the socialist daily, which cried out an alarm. Rather than endure continued imprisonment without trial or hope of justice, 12 of them accepted voluntary deportation, well content perhaps to turn their backs on the Lady of Liberty who had beckoned them years before to the land of freedom. The *Call's* articles were able to effect the freedom of most of the men against whom the embarrassed immigration authorities conceded they had no evidence. Released as penniless as they entered, most managed to work their way back to their homes in the mining camps. Actually only three were deported involuntarily in this single scene from what became known as the Deportation Delirium of 1919-1920.

If one has to go to jail, it should be in the style that the Central Labor Council adopted to say farewell to Hulet Wells, Sam Sadler, and the Pass brothers, convicted of seditious conspiracy in connection with the no-conscription leaflet and, in the case of the Pass brothers, also for failure to register for the draft. Rather as if they were going to Congress instead of prison, a banquet was held in the Labor Temple on June 5, 1919. It was the month of roses in a city noted for roses, and the hall was banked with them. "All Seattle friends of freedom were represented among the guests," reported the *Union Record*, "and many of them had served jail sentences themselves in free speech fights all over the country." Harry Ault of the *Record* served as toastmaster. George Vanderveer, back from the Chicago I.W.W. trial, observed that Americans are "slaves to fashion in the cut of their sleeves, their skirts, their trousers and their ideas — and the last few years they've been wearing them all very short." W. D. Lane, city councilman and acting mayor during Ole Hanson's frequent lecture tours, Anna Louise Strong, and many of those prominent in the union movement paid tribute to the prisoners-to-be. The affair ended with the presentation of gifts and the singing of the "Marseillaise." The next day Miss Strong contributed a "ragged verse," one of her favorite features in the *Record*, written under the pen name of Anise:

> Hulet Wells, the CONVICT
>
> *   *   *
>
> Whose conviction has damned
>
> *   *   *
>
> Judges and courts forever,
>
> *   *   *
>
> And written "PREJUDICE"
>
> *   *   *
>
> Over the gates where once
>
> *   *   *
>
> Was written "JUSTICE."

The labor council set up a fund financed by 50-cent a month pledges from delegates to help the Wells family during his stay at McNeil Island. After the denial of the appeal, the marshals were waiting to conduct the four socialists to the penitentiary.

"American civil liberty is dead," said Wells. "I might as well appeal to the Emperor of Japan." Sadler, who had moved to Tacoma, was given a rousing sendoff by the Workers, Soldiers and Sailors Council of that city.

The Great Red Scare should have taken its greatest toll in Seattle. That penitentiary sentences were awarded only to Louise Olivereau, Wells, Sadler, and the Pass brothers (although scores had been jailed for weeks and even months) was a tribute to the solidarity and power of the radical and labor movements there. Tens of thousands, angry at the war and at the operation of the federal and state sedition laws, formed a solid ring around those indicted. Seattle juries, when honestly chosen, would not convict, whether in the Everett Massacre trial, in the criminal anarchy farce, or in any other cases. Only the blue-ribbon juries handpicked in federal courts could be relied on, at the behest of the Department of Justice, to scrap the First Amendment and traditional American freedoms.

Cheated of sacrificial victims for the Seattle "revolution," the lords of industry and commerce decided to take the straight road toward retribution. The labor movement itself, and not the fringe groups around it, was the real enemy in the eyes of the Chamber of Commerce. It must be destroyed as a militant force. At first the business dailies demanded that the labor movement purge itself. Cried the *Times:* "A handful of radicals put Seattle in the position of staging a revolution against the government of the United States. These radicals must go and it is the business of employers to *See That They Do Go,* by co-operating with conservative labor in the reconstruction." The *Star* fulminated: "Temporarily misled by a gang of criminal, un-American leaders, Seattle union labor can be depended upon not only to repudiate the false leadership, but to see that punishment goes with repudiation."

But the conservative element in the Central Labor Council, which had never believed in the general strike to begin with, had sought to delimit it and helped to end it as soon as possible, refused to fall into the trap laid by the business dailies. Whatever their disagreements with the majority in the Council, they were not discussing them in public for the benefit of the enemy; to the eternal credit of organized labor not a single delegate could be found to echo the editorial cries of the commercial press. Years of experience had taught conservatives as well as progressives and radicals that there was no friendship behind honeyed words.

The Central Labor Council on March 6, at the height of the "clean house" clamor, declared:

> We hasten to assure the draft-slacking publisher of the *Star*, all the employers who hate labor, and all those who love to lick their boots, that we know exactly what they mean by "reds," we know exactly what they mean by "bolsheviki," exactly what they mean by "cleaning house"; that organized labor in Seattle was never so proud of itself, that it appreciates the reds more for the enemies they have made, that it has no intention of cleaning house to please its opponents, and that the general strike is permanently in the arsenal of labor's peaceful weapons.

When it became obvious that the labor movement could not be split and torn to pieces, the powers-that-be organized the Associated Industries, dedicated to the open shop. By "open shop" employers meant, they said, that they would hire and deal with both union and non-union men, on a basis of equality. That meant there would be little point in belonging to a union. In the phrase of Judge Elbert Gary of United States Steel, facing a showdown with unions in his mills, he had no objection to unions "as such" — he just wouldn't enter into negotiations with them or bargain collectively with them. If a worker cared to, he could join the union, just as he could join the Elks or the Seventh Day Adventists, so long as he didn't intrude his union into the mill.

During the war Seattle had operated largely on the union shop principle, and especially in the shipyards. The Employers Association, dedicated to the open shop, had decayed into a rump organization dominated mainly by the lumber interests. As soon as it was safely launched the Associated Industries came out for the "American Plan," a euphemism for the open shop that was being pushed nationally to combat organized labor. In its sales talk to business executives, the Associated Industries offered its own view of recent history. During the war there was "a widespread revolutionary minority in the Pacific Northwest," particularly in the logging camps. The government cleaned them out of the camps, whereupon they descended on the shipyards. Seattle, with New York and Chicago, were the three great centers of radicalism in the United States. The Secret Service estimated there were "500 Reds of national and international reputation" in Seattle. It was because of all this that in ten minutes, according to the Associated Industries, business men gave $110,000 to establish the anti-union organization and that within a short time $200,000 had been put into the war fund.

From the beginning the Associated Industries could boast of substantial victories. Under threat that their charters would be revoked by the international unions, the locals in the shipyard industry returned to work March 11, their demands not granted. As ships on the ways were completed, it was noted that few new contracts were being signed. The Associated Industries put up no battle for more ship construction; it was anxious to see the army of shipyard workers demobilized. During 1919 there was a steady exodus of men back to the interior whence they had come, as jobs disappeared in the yards. In May the building trades were forced into a strike and obliged to return under open shop conditions. The printing trades struck in the job shops; this strike went on for months without clearcut victory for either side. The tailors struck and also faced the united front of the Associated Industries.

In this period the longshoremen made international history, much to the discomfiture of the Associated Industries. They had bucked the tide and won the union shop on the waterfront in midsummer of 1919. And then, early in October, came a mysterious shipment by rail, a trainload of 50 freight cars, destination Vladivostok, and labeled "sewing machines." It seemed a curious export to a country in the throes of civil war.

A longshore crew, suspicious of the cargo, allowed a crate to crash on the dock. Out spewed stacks of rifles, bound for the Kolchak counter-revolutionary government. Upon inquiry it became evident that this was no mere private shipment of "hardware." The United States government, no less, had chartered a ship, inappropriately named the "Delight," to take this cargo of munitions consigned by Remington Arms to Kolchak. The longshoremen's union announced that its members would not touch the hot cargo and that any dock that attempted to move it would be put under permanent boycott. The news sped over the wires to New York and Europe; in Petrograd and Moscow it was hailed as evidence that the hearts of American workers were with their union brothers in Russia.

The Central Labor Council backed up the longshoremen while the business press howled in anguish and Senators fumed in Washington. The *Union Record* found it needful to say in a page-one editorial that "the *Times,* the Associated Industries, Senator Hiram Johnson, Senator Miles Poindexter, the *P-I,* the *Star,* and all the rest of the spokesmen for the ruling class are busily engaged in peddling the only genuine blown-in-the-bottle brand of Kickapoo Sagwa 'Americanism,' in an effort to divert the minds of the workers along alleged patriotic lines. . . . We do not accept flag-waving as a substitute for common sense."

The "Kickapoo Indian Sagwa" was widely advertised in the labor press, as purported to be sold by a medical firm in Seattle. It was touted as "a famous cure for Incipient Revolution and Bolshevism." "Are you troubled," the ad inquired, "with a Russia blood to the head? Do red spots appear continually before your eyes? Are you unable to sleep after ten in the morning? Does the whole world seem Wobbly?

"The first dose turns you into a 'booze-wah.' The second makes you a 'pay-to-riot.' The third makes you want to hang workingmen to lampposts."

A minor hero of the general strike, Paul C. Bickel, paid for his loyalty to principle with his job. A high school teacher of

mathematics and a long-time socialist, Bickel on the eve of the
general strike spoke at a meeting of the streetcar men, urging
them to join the walkout. "Thinking it over," he told the
school board later, "it seemed to me that I ought to do what I
urged others to do, so I went out in sympathy with organized
labor." With only former socialist Judge Winsor voting no, the
board fired him. Bickel had worked in the shipyards in spare
time, in accordance with the government's urging on one and
all, and was a member of the machinists union. Under the name
Mark Stone, he had written for the *Call* from time to time.
Blacklisted in his profession, he went to Oakland, worked in the
shipyards awhile, and then on the *World,* the socialist weekly
there. When that paper folded he was on the point of destitution
for years until he got a job in a small high school in northern
California. Rehabilitated, he taught mathematics later in a
suburban high school in Oakland until his death.

The censors began combing the schools for other victims and
came up with Charles H. Niederhauser, a pacifist who taught in
the West Seattle High School. The editor of the *Post-Intelligencer* urged readers to demand his discharge as "an atheist,
anarchist, German by name, Hun by instinct, and Boche by
choice . . . a conspirator in an attempted bolshevik revolution."
The High School Teachers rallied to his defense, claiming him
to be a true patriot.

Another target for the patriots was Mrs. Anna Falkoff, of
Russian origin and for a time a dweller in Home Colony. A
teacher and an anarchist, she was attracted to the educational
ideals of Francisco Ferrer, the Spanish educator executed in
1909 by the Spanish government. Of Tolstoian cast, Mrs. Falkoff
plodded about barefoot in her garden in the University district
and conducted a modern school for children. The inquisitors
were certain that this was a hotbed for young revolutionists.
Didn't she teach her charges Marxism? "But I am no Marxist
and I have never studied Marxist economics," she protested.
"And anyway, I doubt if it would be worthwhile to teach Marxist economics to such young children." But certainly some in-

doctrination was going on in her school? "Yes," she replied, "I try to teach them to be free."

The heat of persecution fused the lights of *Freedom*, the socialist weekly, which was succeeded by the *Forge*, weekly organ of the Workers, Soldiers and Sailors Council. This Council, endorsed by the Metal Trades and Central Labor Councils, received wide support in the beginning when fears ran rampant that returning veterans might be mobilized into an anti-labor army. But the ex-servicemen seemed more inclined to return to whatever niche in civilian life they had occupied before and were in no mood to be used to break down their own living standards. As work in the shipyards declined, so did income from the shipyard unions and the Workers, Soldiers and Sailors Council lost most of its active union support, continuing as a forum for radical ideas. The *Forge* began seriously to consider ways of tightening union organization through the shop steward system that was sweeping Britain. This system bypassed the top union leadership and aimed to place effective controls in the rank and file through shop stewards elected directly in the various departments in mine, mill, and factory. Many shipyard workers were still angry about the "sell-out" of their strike by the international unions. They preached the futility of craft division and especially saw the weakness in the Seattle situation where workers had struck without the support of shipyard unions elsewhere.

In such a loose organization, spies and Minute Men, the amateur patriots, were rampant. Indeed the Minute Men picked on the Council as a point of concentration and nearly took it over; at that point the Central Labor Council lost interest and turned its attention to the Private Soldiers and Sailors Legion, a national outfit whose local chief was Frank Pease. The industrial spies operated under grants from interests affiliated with the Associated Industries. After the death of the spy chief, his widow deposited his papers with the University of Washington library and as a result a wealth of information and misinformation is available to those concerned with labor affairs of 1919-1920. It

was obvious that at least one spy was well-connected at the Labor
Temple, with easy access to its officials. Fortunately an organization which thought enough of publicity to publish its own daily
newspaper had little to hide, and so this spy's reports added
little to what was readily available to anyone in the columns of
the *Union Record* and the open sessions of the Central Labor
Council.

Other spies ran truer to form, with lurid reports. They operated in the Workers, Soldiers and Sailors Council and among the
I.W.W.'s. Because of the migratory nature of I.W.W. membership, it was easier for spies to penetrate and even to occupy the
desired posts of secretaries in the industrial union branches.
Wild exaggerations of I.W.W. strength featured most such
reports; the Lumber Workers had 46,000 members, there were
12,000 Wobblies in Seattle and 100,000 on the Pacific Coast, and
30,000 in shipbuilding.

The war was long over when McNeil Island penitentiary absorbed Hulet Wells, Sam Sadler, Morris and Joseph Pass. It was
symbolic of the cold fury of the Great Red Scare that it demanded victims long after the occasion for their imprisonment
— opposition to the war — had passed. If it were not a prison,
McNeil Island would be another gem in the expanses of Puget
Sound. This was a prison without walls; passersby on the Sound
saw only a half dozen tall towers manned by armed guards. At
the time it housed nearly 250 prisoners. Many of the politicals
were in for violation of the espionage law; they looked around
to see if there were any German spies or saboteurs. But no, somehow the federals had concentrated only on socialists and
Wobblies.

Among the politicals was Ricardo Flores Magón, the Mexican
anarchist revolutionary who had led an armed expedition from
United States territory to free his country. There Magón sat,
dying of tuberculosis and nearly blind, peeling potatoes, discussing the uneven fortunes of the Mexican Revolution, hungry
for any scrap of news from the struggle there. The Mexican
government had offered him a life pension but politely he

turned it down because as an anarchist he could accept no favors from any government. His companion, Librado Rivera, was a more proletarian type, the prisoners' "military expert," who had been in many a battle. Later Magón was transferred to Leavenworth penitentiary where he died November 21, 1922. His body was shipped in an express car to the border where a great throng of unionists, with red and black flags flying, awaited its arrival. There on a special train Magón's flower-enshrouded coffin went from city to city, everywhere to be greeted by thousands, and on to Mexico City where he was enshrined in the national Pantheon. Today, everywhere in Mexico, streets and plazas are named for Ricardo Flores Magón, and his anniversary is commemorated each year to honor the intellectual father of the Mexican Revolution, who died the death of a dog in an American prison.

Emil Herman, state secretary of the Socialist Party, was serving time on McNeil Island too, along with two Wobblies and an Irish revolutionist whose crime was sending arms to his country, then fighting against the Black and Tan terror. To "Sean" the Irish revolutionary movement had assigned its most important task in the United States; small wonder that he was transferred to the penitentiary farthest away from New York and Ireland. Sophisticated, at home in economics, literature, world affairs, and at ease in seven languages, this intellectual was loved by his fellow-prisoners — most of them poor and uncultured men — for his Irish humor, his humanity, and his knack of being able to get things done for them. For his protection, some of the most eminent figures in Irish-American political life corresponded with him; as a result the prison authorities handled him with silk gloves.

After their arrival on the Island, Wells and Sadler were lodged for a time in the same cell. Sadler, longshoreman, machinist, and tireless socialist agitator, was a quiet, nerveless man, dark-complected, with small powerful shoulders and arms, who held himself stiffly erect, perhaps from his pugilistic training. An orphan in Philadelphia, he had been taken into the Van Dyke home. A relative of the family, Henry Van Dyke, occasionally brought a Princeton professor by the name of Woodrow Wilson to visit in the Philadelphia home. Sam used to take him fishing on the Schuylkill; later he was to say sardonically that it was his own fault he was on McNeil Island; if he had used his wits on the Schuylkill, the professor would never have had a chance "to keep us out of war."

For Morris Pass, the artist, the counterfeiters were a special revelation. They were artists, too, in their fashion. Two of them were far more creative in their prison drawings than many who exhibit in the New York galleries. Because of their skill, imagination, and brains they often took the lead in the good causes in prison.

One night a new guard appeared, about 50 years old. He talked often to the Pass brothers and revealed that he had been a member of Debs' American Railway Union. Blacklisted, he had drifted from job to job. The man was filled with marvellous tales of working-class life and when he spoke of Debs it was with tears in his eyes. When the guard volunteered to bring in material from the outside on his trips to town, the Pass brothers were justifiably suspicious. But no, he visited their families and returned each time with copies of the *Liberator,* the national radical monthly, John Reed's *Ten Days That Shook the World,* the Wobbly and socialist papers, pamphlets, and books. For a solid week thereafter prison didn't matter as the politicals renewed their contact with the world outside, free again although in prison.

For an artist and a writer, the worst of prison was lack of paper. Everything blank was used, even toilet paper. Morris Pass decided to try his hand at sculpture. Where to get the clay and tools? The warden bellowed a loud "No!" The defense committee got in touch with New York artists and with prison bureau authorities in Washington. Even President William Short of the State Federation of Labor, no great admirer of radicals such as the Pass brothers, interceded. Sean, the Irishman, got busy and within 72 hours Morris Pass had his raw materials.

Then came a routine check of the cells; the warden was furious. Pass faced loss of all good time and the hole, to boot. It happened that the chaplain was a pacifist and a Christian as well. Morris said to him in the warden's presence: "Reverend, you gave me this clay and the tools yesterday morning." The chaplain, looking straight at the warden, replied: "I think I did, I think I did." That saved Morris from the hole; in any event permission had come from Washington for him to have the materials he needed.

The constant atrocity at the prison was its fare. Bread, potatoes, and a sludge called coffee; the stew was usually inedible. It was this, among other things, that drove Hulet Wells to an act of desperation. He was assigned to the wood crew which went out and felled timber and sawed it for prison use. The work arduous, the food inedible, Wells felt his strength slipping. As a good union man, his requests for transfer to other work having been ignored, he decided to go on strike. In a prison, that is sheer madness; but Wells had reached the point of despondency where life and death mattered not. To Warden O.P. Halligan, a hard, ignorant autocrat, he wrote: "Since you have not had the courtesy to reply to my request for a change in work, I am quitting the job, and you can proceed with whatever brutalities are usual in such contingencies."

On August 22, 1919, Wells was thrown into the black hole. Handcuffs about his wrists were chained to the bars at the level of his head and he was forced to stand in that one position eight hours a day. For food there were two slices of bread a day until Sean, the Irish revolutionist, was able to arrange that food be sent him from the warden's kitchen. When unchained, Wells poked about the bare cell, found a hole and from far up in its interior he rescued a copy of the *Saturday Evening Post* which carried a story, "The Enchanted Hour," by the then little known writer Sinclair Lewis. The story was about a radical colony in California, somewhat like those that had flourished in Washington State. When news leaked out from McNeil Island that Wells was standing chained to his bars eight hours a day, a storm of protest welled up in both the Seattle and Tacoma labor councils. The *Union Record* published on its front page an artist's illustration of Wells in his black hole, manacled, and a replica of the cell was exhibited in the lobby of the Labor Temple.

The Central Labor Council held an open air rally for Debs, Mooney, and the Seattle prisoners on September 7, 1919. Three thousand turned out at Fourth Avenue and Virginia Street on an open lot to hear Bob Minor, world-famous cartoonist and correspondent. "Men like Hulet Wells, Gene Debs and Tom Mooney, who are in jail today for you and me," he said, "are the men who shape tomorrow for liberty and justice." Minor reported on his European trip, where he had interviewed Liebknecht, Lenin, Bela Kun, and other revolutionary leaders. C. J. France, attorney for the Port Commission, and brother of Senator Joseph Irwin France of Maryland and of Royal France, endorsed the demand for liberation of all political prisoners. "We have forgotten," he said, "the principles of the origin of our nation if we have forgotten how to object, to agitate and rebel." At another meeting in the Arena a few days later 6,000 turned out to hear continuing reports from McNeil Island. The longshoremen adjourned their own meeting and marched in a body to the Arena. Endorsing the campaign for release of political prisoners, the Central Labor Council commissioned Anna Louise Strong and Phil J. Pearl of the barbers union to attend the Chicago convention of the American League to Preserve Civil Liberties.

It was about this time that President Wilson was making his final swing around the nation. The labor movement had prepared a special reception for the President, a "silent protest." The Central Labor Council had 100,000 badges printed reading RELEASE POLITICAL PRISONERS. As the parade came up Second Avenue, the President and his party could note block after block of people standing with folded arms, silent and reproachful, their badges fluttering in the breeze. Instead of the roar of applause with which his cavalcade was usually greeted, Wilson got the ominous silent treatment. At the great meeting that night, perhaps half the audience wore the badges in their lapels and sat on their hands during the President's speech. It was the "Seattle treatment" and it received nation-wide attention as another evidence that the city on the Sound was indeed unique. The following morning a delegation from the Central Labor Council, the State Federation of Labor, and the Triple Alliance — representing labor and the farmers — waited upon Wilson with a plea for the release of Wells, Sadler, and the Pass brothers. The President said he would study the petition.

After several weeks of being chained, and convinced that he was alone in the world and forgotten, Wells suddenly was released from his shackles, light was permitted in his cell, and the food was improved. Then came delegations from the Seattle and Tacoma labor councils, permitted by Warden Halligan to see that Wells was receiving quite humane treatment for a man who had defied prison rules by striking. After their departure, the manacles went on again; a committee of doctors who made a surprise visit to the penitentiary September 23 found him strung up. A grand jury investigation was ordered, and the heat was on Warden Halligan.

The case presented a nice dilemma for the prison authorities. It would never do to permit a federal prisoner to win a strike; on the other hand the Puget Sound labor movement was screaming about black torture in the black hole in the black hell of McNeil Island, and the publicity did the Wilson Administration little good. A face-saving device was discovered; Wells was transferred to Leavenworth penitentiary — chained to three other prisoners for the long journey — and Warden Halligan somewhat later was eased out of his job. Wells, by iron determination and an indomitable will, had won his strike in principle — he had escaped the wood gang. It was one of the few examples of solitary action, backed by an aroused labor movement on the outside, winning out against prison authorities; the Wobblies repeatedly won their demands by "battleshipping" the jail, but Wells was no Wobbly, either by conviction or temperament.

At Leavenworth, Wells moved with as distinguished a company of men as could be found behind the bars anywhere. I.W.W. members from all over the country were in one huge cellhouse which they converted into a proletarian university. In the Kansas contingent were the three Browder brothers; other contingents came from jails in California, Oklahoma, and other points where the Wobblies had been concentrated for their trials. Socialist farmers from Oklahoma who had taken part in the Green Corn Rebellion, socialist workers, draft-resisters, and religious objectors to war swelled the ranks. Carl Haessler, the Ph.D. from Illinois, Charles Ashleigh, the English poet, Brent Dow Allison, the Chicago pacifist, Maurice Becker, the artist, and others organized lectures and courses in the learned disciplines while expert mechanics gave instruction in electrical and machine trades.

Wells was asked by prison authorities to petition for a parole; he replied that what he wanted was not a parole but an apology from the President. Nevertheless he with Sadler and the Pass brothers were released at various times from October to December, 1920. News of Wells's release had been wired ahead and there were a thousand people at the railroad station to greet him. Hundreds later attended a luncheon given in his honor by the Central Labor Council. Louise Olivereau, the other Seattle federal prisoner, had been released in the spring of 1920.

The Seattle socialists who had given nearly two years of their lives for their opposition to the First World War could find sour satisfaction in the nation-wide revulsion that swept the country a few years later. Such an eminent authority on Anglo-American relations as Winston Churchill, discussing the question of repayment of the British war debt, expressed himself in words that would have gotten him 10 to 20 years in an American penitentiary: "Legally we owe the debt to the United States, but logically we don't, and this because America should have stayed out of the World War. If she had done so, the Allies would have made peace with Germany in the spring of 1917, thus saving a million British, American, French and other lives and prevent-

ing the subsequent rise of fascism and Nazism." And, the former
Prime Minister might have added, the rise of Soviet Russia.

To that estimate General Hugh S. Johnson, the director of
the draft, later to be head of Roosevelt's NRA, added his comment: the First World War, he said, was "the most disastrous
gamble this nation ever made. We were disillusioned in our
ideals, two-timed in our agreements and understandings, frus-
trated in our aims, rooked in our financial dealings and left with
a burden of debt and depression which has mortgaged our future, vastly impaired our national heritage and still threatens
our whole political, social and economic structure as we and
our fathers had known it for 150 years." Acid words, easily written at so much a line for a nationally-syndicated column, but
when socialist and I.W.W. workmen said much the same thing
at a time when it could have changed history, the penitentiary
doors swung open for them.

8

Tragedy in Centralia

So fiercely did the flames of persecution lick around the I.W.W. late in 1919 that only two halls in the entire state of Washington were open, in Seattle and Centralia. Continued police raids on the Seattle hall had led Lumber Workers Industrial Union 500, representing some 20,000 loggers in the Pacific Northwest, to canvass its membership on methods of protecting that hall, the nerve center of the union and its central means of contact with the men as they came in from the camps and returned to them. Active members, passing through the Seattle hall, voted 1,021 to 233 to call a general strike in the woods if the hall were closed.

The loggers also voted by 1,282 to 34 to enforce the eight-hour day from the time of leaving the bunkhouse till the return. In the bigger camps it took 30 minutes to an hour to get from the camp to the scene of logging operations — "dead time" for which the men got no pay. They also voted overwhelmingly to ban overtime work except in emergency, to provide more jobs at a time when unemployment was mounting. In the big camps along the slopes of the Cascades and the Olympics, the I.W.W. was a potent force in holding the basic eight-hour day and working conditions against postwar pressures. But by its nature the I.W.W. was more of a movement than an organization; in confronting the companies, most of which were implacable in their opposition to any form of unionism, and particularly to it, the I.W.W. maintained conditions only by an incessant guerrilla struggle.

In the Grays Harbor region and the rest of southwest Wash-

ington the I.W.W. was by no means so well entrenched. No
Wobbly halls were tolerated in Aberdeen, Hoquiam, and the
other mill towns. In Raymond, a sad little sawmill town, Wobblies were rounded up early in 1918 and tried en masse in the
Commercial Club on charges of vagrancy. Their crime — refusal to work 12 hours a day in the woods. Mark Litchman, the
doughty Seattle socialist lawyer, faced not only the hostile court,
a battery of lumber company lawyers, but also a hundred soldiers compelled to attend the trial in an effort to terrify the
I.W.W. and their attorney. The soldiers however enjoyed their
respite from working the twelve-hour day in the woods, to which
they had been consigned to break the I.W.W. general strike for
the eight-hour day. Many of the soldiers said after a taste of logging that they too would have struck if they could have. Ironically, only a few weeks after the vagrancy trial the eight-hour day
was decreed by the government.

In the fall of 1919 unemployment was spreading and wages
were slipping. A labor market report in *New Solidarity*, the
I.W.W. weekly, read:

> ABERDEEN, Oct. 16 — The market
> this week is noticeably sluggish and
> buyers are very cautious because of the
> large number of slaves offered.
> It is the general opinion that the mas-
> ters will, if the offerings continue so
> heavy, dispose of their old stock and
> supply themselves in a cheaper market.
> On the other hand the slaves, not being
> able to sell their services, are consider-
> ing reducing the labor supply by con-
> tinuing with the I.W.W. and creating
> a shortage by establishing the six-hour
> day.
> Good strong young common labor
> slaves are selling for $4.50 and $5 a day;
> semi-skilled and skilled, $5 to $7; runts,
> cripples and old slaves find few buyers.

About midway between Seattle and Portland lies Centralia,
then a town of some 7,000, a lumber, railroad, and trading cen-

ter for Lewis County, which sweeps down from the summit of
the Cascades to the Grays Harbor country. In September, 1919,
Britt Smith leased a store-front hall in the two-story wooden
Roderick Hotel, a workingmen's rooming house on drab Tower
Avenue, for an I.W.W. hall.

It took a man of uncommon courage to consider opening an
I.W.W. hall in Centralia in 1919. There had been a Wobbly hall
a few blocks away the year before but during a Red Cross parade
April 30, 1918, a group of business men stormed it, smashed
doors and windows, piled furniture and files in the street and
beat up the Wobblies inside. After setting fire to the hall, the
hoodlums then lifted the I.W.W. by the ears onto trucks and
took them out of town, where they were dumped into a ditch,
beaten again, and warned never to return.

An old blind news vendor named Tom Lassiter had a little
stand where he sold the *Industrial Worker,* the *Union Record,*
and other labor and radical papers. One night in June, 1919, a
bunch of men overturned his stand, destroyed his papers and
warned him to quit. Undaunted, Lassiter re-established his
business. On June 13 he was seized at his stand, thrown into an
auto and dumped into a ditch at the county line and warned
not to return. At that the *Union Record* up in Seattle became
interested and sent a reporter to inquire into the state of affairs
in Centralia. Later, even more disquieting news reached Seattle.
The *Record* reported on October 24:

ANARCHY URGED
BY CENTRALIA
BUSINESS REDS

Prepare to Ignore Law in
Hysterical Plan of Direct Action

CENTRALIA — The "business reds"
of this city are again preparing to drive
out the "wobblies" and at a recent meeting organized a secret committee of ten
who are said to be pledged to drive
every member of the organization and
every citizen who sympathizes with it
out of the district.

The alleged action was taken at a
meeting of the Centralia Citizens' Protective League, held in the Elks' hall
and presided over by William Scales, a
grocer who was accused of playing a
leading part in the kidnapping of
Thomas Lassiter, *Union Record* agent,
last June. F. B. Hubbard, the so-called
"busted lumber baron of Southwest
Washington," is said to have taken an
active part in the meeting and to have
clashed with members of the city council and the chief of police over methods
to be employed in forcing the I.W.W.
out of town.

Hubbard, it is said, declared if he
were chief he would rid the town of
"wobblies" in 24 hours. This statement
is alleged to have been made after the
chief of police had declared there was
no law under which he could drive the
organization out of the city. Scales is
reported to have advocated direct action, declaring that he did not believe
any jury would be obtained that would
find those taking part in a raid on the
I.W.W. hall guilty of violating the law.

Every "wobblie" is to be listed, business men themselves to refuse to em-
ploy any man known to be a member
or suspected of sympathizing with the
organization. The gathering of these
lists has already started.

Reports of this meeting excited the admiration of the Tacoma
News-Tribune, which applauded the good old vigilante spirit,
in the tradition of the West of yore. It appeared that after the
various acquittals in trials of radicals, the Employers Association
of Washington, dominated by the lumber interests, was through
with legality. The I.W.W. must go; if juries chosen from the
people wouldn't do their duty, then it was time for the torch and
the noose!

The secret committee, composed of employers, businessmen,
and American Legion officials, laid its plans, which were an-

nounced November 7. The Legion post was to parade Armistice Day, November 11, and its route included that part of Tower Avenue where the I.W.W. hall was located. As that section of town consisted of third-rate hotels, pool halls, cheap restaurants, and nondescript stores, the choice was ominous. In alarm Mr. and Mrs. James McAllister, proprietors of the Roderick Hotel, in whose building the hall was rented, appealed to the police chief for protection. He replied quite coolly that there weren't enough police in Centralia to stop the marchers if they decided to invade the hall.

The group of I.W.W., some dozen or more then in town, gathered with Secretary Britt Smith to consider what to do. There were three choices before them: Close the hall on Armistice Day and allow it to be sacked, as the earlier one had been in the previous year. Stand by in the hall and be beaten up by the Legionnaires and deported — the Everett treatment. Or they could defend their hall. The I.W.W. conferred with a young attorney, Elmer Smith, who had incurred the wrath of the upper crust by defending workingmen against employers in wage and other claims. Smith told them that under the law they were within their rights in defending the hall against attack, even with guns.

Prudent men, valuing their own skins, would have closed the hall in the face of the obvious threat. But prudence was not a Wobbly trait. Rather their shining glory stood out in audacity, courage, and stubbornness in defense of their rights, and for that they are remembered in history. It was typical too of their utter decentralization and local autonomy that apparently it did not occur to any of them to get in touch with the western headquarters of the I.W.W. in Seattle on a matter which was to prove of transcendental importance to the entire I.W.W. movement.

Nearly all the I.W.W. in Centralia were loggers, young men, and some were returned servicemen — all familiar with weapons. In those days knowledge of firearms was not the monopoly of sportsmen and soldiers; on the western frontier guns were the common equipment of the pioneers, and Washington was still near the pioneer days. The returned soldiers among them considered the best methods of defense. On the other side of the street in the next block and some 300 feet away was the Arnold Hotel, another workingmen's place, and down Tower Avenue, near the intersection of Second Street, was the Avalon House. At some distance from the Roderick Hotel was Seminary Hill which overlooked the avenue. From the hall itself and from these vantage points, the hall could be protected if need be.

The I.W.W. printed a thousand copies of a circular which was widely distributed in Centralia November 4, a week before the parade. It read:

TO THE CITIZENS OF CENTRALIA WE MUST APPEAL

To the Law-Abiding Citizens of Centralia and to the Working Class in General: We beg of you to read and carefully consider the following: The profiteering class of Centralia have of late been waving the flag of our country in an endeavor to incite the lawless elements of our city to raid our hall and club us out of town. . . . These profiteers are holding numerous meetings to that end, and covertly inviting returned service men to do their bidding. . . . These criminal thugs call us a band of outlaws bent on destruction. This they do in an attempt to hide their own dastardly work in burning our hall and destroying our property. They say we are a menace; and we are a menace to all mobocrats and pilfering thieves. Never did the I.W.W. burn public or private halls, kidnap their fellow citizens, destroy their property, club their fellows out of town, bootleg, or act in any way as lawbreakers. . . . Our only crime is solidarity, loyalty to the working class, and justice to the oppressed.

It was no secret on the streets of Centralia that the I.W.W. hall was to be raided Armistice Day. The weekly meeting of the Lewis County A.F. of L. Trades Council was troubled by these reports; Vice President William Dunning got in touch with Warren O. Grimm, who had just been elected commander of the Legion post, and told him that the labor unions strongly disapproved of such lawlessness. "You fellows are making a mistake," Grimm replied. "Decent labor should keep out of this."

Clearly there was no "third force" to stand between the Legion and the I.W.W. Ministers of the church either whooped it up for violence or were silent; the "better element" was all for blasting the I.W.W. out of town; the ordinary working people didn't count for much. The Legionnaires were determined to clean out a nest of vipers; the Wobblies were just as determined not to permit a second sacking of their hall.

The parade formed downtown about 2:00 P.M. on November 11, a drizzly day that cut down attendance a good bit. After traversing the main streets, the line of march led off to Tower Avenue. With the Legionnaires at the head, the marchers passed the I.W.W. hall, its window emblazoned with the three-star Wobbly emblem in red, and then stopped at the next cross street where the Legionnaires held back as the rest of the parade formed ranks and reversed its march to pass the I.W.W. hall again.

Watching carefully in the I.W.W. hall were Wesley Everest, Britt Smith, Ray Becker, James McInerney, Tom Morgan, Bert Faulkner, and Mike Sheehan. On Seminary Hill were Loren Roberts, Bert Bland, and Ole Hanson; in the Arnold Hotel, O. C. Bland and John Lamb; in the Avalon House, "John Doe" Davis. Eugene Barnett was in the office of the Roderick Hotel. The Elks in the parade and some youngsters, headed by the color guard, passed the I.W.W. hall for the second time and then the Chehalis Legion post, followed by the Centralia Legion men, formed the tail of the procession. The Chehalis contingent had already reached the next cross street beyond the Wobbly hall when the Centralia group stopped in front of the hall. The postmaster of Centralia and a minister who had opposed state abolition of capital punishment both dangled ropes in their hands. Annoyed by the progress of the Chehalis Legionnaires, the parade marshal rode up to them on his horse and challenged: "What is the matter with you fellows! Aren't you in on this?" He signaled with his whistle and from the Centralia marchers rose the cry, "Come on, boys! Let's get them." There was a dash toward the hall, the window with the infuriating I.W.W. emblem came crashing down, and men surged forward against the sagging door, which yielded.

Shots rang out from inside the hall, from Avalon House and the Arnold Hotel, and from Seminary Hill. Post Commander Warren O. Grimm was shot in the abdomen and staggered to a nearby store. Arthur McElfresh, shot in the head, died almost instantly. Ben Casagranda fell on the street, mortally wounded. Several paraders received minor wounds. The Legionnaires swarmed into the hall; the Wobblies retreated to a disused ice storage compartment in the rear. After wrecking the hall, the Legionnaires forced open the ice compartment and dragged out the I.W.W. But one, Wesley Everest, an ex-serviceman, had darted out the back door, firing his .45 Colt as he went. Everest fled down an alley, pursued by rifle bullets, and gained the bank of the Skookumchuck River, which he attempted to ford. It was too deep and swift, and he came back up the bank, revolver still in hand. Dale Hubbard, nephew of F. B. Hubbard of the Eastern Railway & Lumber Company and former president of the Employers Association of Washington, headed the mob. Everest shouted that he would surrender to an officer of the law, but not to the mob. He fired and Hubbard fell, mortally wounded. His revolver hot and empty, Everest was seized by the mob, his teeth were knocked out, and he was led to jail with a belt around his neck. "You haven't got the guts to lynch a man in broad daylight," he jeered through bloody lips. He was right.

That night at 8 o'clock the lights went out all over Centralia. Soon thereafter a group of men drove up to the jail, smashed in a door and dragged Everest out. They threw him into a car which headed a procession to the Chehalis River bridge on the outskirts of town. The lights then went back on in Centralia.

Badly beaten again, Everest would not give up. From his position on the floor in the back of the car he hit out at his assailants. Someone in the back seat then proceeded to castrate Everest as the others held the screaming man. "For Christ's sake, men," he pleaded, "shoot me — don't let me suffer this way." Years later a visiting Legionnaire who was looking into the events of that horrid night interviewed the castrator. Every few minutes, the visitor said, the man got up and washed his hands.

In any event his business shrank, for self-respecting workers said they'd rather die than have anything to do with *him*.

At the bridge Everest was dragged out and a rope knotted around his neck, and his body flung over. Everest clutched at a plank; Legionnaires stamped on his fingers, and he fell. Dissatisfied with the knot, the lynchers pulled the body back up and used a longer rope, and hurled the body over again. Still dissatisfied, they hauled Everest's body up a third time — by then he must have been dead — and tied a more professional knot on a longer rope and flung the body over. Then, with car lights playing on the scene, they amused themselves awhile by shooting at the swaying body. Satiated at last, the mob left and darkness returned. Next morning somebody cut the rope and the body fell into the Chehalis River.

Fearful that friends of Everest might rescue the corpse and bear it away, a posse searched the river and recovered it. Then they dumped the horribly mutilated body on the floor of the jail where the Wobblies from their cells could see it, and there it stayed for two days. Finally the deputies on November 15 gave shovels to a detail of four imprisoned I.W.W.'s and took them to a field on the outskirts of town where they were forced to dig a grave into which the body was flung. Such was the end of Wesley Everest, who died grim, game, and staunch in his principles.

A grisly kind of perverted humor marked the coroner's report on Everest's death. Everest had broken out of jail, the coroner said, and taken a rope with him to the bridge. There he tied the knot around his neck, jumped off, but failing to kill himself, climbed back up and jumped off a second time; still alive, he climbed back up, shot himself in the neck and jumped off the bridge again; woke up at seven in the morning, cut the rope, fell into the river, and was drowned. The coroner's grim whimsy was no surprise to townspeople who knew what had gone on the previous night. This joker was rewarded by being made superintendent of the state insane asylum in Steilacoom.

Followed days of horror and nights of terror for the imprisoned I.W.W. By day they were grilled incessantly by prosecutors, kept incommunicado and denied legal counsel. By night the mob gathered outside the jail, cursing, blowing auto horns, flashing lights into the darkened jail room, throwing various missiles through the windows, pointing loaded guns through the bars. In the cold November nights there were neither mattresses nor blankets. Loren Roberts, a youngster of 19, went insane. For ten nights the hellish scenes were re-enacted.

In the meantime posses searched the hills around Centralia for those who might have escaped. The American Legion took over control of the region from the police and sheriff. On November 15 a posse came across a lone armed man, John Haney. They shot and killed him; it turned out that he too was a posseman, out hoping to bag a Wobbly. The first reports said he had been killed by roaming I.W.W.'s and these made the headlines across the nation; later reports of the truth were buried on inside pages.

Across the state more than a thousand were arrested in the various man hunts for Wobblies. They were supervised by the county prosecuting attorneys who had been called into session by the state's attorney-general and instructed to hunt down every Wobbly, and use the criminal syndicalism statute to try them en masse. Federal warrants were issued for T.F.G. Dougherty and Walker C. Smith to impede publicity for the defense. Dougherty left for Canada and Smith went into temporary seclusion to carry on his mission.

The nation was stunned by the news that came over the wires from the Associated Press in Centralia. Armed Wobblies had deliberately and wantonly fired into a parade of Legionnaires, killing four. Even Big Bill Haywood, out on bail in Chicago, was said to have blanched. He was quoted as saying that the I.W.W. did not condone murder. From one end of the nation to the other came cries for the extermination of the I.W.W., with or without waiting for due process.

The news appalled the editorial staff of the Seattle *Union Record*, too. Two reporters were sent posthaste to check the facts, in a flivver flying side curtains to shield them from the rain.

They found Centralia beleaguered by the Legion, the jail out of bounds, and they felt fortunate to escape with their lives.

The inquest over the bodies of the four Legionnaires was held November 12, and by the next day the Centralia tragedy began to take on another aspect. The Associated Press reported:

> CENTRALIA, Nov. 13 — Testimony tending to show that the marching ex-service men started toward the I.W.W. hall before shots were fired from the building or from the Avalon hotel opposite, featured the coroner's inquest over the bodies of four former soldiers killed here last Tuesday and is said to have been responsible for the failure of the jury in rendering its verdict to fix responsibility for the shooting.
>
> Dr. Frank Bickford, one of the marchers, testified that the door of the I.W.W. hall was forced open by participants in the parade before the shooting began through the doorway or from the Avalon hotel opposite. Dr. Bickford said he was immediately in front of the I.W.W. hall at the time and that during a temporary halt some one suggested a raid on the hall.
>
> "I spoke up and said I would lead if enough would follow," he stated, "but before I could take the lead there were many ahead of me. Some one next to me put his foot against the door and forced it open, after which a shower of bullets poured through the opening about us."

The AP reported that Dr. Herbert Y. Bell, also a marcher, said the surge toward the hall and the shots were "as nearly simultaneous as any human acts could be." The correspondent who had blurted out the truth was hounded out of Centralia. The lumbermen back of the Legion wanted no more of that kind of reporting.

One lone Legion voice spoke out against the hysteria. Commander Edward F. Bassett of Silver Bow Post in Butte, Montana, said:

> The I.W.W. in Centralia who fired upon the men that were attempting to raid the I.W.W. headquarters there were fully justified in their act. Mob rule in this country must be stopped, and when mobs attack the home of a millionaire, or of a laborer, or of the I.W.W., it is not only the right but the duty of the occupants to resist with every means within their power. If the officers of the law cannot stop these raids, perhaps the resistance of the raiders may have that effect.

To the Employers Association of Washington, which had masterminded the attack, the blood on the streets of Centralia must have seemed a cheap price to pay if it helped achieve the ultimate goal — the destruction of all organized labor in the state. Still smarting under the fiasco of Mayor Ole Hanson's "revolution" after the Seattle general strike earlier in the year, which had failed to smash the labor movement or even to convict a single victim, the employers wheeled in quickly for the kill this time. Their favorite organ, the Seattle *P-I*, sounded the shrill warcry the day after the Armistice Day tragedy. In a lengthy editorial November 12, it said:

BACK TO THE SOURCES

The blood of our servicemen assassinated in Centralia demands some plain speaking. The Centralia outrage is the culmination of a long series of events, in which several agencies have played a disloyal, a discreditable and a hypocritical part.

Frankly, we charge:

That organized labor in Seattle and in the state of Washington has given aid and comfort to the I.W.W. and to every anarchistic organization and influence within the state;

That the Seattle *Union Record*, the official organ of organized labor, has given every encouragement to the I.W.W.; has used every artifice of propaganda to incite them to violence in peace and to sedition in war....

The *Union Record* is today an I.W.W. organ, and every union man in this city and in this state knows it. It stands for revolution, soviets, proletarian dictatorships; and by every art of suggestion, innuendo and falsehood it seeks to bring these things to pass. During the war it was just as disloyal as it dared to be, and now it is just as anarchistic as it dares to be.

The same day the *Union Record* replied to this attack in an editorial to become nearly as famous as the "We are on the road — NO ONE KNOWS WHERE" editorial before the general strike. It was headed:

DON'T SHOOT IN THE DARK

Violence begets violence.
Anarchy calls for anarchy.
That is the answer to the Centralia tragedy.

And the reason for it is found in the constant stream of laudation in the kept press of un-American, illegal and violent physical attack upon the persons of those who disagree with the powers that be.

The rioting which culminated in the deaths of three of our returned service men at Centralia last night was the result of a long series of illegal acts by these men themselves — acts which no paper in the state was American enough to criticize except the *Union Record*. . . . Organized labor has had no connection with nor had it any sympathy for the perpetrators of the violence at Centralia, NO MATTER WHOM THEY MAY BE, and from the facts at hand both sides have earned the severest condemnation of law-abiding people.

We advise all to await with us the development of the truth about the whole affair.

Such counsel did not please the choleric Seattle *Times*. In a flaming editorial, it declaimed:

There is but one effective answer to the methods employed by the I.W.W.
TERRORIZE THE AMERICAN BOLSHEVIKI! . . . .
Organized labor must be made to understand that unless it CLEANS HOUSE there will not be, anywhere in this section, any of organized labor left!

It was at this point that the roof fell in on the *Union Record*. On November 13, two days after the Armistice Day tragedy, the Department of Justice seized the *Record*'s plant and arrested Editor Ault and Frank A. Rust and George P. Listman of the *Record*'s board, on charges of sedition. Barrels of documents were carted off to the federal building for examination.

The *Record* staff moved fast. As soon as the marshals had departed an extra edition was prepared that came rolling off the press at 9:00 P.M. Some 25,000 copies were sold that night — the biggest "extra" in Seattle history. The next day the marshals appeared again and padlocked the plant. On a flatbed press of a suburban paper the *Record* then published a bob-tailed edition by running the machinery day and night. The copies sold like hotcakes for a nickel a copy, though the regular price was two cents. The "extra" carried this editorial:

REASON WILL TRIUMPH
"Terrorize the Reds," they say, and describe all who venture to hold different opinions from themselves as "Reds."
From news reports of latest events in Centralia it appears that the I.W.W. hall was attacked before the fatal shots were fired. The coroner's jury, because of the testimony of competent witnesses, has failed to fix the blame for the shooting.
These developments do not justify the shootings. They do justify the stand taken by the *Union Record*, when the first reports of the tragedy arrived. We told the truth then and we will continue to do so always.
Just as long as the "kept" press of the city incites to riot, just as long as they continue to lie, there will be little social and industrial peace here.

On November 21 the U.S. Commissioner ordered the *Union Record's* plant returned, holding that the warrant was faulty. Embarrassed perhaps by the too-flagrant show of prejudice against the labor paper, the Department of Justice even-handedly cracked down also on the *P-I* and the *Star*. The federals did not go so far as to seize their plants but merely suppressed editions in which appeared an unusually virulent paid advertisement by Edwin Selvin, editor of the *Business Chronicle*. Among choice items from Editor Selvin's editorial statement were these:

Real Americans must rise as one man in the righteous wrath of outraged patriotism. First, invoke such legal machinery as we have, and if that is not sufficient, then hastily construct something foolproof. We must smash every un-American and anti-American organization in the land. We must put to death the leaders in this gigantic conspiracy of murder, pillage and revolution. We must imprison for life all its aiders and abetters of native birth. We must deport the aliens.
The I.W.W., the Nonpartisan League, the so-called Triple Alliance in the state of Washington, the pro-German Socialists, the Closed Shop Labor Unions, the agitators, malcontents, anarchists, syndicalists, seditionists, traitors — the whole motley crew of Bol-

shevists and near-Bolshevists — must be outlawed by Public Opinion and hunted down and hounded until driven beyond the horizon of civic decency.

Selvin included in his devil-list President Wilson whose New Freedom had unlocked the treacherous chain of events, President Samuel Gompers of the "Un-American Federation of Labor," and Louis F. Post, the assistant U.S. Secretary of Labor who "came to the Pacific Northwest on a speaking tour inflaming the masses and inciting to resistance to law by his preachments of Sovietism and Bolshevism." "The whole Labor Movement," cried Selvin, "is putrid, its rottenness taints the atmosphere of every industrial center. . . . The chief exponent of anarchy in this community is the *Union Record* . . . a journalistic sewer into which flows all the slime of moral perverts. . . . Public policy requires that the mouthpiece of applied anarchy cease to exist."

Selvin was arrested for mailing unmailable matter. His bail was set at only $1,000, although the *Union Record's* officials had had to post bail of $5,000 and $6,000 each.

When Selvin's ad appeared in the early edition of the *P-I*, the chapels of the printing trades met hastily at 10:30 P.M. and notified the management that no union man would touch type or press if subsequent editions carried the Selvin outburst. The printing trades resolution, presented to the management, read:

As members of the several trade unions employed in the production of your newspaper, the Seattle *Post-Intelligencer*, we make the following representations:

We have been patient under misrepresentation, faithful in the face of slander, long suffering under insult; we have upheld our agreements and produced your paper, even though in so doing we were braiding the rope with which you propose to hang us; day after day we have put in type, stereotyped, printed and mailed calumny after calumny, lie after lie, insult after insult.

Little by little, as our patience seemed to be unbounded, your editorial and business policy has encroached upon and further and further overstepped the bounds, not only of fairness and truth, but decency and Americanism itself. We have even meekly witnessed your unfair and reprehensible campaign of falsehood and ruin result in the suppression of the last medium of honest expression for our cause in Seattle, not only denying our brothers the means of livelihood, but denying us a far greater boon — the American right of a free press.

So long as these things appeared to be a part of your unfair fight against organization — our organization and others — we have been able to endure them in the hope that at last truth might prevail. But there must be a limit to all things.

In the page advertisement in the *Post-Intelligencer* of November 18, 1919, purporting to have been written and paid for by one Selvin, but which had as well have occupied the position in your paper usually taken up by your editorial page, your utter depravity as a newspaper, your shameless disregard of the laws of the land, your hatred of opposition, your reckless policy of appeal to the passions of citizenry, reached depths of malice and malignancy hitherto unbelievable. It is nothing less than excitation to violence, stark and naked invitation to anarchy.

Therefore, be it resolved, by the whole committee of your organized employed in meeting assembled, That if your business management cannot demonstrate its capacity and sagacity, if your editorial directing heads must remain blind to the thing they are bringing us to; if together you cannot see the abyss to which you are leading us — all of us; if you have no more love for our common country than is manifested in your efforts to plunge it into anarchy, then as loyal American citizens — many of us ex-service men who very clearly proved our faith in America and its institutions — we must, not because we are unionists but because we are Americans, find means to protect ourselves from the stigma of having aided and abetted your campaign of destruction.

J. M. HERSHEY, Chairman; JOHN J. WENNER, E. A. GRABER, M. OLNEY, ALVARO C. SHOEMAKER, Committee.

The offending ad was dropped from subsequent editions. It was perhaps the first and only instance in American journalistic history when the union printing trades staff presumed to reprimand their employers.

The Department of Justice scrutinized the *Union Record* to obtain evidence to support its charge of sedition. To strengthen the indictment, Anna Louise Strong was also arrested. The Department charged that Ault, Listman, Rust, and Miss Strong had tried to

incite, provoke and encourage resistance to the United States by the following means and methods, among others, to wit: by presenting and purporting to advance the interests of the laborers as a class and giving them complete control and ownership of all property and of the means of producing and distributing property through the abolition of all other classes of society described as "capitalists," "the capitalistic class," "the master class," "the ruling class," "exploiters of workers," "Bourgeois," such abolition to be accomplished not by political action, or with any regard for right or wrong, but by the continual and persistent use and employment of unlawful, tortuous and physical means and methods involving threats, assaults, injuries, intimidations, and murder upon the persons, and the injury and destruction (known to said defendants and their said confederates and associates as "sabotage," "direct action," "working on the public," "wearing the wooden shoes," "working the sab cat," and "slow down" tactics) of the property of such other classes, the forcible resistance to the execution of the laws of the United States and the forcible, revolutionary overthrow of existing Governmental authority in the United States, use of which said means and methods was to accompany, and to be accomplished in part by, local strikes, industry strikes and general strikes . . . depicting as heroes and martyrs Kate O'Hare, Eugene V. Debs, Hulet M. Wells, William D. Haywood. . . .

As if all this were not enough, they were also accused of using the post office to distribute "indecent and unmailable matters, to wit: printed matter of a character tending to incite arson, murder and assassination. . . ."

The indictment read like a paraphrase of Edwin Selvin's most lurid prose; indeed instead of indicting Selvin on a parallel charge it would have seemed more logical for the government to subpoena him as its chief witness.

This farrago was filed in federal court December 2. A month later Judge Jeremiah Neterer took a look at the mess of evidence handed up to him and decided that "nowhere is there apparent any statement advocating any change other than by constitutional methods . . . nor is there anything printed which would tend to support Germany and Austria-Hungary." Case dismissed. So was Selvin's.

Thus once again the open-shop forces of the state had overshot their mark, in trying to crucify the whole labor movement for the Centralia tragedy, after failing to destroy it at the time of the general strike nine months earlier in 1919.

But in Centralia it was quite otherwise.

There the imprisoned Wobblies stood alone, physically at any rate. The only man in Centralia who might have helped them legally, Elmer Smith, their attorney, had been thrown into jail with them. The Lewis County Bar Association voted to ban any legal assistance from its members. The prisoners were sealed off from the world — it was revealed only that one by one they were being questioned by a staff of prosecutors recruited around the state, some of them attorneys for lumber companies. Tom Morgan yielded to the inquisition and confessed. In the main what he revealed could be assumed logically by anyone, that the I.W.W. had planned to defend their hall, but his confession enabled the state to pinpoint the location of the various defendants on the fateful day. The 19-year-old Loren Roberts collapsed into insanity, clouding his confession. Eleven men were indicted for the first degree murder of Warren O. Grimm, among them Elmer Smith, for advising them of their rights. As late as November 21, the Centralia *Chronicle* reported: "Centralia police affairs are still under complete control of the American Legion, a special committee of the local post, headed by Lt. Frank Van Gilder, directing all investigations of Wobblies arrested and organizing the man hunts."

In this case the prosecution was taking no chances, such as a trial in a big city where organized labor had influence. A change of venue was granted to Montesano, the county seat of adjoining Grays Harbor County, a town of some 2,000, innocent of any vestige of labor organization. This change was granted over the vehement opposition of the Centralia Legion, which wanted a legalized lynching party right at the scene of the tragedy. Attorney George F. Vanderveer, who was busy in Chicago handling appeals of the national I.W.W. prisoners, hurried to Montesano to plead for a second change of venue to Olympia or Tacoma, farther removed from the scene of passion. Judge George D. Abel agreed with him; the prosecution then retained the judge's brother as associate counsel so the judge had to disqualify himself. The other Grays Harbor judge was held to be too favorable to labor, so Governor Hart named Judge John

M. Wilson, who had delivered a eulogy of the dead Legionnaires. He promptly vetoed a change in venue.

Montesano was bursting at the seams when the trial opened
January 25. The Legion had raised a fund of $11,750 among em-
ployers — mostly lumber companies — to pay some 50 Legionnaires at $4 a day and keep to attend the trial in uniform, and
they occupied the front of the courtroom. Because, the state said,
the I.W.W. might descend en masse on the little town to free the
prisoners, a troop of federal soldiers was encamped on the courthouse lawn; their martial music floated in to add to the tension.

Vanderveer's case rested upon the arguments that the I.W.W.
had defended their hall, as they were entitled to do by law, and
that they had every reason to fear violence from the Legion parade. He was alone, pitted against six attorneys for the prosecution. In his opening statement he cited the demolition of the
earlier hall in 1918; organization of the citizens' committee in
June, 1919; the kidnapping of Tom Lassiter; the vote to set up
a secret committee with the open aim of driving the Wobblies
from Centralia; the articles in the Centralia papers openly proclaiming that purpose; the I.W.W. circular pleading with townspeople to avert the attack; and numerous placards posted around
the I.W.W. hall and elsewhere threatening violence.

Curtly Judge Wilson demolished practically all of Vanderveer's case by ruling that evidence of the attack on the earlier
hall and of all the ominous preparations for repetition of that
act on Armistice Day was irrelevant. The sole question before
the jury was, Who murdered Warren O. Grimm? Vanderveer
sought by every legal stratagem to connect Grimm with the
attack on the hall and indeed what was presented in court would
have satisfied most. But what could be done in Montesano?
Three witnesses who testified to Grimm's attack on the hall were
promptly arrested for perjury as they left the stand. At that
Vanderveer almost came to blows with the sheriff. Though arrested, the witnesses were never prosecuted, but the threat of
instant arrest threw a pall over efforts to obtain more defense
witnesses.

Who were the men in the dock?

First, there was Eugene Barnett, charged directly with the murder of Grimm — the rest being accomplices. He was a coal miner and member of both the I.W.W. and the United Mine Workers. He had not been in the hall at all but in the adjoining Roderick Hotel, unarmed. When he heard the shooting, he slipped out by a back door and went home. Escaping to the woods, he was captured in the manhunt.

Ray Becker, logger, age 25, had studied for the ministry and his father and brother were preachers. He joined the I.W.W. in 1917. Armed with an Ivor Johnson .38 revolver, he defended himself in the hall until his ammunition was exhausted.

James McInerney, logger, born in Ireland, joined the I.W.W. in 1916 and was wounded on the "Verona." He was in the hall and resisted with arms.

Britt Smith, I.W.W. secretary, who lived in the hall. A logger, age 38, he was the man the mob was looking for when they lynched Wesley Everest by mistake. He was armed.

Bert Bland, logger, joined the I.W.W. in 1917. He fired from Seminary Hill and took to the woods, being captured a week later during the manhunt.

Loren Roberts, logger, age 19, who broke down under prison treatment and went insane. He fired from Seminary Hill.

O. C. Bland, logger, resident of Centralia for many years. A brother of Bert Bland. He was in the Arnold Hotel, armed.

John Lamb, logger, joined the I.W.W. in 1917, a resident of Centralia. He was in the Arnold Hotel, unarmed.

Mike Sheehan, 64, born in Ireland, and a lifetime union man. He was arrested, unarmed, in the union hall.

Bert Faulkner, 21, a logger, member of the I.W.W. since 1917, and an ex-serviceman. He was in the hall, unarmed.

Elmer Smith, lawyer, who advised the I.W.W. about their legal rights.

Ole Hanson, who was on Seminary Hill, made his getaway and disappeared. "John Doe" Davis, in the Avalon House, armed, also escaped. Tom Morgan, who was in the hall, unarmed, turned state's evidence and was not indicted.

None of the indicted men, aside from Britt Smith and Elmer

Smith, could be called leaders. They were rank-and-file union men, loggers, imbued with a faith in their class and with the high courage to defend their rights against odds which in reality were insuperable. Their dogged determination was of a piece with that of the martyrs in all ages.

The press table at Montesano was crowded; never before had there been a time when the name of the sleepy little courthouse town had appeared in the nation's press. Side by side with the correspondents for the big news services and the Pacific Northwest dailies was a new type of correspondent — the labor reporter. The Seattle *Union Record* sent its ace reporter, Frank Walklin. And the New York *Call,* socialist daily, assigned a staff member, John Nicholas Beffel, to cover the trial. Thus Eastern readers were given a telegraphic report of the proceedings. Not daring to send a representative into Montesano, the I.W.W. weekly in Chicago, *New Solidarity,* enterprisingly reprinted all of Beffel's dispatches. Meanwhile the Wobblies' weekly paper in Seattle, the *Industrial Worker,* managed somehow to obtain regular and comprehensive unsigned accounts of the trial.

Montesano's atmosphere in those weeks was tense, and Walklin, Beffel, Attorney Vanderveer, and three defense investigators found it prudent to go back each evening to a hotel in Aberdeen, 13 miles west, rather than to trust to the mercies of the Legionnaires who seemed to be everywhere in the county seat day and night.

Walklin's reports were later republished in a pamphlet, *A Fair Trial? — A Record of the Prejudice and Passion that Dominated the Legal Profession and the Press in the Famous Centralia Labor Case.* Walklin, a seasoned newspaperman from the East with no radical background, concluded:

> I found that nowhere else on earth is there such evidence of the methods of the abysmal brute as in Southwest Washington. There are hundreds of men there who are identified with the lumber interests in all capacities from wage slaves to managers, who understand nothing but brute force and money gained from the blood of others. . . . I am convinced that nothing, not even arson, rape or murder, would deter these lumber barons if they thought it would bring their desired financial ends.

He described Judge Wilson as "perching above the courtroom like a black bat ready to spring over a ruined wall."

On the night of March 12 the fate of the indicted men was given to the jury, the State having presented all of its evidence, and the defense that portion of testimony which the court would tolerate. After 20 hours the jurors returned with a verdict finding Eugene Barnett, accused of firing the shot that killed Grimm, and John Lamb guilty of third-degree murder, a non-existent crime in Washington State. They acquitted Elmer Smith and Sheehan, found that Loren Roberts was insane at the time of the shooting, and adjudged Britt Smith, the two Blands, Becker, and McInerney guilty of second-degree murder. Faulkner had already been freed for lack of evidence at the end of the State's presentation.

The verdict threw the courtroom into an uproar, Judge Wilson being covered with confusion. He had instructed the jury that only three verdicts were admissible, murder in the first or second degree, or acquittal. The first degree charge covers premeditated murder; second degree, intentional but unpremeditated. Vanderveer, in his closing address to the jury, had emphasized that only two verdicts were possible, first-degree murder or acquittal, as the charge against the men was premeditated murder. Recovering his composure presently, Judge Wilson refused to accept the jury's findings, and sent it out again to reconsider. Two hours later it returned, and now found Barnett and Lamb guilty, like the other five, of second-degree murder. Ironically the court accepted that finding.

To the new verdict the jury unanimously added this plea: "We the undersigned jurors respectfully petition the court to extend the leniency to the defendants whose names appear on the attached verdict" — referring to all who were found guilty. The contradictions in the verdict reflected the mixed thoughts and emotions of the jurors. Some wanted outright acquittal, others a first degree verdict. The attack by the Legionnaires on the hall influenced those favoring acquittal; the dispersion of the I.W.W. in hotels and on Seminary Hill seemed to others not to be a genuine defense of the hall. The unanimous plea for mercy was wrung from these latter by those favorable to the defendants on the threat that otherwise they would "hang" the jury.

The rage that swept the ranks of the Legionnaires and the business press would have seemed to indicate that the I.W.W. had won a great victory. Outright hanging had been demanded as the only possible penalty; refusal of the jury to give them the blood they demanded seemed grotesque. The Legion declared the verdict to be "an impossible, monstrous miscarriage of justice." The jury was "incomprehensible." The state insisted that all the men would be tried anew, for the murder of McElfresh, and Elmer Smith and Sheehan were rearrested immediately upon their acquittal. "The verdict," said the prosecutor, "is a travesty on justice. We shall continue to prosecute these men until a proper conviction is procured."

But all was not lost for those who lusted for blood. On April 5 Judge Wilson, who had presided with such cold fury during the trial, evened the scales of justice to his own satisfaction. The jury's unanimous plea for mercy was tossed into the wastebasket. Each I.W.W. was sentenced to the maximum, 25 to 40 years, the equivalent of a life sentence. The law provides a minimum of ten years for second-degree murder and many legal experts contend that the Washington law did not permit more.

No effort was ever made to prosecute the lynchers of Wesley Everest although their names were well known in Centralia. The deadly contrast between freedom for the perpetrators of this peculiarly revolting crime, and the long imprisonment for the men who were defending their union hall, is too obvious to underline. But there is no statute of limitations for murder, and who knows. . . .

The savage sentences imposed on the defendants were a lethal blow to the I.W.W. Even the Chicago defendants had been given maximum sentences of only 20 years, and most were much less. All the Chicago defendants were freed by 1923. But the Centralia prisoners endured imprisonment in Walla Walla state penitentiary until 1933. Five of the jurors in 1922 signed affidavits that the conduct of the trial had been unfair and that pertinent information had been withheld from the jury. They would have stood out for acquittal, they swore, if they had known that their plea for leniency would be ignored. Four other jurors agreed in part with the five but declined to sign affidavits, perhaps because of fear of economic reprisal. The five jurors pleaded personally with the governor for a pardon.

Walker C. Smith, the indefatigable Wobbly editor, lampooned the Montesano trial in a pamphlet, *The Kangaroo Court of the State of Lumberlust*. The defendant, A. Wise Wobbly, was charged with comical syndicalism and ten thousand crimes in the Inferior Court of Sawdust County, Judge Lynch presiding. Proceeds of this pamphlet and of innumerable affairs held throughout the Puget Sound country went into the coffers of the Prison Comfort Club, which furnished tobacco and other small amenities to the Centralia prisoners.

In response to an appeal by some church groups in the state, the Federal Council of Churches, the National Catholic Welfare Conference and the Central Conference of American Rabbis in 1930 conducted an investigation. Their careful report ended on the note: "The six I.W.W.'s in Walla Walla Penitentiary are paying the penalty for their part in a tragedy the guilt for which is by no means theirs alone. They alone were indicted; they alone have been punished."

James McInerney died in prison in 1930. Barnett became a fur rancher in Idaho, was an organizer for the CIO International Woodworkers Union (an old fighter in the I.W.W. Lumber Workers Industrial Union 500 must have had some qualms in joining the new CIO union!) and was active in the Progressive Party in 1948 (another deviation from the Wobblies' resolute anti-political position). John Lamb, upon his release, returned to Centralia where "he continued," according to the *Industrial Worker*, "to work for the cause of human freedom by speaking up on every possible occasion for the I.W.W." He died in 1948 when his house burned down under mysterious circumstances, his family barely escaping with their lives. Britt Smith returned to his work in the woods and joined the CIO Woodworkers Union; in his later years he was active in the Washington Pension Union, a radical until his death. Ray Becker, the indomitable one, scorned the parole offered in 1933, on the ground that he was not guilty, and remained in prison until 1939, when he won a complete pardon. After his release Becker opened a small leather goods store in Vancouver and when he died in 1950 the Portland *Oregonian,* which had wished them all hanged in 1920, ran a quaintly nostalgic obituary.

Elmer Smith, the lawyer, devoted the rest of his life to freeing the Centralia Seven. Although after their acquittal the state reindicted him and Mike Sheehan for murder again, the fire had gone out of the Legion-lumber authorities, and the charge was never pressed.

Young Smith, a red-headed six-footer of athletic physique, had come from Minnesota after graduation from McAlester College where he had prepared for the ministry, and the St. Paul College of Law, to practice in Centralia where his father had gone. Soon he earned the enmity of the business interests by taking cases of workingmen defrauded of wages, or seeking compensation for accidents, or suffering violations of labor legislation. A girl on the Centralia *Chronicle* who had been working for $3 a week in violation of the minimum wage law went to him for help and he won her case. After that the *Chronicle* took a dark view of the young lawyer. One case in particular aroused his indignation — a worker with a large family who held he had been defrauded by a subsidiary of Hubbard's Eastern Railway & Lumber Company. A small daughter died of malnutrition during her father's unemployment and Smith charged that Hubbard's firm was responsible for her starvation. A suit for libel and the threat of disbarment failed to deter him in that case. When an out-of-town speaker came to a meeting at the Wobbly hall, a vigilante committee was in the audience. Sensing the danger, Smith after the meeting sauntered to the railroad station with the speaker to see that he got out of town safely.

Warren O. Grimm warned Smith that he was playing with the

wrong crowd. "You'll get along all right if you will come in with us. How would you feel if one of your clients would come up to you in public, slap you on the back, and say, 'Hello, Elmer'?" "Very proud," replied Smith. He handled the case of Tom Lassiter, the blind news vendor. Gathering affidavits concerning the men who kidnapped him, Smith went to the Lewis County prosecutor, but that worthy was too busy to concern himself with such petty matters. The affidavits were taken to the Governor for action, and were duly filed away.

"Handle these I.W.W. cases if you want to," a brother lawyer told him, "but sooner or later they're all going to be hanged or deported anyway."

After his imprisonment for three months awaiting trial, Smith was broke, his law office gone, and he was disbarred from practicing in state and local courts. Grateful Centralia workers, among them many railroad men (for Centralia was a division point), chipped in to buy building materials and took part in erecting a small law office, where he worked with a partner who could practice. There was little prospect of affluence for such a man, and on the one chance, the disposal for $25,000 of a timber claim that he owned, all his family got was a piano, a set of dishes, and payment of back bills. The rest went into the campaign for freeing the imprisoned I.W.W. and for cases of working people seeking redress of injustices.

In the summer of 1920 Smith decided to run for prosecuting attorney of Lewis County on the new Farmer-Labor Party ticket. As no paper in the county would even carry news about the Party, Smith decided to start a weekly paper. In the backwoods town of Toledo, once important, before the coming of the railroads, as the head of navigation on the Cowlitz River, he acquired the printing equipment of the defunct Toledo *Messenger* and moved it to Centralia for the new *Farmer-Labor Call*. A quaint old editor was installed who distinguished himself in one issue by running a top headline — CAPITALISM THE ABOMINATION OF DESOLATION. After that Smith consulted with Editor Ault of the Seattle *Union Record* and obtained the services of a young *Record* reporter. Smith campaigned up and down Lewis County, basing his talks on the need for an honest enforcement of the law for farmers and workers. In the election of November, 1920, Smith and the Farmer-Labor Party carried every rural precinct in Lewis County and lost only because of the adverse votes in Centralia and Chehalis, the business centers.

By 1921 another Wobbly hall had been opened in Centralia, built by members on land donated by Elmer Smith. Whether from consciousness of guilt or because they had an awesome respect now for the Wobblies' determination to defend themselves, the Legionnaires did not molest the hall, aside from occasional hooliganism. For many years, too, hoodlums would heave rocks and bricks through the windows of Smith's home, often following up with gobs of mud. But by 1927 the persecution had died down. Despite everything, he maintained an even-tempered good nature: friends remember that "he never said a mean word." They can still see the tall, red-headed fellow, doing square dances like a big teddy bear in the Wobbly hall, graciously whirling little old Miss Young, who picked him for every square she could. In 1929, when the Centralia prisoners became eligible for parole, he and Captain Edward P. Coll, a Legionnaire, arranged a meeting attended by 1,200 townspeople in the Labor Temple to petition the governor for release of the seven men. Captain Coll had been Commander of the American Legion in Hoquiam, Washington, and had made several visits to Centralia to get the facts for a fair history of the case. He stated, "Breaking into the workers' hall was a felony, and he who perpetrates a felony and in so doing causes others to lose their lives is also guilty of murder."

Smith died in 1932 of a hemorrhaging ulcer, at the age of 46, at the Puyallup "sanitarium" run by a man who years later was imprisoned for practicing medicine without a license. His memory is still green in Centralia and among friends scattered to the four winds — memory of an incorruptible, able, friendly man who dedicated his life to his principles. True to its principles, too, in a way, was the Centralia *Chronicle,* which did not even carry a notice of the death of one of the city's most notable residents. Ironically, the day he died, Elmer Smith's disbarment was rescinded.

On Memorial and Armistice Days school children are still herded to City Park where a monument to the four Legionnaires bears the legend: "Slain on the streets of Centralia, Washington, while on peaceful parade wearing the uniform of the country they loyally and faithfully served." There is no corresponding monument for Wesley Everest who also, according to his lights, served his country and his fellow workers loyally and faithfully, overseas and in Centralia. The last memorial services held for Everest were conducted in 1939 at the bridge where he was hanged. The Washington Commonwealth Federation, successor of earlier radical and progressive movements, joined with the CIO International Woodworkers Union in sponsoring the memorial meeting, attended by hundreds of union people.

9

Ebb and Flow of Radicalism

A novel feature of the Montesano I.W.W. trial was the presence of an extra-legal jury representing labor of the Pacific Northwest. The legal farce being conducted in Judge Wilson's courtroom was of immediate concern to the national I.W.W., the culmination of the savage blows rained upon it by federal, state, and local authorities. But the A.F. of L. unions, too, saw the wide implications of the judicial lynching party. The fate of all organized labor would be profoundly affected by the outcome of the trial. Already the *Union Record* had been temporarily seized and suppressed; the Associated Industries was waiting to administer the lethal blow to wages and working conditions so laboriously safeguarded by years of struggle and sacrifice. The Seattle general strike, with its attendant Ole Hansonized "revolution," had first brought to national attention the presence within the United States itself of the very forces that had produced a worker-peasant upheaval in Russia and were convulsing Europe. Reaction fought back with the "red" scare against labor's aspirations by painting them as plots and conspiracies hatched in faraway Petrograd and Moscow. The great steel and mine strikes of 1919 against intolerable conditions were declared to be manifestations of this gigantic world-wide revolutionary surge, and were fought as such by the federal government through injunctions and troops, by terrified state and local authorities, and by the resolute masters of steel and coal.

And it was exactly at this time that Centralia shattered whatever composure remained on the national scene. The tragedy and its aftermath surpassed all other outbreaks of passion in the

1919-1920 period in its calculated brutality and savagery and
became the classic example of anti-radicalism whipped into a
maelstrom of unprecedented hysteria, hate, and intolerance. If
fear of the weak and insecure Russian Soviet Republic, in its
first years, could so shake the very capital country of capitalism,
it was hardly surprising that a generation later its subsequent
growth would develop in this country a national malignancy,
tearing at the basic concepts of democracy and freedom upon
which the Republic had been founded. The indifference toward
civil liberties and violence exhibited in Centralia foreshadowed
the rise of McCarthyism in the 1950's. At the height of the Great
Red Scare, which may be placed at the beginning of 1920 during
the Deportation Delirium, it was estimated that 1,400 had been
arrested under criminal anarchy and syndicalism laws, of whom
300 were convicted and jailed; and these figures were necessarily
a minimum for much of the violence that was vented on hapless
radical workers went unreported and unrecorded.

As a result of the Great Red Scare, Attorney-General Mitchell
Palmer established the General Intelligence Division within the
Bureau of Investigation of the Department of Justice and to
head it appointed a young policeman, J. Edgar Hoover. That
started the FBI on its way, and it was to be said a generation
later that six Presidents had served under Hoover. Within a
year he claimed to have the names of 200,000 radicals in his card
indices.

Small wonder then that organized labor sent a special jury to
give its own verdict on the macabre proceedings in the little
county seat of Montesano. The Central Labor Councils of Seattle, Tacoma, Portland, and Everett, the Seattle Metal Trades
Council, and the Centralia lodge of the Brotherhood of Railroad Trainmen sponsored the jury. Its foreman was Paul K.
Mohr, charter member of the Seattle bakers union in 1889, one-
time president of the Seattle council, and an old-time socialist.
The jury met March 15, 1920, in the Tacoma Labor Temple
and agreed unanimously on a not-guilty verdict. The jurors said
that there was a conspiracy to raid the I.W.W. hall and that

Grimm took part in it. They denounced Judge Wilson's conduct
of the trial as unfair and prejudiced. The verdict was approved
by the Lewis County Trades Council, composed of men and
women who knew far more about the facts than any other body
in the country. The Seattle council sent the labor jury's verdict
to all A.F. of L. city councils in the United States, and endorsed
a proposal by the Everett council that $3,000 be raised as a re-
ward for the arrest and conviction of Everest's lynchers.

It was about this time, when hundreds of foreign-born workers were being deported, that a meeting representing 12,000
Russians in the Pacific Northwest asked that they be permitted
to return voluntarily to their home country if the federal authorities were displeased by their presence in this country. Either let
us go, or let us alone, they pleaded. The government much preferred to terrorize them. The Seattle labor council endorsed the
Russians' plea, asked other central labor bodies to stop their
members from making and handling munitions to be used
against the Soviet Republic, and urged the American government to recognize the worker-peasant government. Concerned
over the national hysteria, the council set up a committee on
class war prisoners and constitutional rights headed by Phil
Pearl of the barbers union, and voted $100 for the "Debs Spe-
cial" of the *Appeal to Reason,* a 2,000,000-copy special edition
urging his release from prison.

In 1919-1920 the *Union Record* reached the height of its
prestige and circulation. During the periods of the general strike
and the Centralia tragedy, circulation shot up to 100,000, and
was limited only by the capacity of its press. The *Star,* which
before the *Record* had been regarded as friendly to labor, shrank
in circulation and eventually disappeared. The *Record* published special editions for Tacoma and Everett, and reached
throughout the Puget Sound country as the unchallenged
spokesman of labor. An Associated Industries spy reported that
the unions "have something now that they never had before in
the line of propaganda — this is the *Union Record.* No one can
fully realize the tremendous influence this paper carries among

the workers and even among a large body of small business men." Referring to plans to establish a Sunday edition, the spy added that "I hate to think of what will happen on account of the influence a Sunday paper of this kind would have. . . . Anyone by investigating the workers of today can readily see their friendly feelings and sympathies toward the Russian government, and if this thing continues for another ten years we will find that the government of this country will be thrown over by their political and economic strength."

After the general strike the Chamber of Commerce imposed an advertising boycott on the paper which became even tighter after the Centralia tragedy. This was the most effective blow that could have been struck. Money was always tight; there was nothing for bigger presses or expansion, and certainly no possibility for the Sunday edition which Editor Ault planned. Circulation in these years ran normally around 50,000, ranking the *Record* with the *Times,* and ahead of the *P-I* and the *Star.*

The growth of the daily radical press around the country and the failure of the standard press agencies to report labor news except in a sensational or malicious manner, led Editor Ault to join with others in establishing the Federated Press, with headquarters in Chicago. William F. Dunne, the courageous editor of the Butte *Daily Bulletin,* the only other union-owned daily, added his support. The *Bulletin* was published in a raw frontier mining camp whose only industry was copper. Violence, highlighted by the shameless lynching of Frank Little, the I.W.W. representative, was the order of the day in Butte. Dunne and his co-workers went constantly armed, with a guard in the plant of the *Bulletin* to discourage raids such as at Centralia. There were socialist and radical dailies in New York, Milwaukee, Minneapolis, and Oklahoma City; an I.W.W. daily in Duluth, and a dozen dailies published in Yiddish, Russian, German, Finnish, and other languages. They joined in Federated Press, with several score weekly papers of labor, farmers, cooperatives, working-class political parties, and independent groups. From bureaus in Chicago, New York, and Washington and the reports of scores of correspondents throughout the country, Federated Press published a daily news service. Even though mimeographed and mailed, it regularly scooped the wire services on labor news.

In 1919-1920 the base of the unions shrank as the shipyards closed. The powerful metal trades unions dwindled in size, nor were the commercial interests displeased at the drying up of this source of labor radicalism. David Rodgers, the shipbuilding genius of the Skinner & Eddy yards, biggest in Seattle, was reported to have offered to lease part of the yards to take care of contracts for $40,000,000 in shipping. This would have furnished work for 6,000 men with a payroll of $10,000,000 a year. Open shop forces were able to stymie Rodgers by appealing to Judge Gary to deny him steel.

Seattle unions had made several desultory efforts across the years to create a labor party, and in 1919 the Central Labor Council again endorsed the idea. It was becoming apparent that while the Republican party as usual represented the employers' point of view, the Democrats, shattered by the Wilson debacle, were to offer only a pale reflection of the Republican program in 1920. The Democrats' main issue, the League of Nations controlled by the leading capitalist powers, left the unions cold. This was no genuine federation of the peoples, an idea which had been endorsed repeatedly in state labor conventions.

The Chicago Federation of Labor, which had taken the lead in the national drive to free Mooney and Billings, and had encouraged William Z. Foster, the former I.W.W., to organize the packinghouse and steel industries, took the lead again in 1919 in organizing the Labor Party. The New York central labor body, a dozen state federations, and scores of city central councils and local unions joined enthusiastically. At the founding convention November 29, 1919, in Chicago, Editor Ault and other Seattleites were prominent. There was fire in the bowels of the union movement which the official leadership of the A.F. of L. was unable to quench. The barbarous suppression of the steel and coal strikes, coupled with the worldwide revulsion against the war and the system which had produced it, the betrayal of the fancy promises of Wilson's 14 Points in the so-called peace treaty, and the rise of labor parties to power in various parts of Europe, all flowed together. In the words of Nathan Fine, historian of labor and farmer parties, "hope filled the common man's breast everywhere. He felt a kinship with his fellow-worker. He thought in group and class terms. He believed, in the words of Eugene Victor Debs, that the day of the people had arrived."

The Labor Party adopted a platform calling for nationalization of the basic resources and utilities, the democratic control of industry and a "league of the workers of all nations pledged and organized to enforce the destruction of autocracy, militarism, and economic imperialism throughout the world." "The Labor Party was organized to assemble into a new majority the men and women who work, but who have been scattered as helpless minorities in the old parties under the leadership of the confidence men of big business."

In 1918 the Washington Federation of Labor had joined with the Grange and the independent railroad unions in a Triple Alliance, so named from the current movement in Britain. Also modeled largely on the ambitious post-war reconstruction program of the British Labour Party was a program embodying the ideas of the New Deal, to be enacted 15 to 20 years later in the social security and labor legislation of President Roosevelt. The war, said the State Federation, had made essential "the reconstruction of the whole social and industrial fabric." It was a program, said the *Union Record*, "upon which extreme radicals and more careful conservatives can find agreement — in fact, it was the result of these two groups reasoning together to find a common ground to advance the interests of the workers."

Hand in hand with the Grange, the State Federation endorsed a resolution on "self-evident truths" which stated that "the cause of labor unrest is the exploitation of producers by parasites; the earth belongs to the people thereof and therefore cannot belong to any individual, group or corporation; that all wealth is the labor of hand and brain plus natural resources, and that anything of value belongs to the producer."

To correct the weakness revealed in Seattle's isolated **general** strike, the State Federation convention in 1919 called for a referendum in all local unions for establishing the One Big Union, in which craft unions would be absorbed into industrial unions and use their strength unitedly. This paralleled a movement that was sweeping western Canada and had come to a head in the Winnipeg general strike of 1919, a strike, unlike Seattle's, marked by violence. It became evident that western Canada was on the verge of a revolutionary situation, and the Ottawa government reacted promptly to stamp out industrial rebellion with the Royal Northwest Mounted Police, armed vigilante committees, and indictments for sedition. Nevertheless the O.B.U. persisted on the prairies and in British Columbia, gaining the support of tens of thousands of A.F. of L. workers tired of craft division. The movement swelled across the border into the state of Washington and was reflected in the State Federation of Labor's vote. The national A.F. of L. moved as swiftly into this situation as the Ottawa authorities had in western Canada, and commanded the Federation to call off the referendum for the One Big Union under pain of having its charter revoked.

In March of 1919 the National Civic Federation, composed of leaders of the A.F. of L. and various business elements, published a letter in its *Review* which threw an interesting sidelight on the rebellion against the A.F. of L. leadership. This letter was presumed to have been sent to leaders of the national Mooney convention in Chicago in January of 1919. It said:

We will have representation at Chicago of about 3,000 delegates from the A.F. of L. I understand from the best authority that Samuel Gompers will instruct the Eastern delegates to stay away from Chicago. This will play right into our hands. The convention will be composed of and controlled by the ultra radical element of the A.F. of L. that will vote for the adoption of the new preamble indorsed by the Washington Federation of Labor. We will be able to show that the two factions of the A.F. of L. are irreconcilable and therefore we can slide through a motion to withdraw from the A.F. of L. In so doing, every radical faction west of the Mississippi will join us. We will be able to pull every organization west of Chicago, which will represent over 1,000,000 members of the A.F. of

L. The I.W.W., the Socialists and Non-partisans and the Bolshevists will indorse our preamble and we will be able to control the entire West. . . . Seattle has always revealed a fine spirit, and we can expect to be the majority party in industrial circles of the West in the next six months.

The letter showed internal evidence of the work of some industrial spy but nevertheless it did indicate that the national A.F. of L. had reason to be fearful of the fires of revolt in the West, centering on Seattle. In any event the leaders of the Mooney convention squelched the possibility of a new federation of labor being organized by adjourning after passing the Mooney general strike resolution, over the vehement protests of a majority of the delegates who wanted to debate far wider issues.

When the Labor Party met again in Chicago in July, 1920, the opposition of the national A.F. of L. and the refusal of Senator LaFollette to accept its radical platform cut seriously into its strength. From the sessions arose the Farmer-Labor Party with Parley Parker Christensen of Utah, relatively unknown, as presidential nominee. Nevertheless the Washington State contingent returned home determined to establish the new party as a factor in state politics. C. J. France, attorney for the Port Commission, was nominated for U.S. Senator, Robert Bridges, chairman of the Port Commission, for governor, Secretary James A. Duncan of the Seattle labor council for congressman, Master William Bouck of the State Grange for congressman from northwest Washington, and Homer T. Bone for congressman from the Tacoma district. As many as 6,000 rallied to the campaign meetings. The state topped the nation in votes for the Farmer-Labor national ticket, with 77,000 as contrasted with 50,000 in Illinois, the second highest state vote. Tacoma elected a state senator and two representatives and the vote for state candidates ran around 100,000. In 1922 the Farmer-Labor Party campaigned again and won five legislative seats. In 1924 third-party enthusiasm would not down, and Senator LaFollette drew 150,000 votes on the Progressive ticket against 43,000 for the Democratic presidential nominee. But as with most third-party ventures, the enthusiasm in the campaigns soon petered out when candidates were not elected, and little effort was made to establish a permanent political organization on a ward and precinct basis. Despite its lack of electoral success, the Farmer-Labor Party hung on through 1926 when Hulet Wells was state chairman.

Meanwhile in this period the Socialist Party practically disappeared in Washington. In 1919 the national organization split in three, the Socialist Party retaining the allegiance of the right wing, while the left wing organized the Communist Party, based mostly on the Russian-language federation of the old Socialist Party, and the Communist Labor Party, based more on the native-born sections. In Seattle the Socialist Party vanished as a political factor. Emil Herman, released from McNeil Island, maintained a state office in Everett for a few scattered members. Despite their radical reputation, Seattle workers showed little enthusiasm for either of the Communist parties. The Russians maintained their own party but the native-born and Scandinavians did not rally to the Communist Labor Party in any appreciable numbers, and it was not until many years later, during the Great Depression, that the by-then united Communist Party attracted much notice in the state. Kate Sadler, the flaming evangel of socialism, refused to align herself with any of the factions in the split and withdrew after a few years to Vashon Island, across the Sound from Seattle, to live in practical retirement with her second husband, Charles Greenhalgh. Hulet Wells announced his resignation from the Socialist Party when the Central Labor Council endorsed the formation of a Labor Party in 1919. He had always been critical of the influence of the intelligentsia and professionals within the party and had insisted that a true socialist party must be based on labor, as in Britain. Most socialists threw themselves enthusiastically into the work of the Farmer-Labor Party. As a consequence, propaganda for socialist principles as such began to die out in Seattle. *Freedom*, the last socialist paper to be published there, expired in 1919, and with it ended an epoch that dated from around 1900 and that saw a score or more of socialist papers published in various parts of the state.

The closing of the shipyards and the subsequent decline in membership of the metal trades unions caused a shift in the Central Labor Council. The older building, teaming, and service trades resumed their previous importance while the militant radical delegates found their ranks dwindling. Now that war was over, a large section of the working class was no longer needed for production and reverted to the classic reserve army of the unemployed, their very presence a drag on the ability of the organized employed to forge ahead.

Dissension broke out in the Central Labor Council, not on a straight issue of radical against conservative ideas and programs, but on a factor that caused increasing alarm among the radicals, the rise of what they called labor capitalism within the ranks of unionism. It all started innocently and wholesomely enough, in the creation of labor's own economic institutions. A hard-fought laundry strike had resulted in the organization of Mutual Laundry, cooperatively owned. Rochdale principles had been used to create a sturdy wholesale and retail grocery business, with the support of labor and the Grange. The Union Theater Company was formed, presumably to show labor and progressive films and to help the theatrical trades maintain union conditions. The Trades Union Savings and Loan Association offered to divert the savings of unionists into labor enterprises.

The most ominous move was announced guilelessly in the organization in 1919 of Listman Service, headed by George P. Listman of the *Union Record* board and an old-time union printer. Listman Service was formed "to secure for the working class the ownership of the industries in which they labor." By withdrawing their savings from the capitalist banks and putting them into labor enterprises workers could gradually take over the industries and begin managing them. This was indeed a variant on Lenin's theory of worker management, and by-passed neatly the need for any violent seizure of private property. There arose soon after United Finance Company, General Dis-

tributors, and Federation Film Corporation. Then came Padilla
Bay Land Company, which was developing property near the
Equality Colony of yore. Bottom was reached with Deep Sea
Salvage, which was to raise ships laden with gold which had sunk
along the treacherous Inside Passage to Alaska. Whatever misgivings Editor Harry Ault, the one-time socialist, may have had
about these schemes to lift the working class by its bootstraps
into the promised land, one by-product was welcome — the advertisements for these enterprises which helped tide the *Union
Record* over the boycott imposed by the Chamber of Commerce upon advertising by department stores and the bigger
merchants.

The issue of labor capitalism flared on the floor of the Central
Labor Council and a resolution to forbid any officer from de-
riving a major portion of his income from rent, interest, or
profit carried by 100 to 94. At this, the moderate leaders of the
Council, many of them on the boards of the labor enterprises,
closed ranks with the conservatives and made a determined
effort to get better attendance of delegates from the teaming
and building trades whose appearances on the council floor had
become slack. The resolution was then rescinded by a vote of
123 to 102. The council's sessions, which until 1920 had been
devoted largely to ways and means of advancing labor's cause,
degenerated into wrangles over the probity of many of its
members.

For Anna Louise Strong, the idealist who presided over the
Union Record's editorial page, the experience was shattering.
Her personal allegiance to Editor Ault persevered, but she was
aghast at the corruption of high principles into tawdry salesman-
ship and outright exploitation of the loyalty of *Union Record*
readers, into feathering the nests of a horde of salesmen, high-
pressure financiers, and scheming adventurers. Lincoln Steffens
came through Seattle in 1920, and Miss Strong took him to
Blanc's restaurant, the hangout of the intellectuals. She explained the situation. "So you are siding with Harry?" Steffens
asked.

"Well, no, I can't exactly side with Harry. I think it's terrible the way our paper is going. . . . Harry is between the devil and the deep sea. I think he's not bold enough; he ought to defy these advertisers even if we have to have a smaller paper. But the paper is his child; he dreamed of it when he used to work as a small boy in a printing office and sleep on the table at night. He gave his best years to make this paper; I hate to see these upstarts call him a traitor. But I can't agree with Harry either; he's begun to say the workers are ungrateful. One can't say that."

Talk drifted to Moscow, whence Steffens had just returned. "O, I'd give anything if I could go there!" she exclaimed. "Why don't you then?" asked Steffens.

In 1921 Anna Louise Strong was off to Poland for the Friends Service Committee, the only avenue by which one might hope to slip through the Allied blockade into Russia. Editor Ault announced in the *Union Record* that he had given a leave of absence for a few months to "perhaps the one indispensable person on our staff," but he probably sensed that this ended an era for the *Union Record*. She never returned but gave herself thenceforth to the mission of interpreting the Russian, Chinese, and other revolutions to wondering Americans; eventually she became associate editor of the *Moscow Daily News* in the 1930's when Russia swarmed with engineers and technicians from the United States and British countries, mostly driven from their homelands by unemployment, and in need of news of the world in English. In the 1950's she settled in Peking where, enjoying the confidence of the leaders of the Chinese Republic, she became an interpreter of their ideas and programs to the western world.

Another pilgrim from Seattle showed up in Russia — Hulet Wells. The Red International of Labor Unions had called a conference to meet in Moscow in the summer of 1921 and had sent out invitations to labor bodies throughout the world to attend. The Seattle Central Labor Council, with that of Detroit, accepted, and designated Wells to go as an observer as well as correspondent for the *Union Record*. Furnished with $500 and

a special kind of passport by the Russians under the name of
Alexander Petrov, he sailed from New York on a former Russian vessel where he met Leo Laukki, a friend from Leavenworth days. Laukki had fled Finland after the 1905 revolution,
had joined the I.W.W., and was head of a Finnish labor college
in Minnesota.

From Moscow Wells wrote to the *Record:* "As for myself, I
have seen miracles. The magnitude of the things that have been
done leaves me wondering. I came expecting to see a people
weak from hunger and clothed in rags. I find a people well
clothed and with scarcely any marks of insufficient food. I find
an army of a kind such as there never was in the world before. I
find a system of distribution working with a machinery so
elaborate, that with such otherwise strained resources, I would
not have believed it possible." This preliminary impression he
later revised as somewhat too enthusiastic, particularly in regard
to the food situation when he traveled subsequently in the Volga
famine districts.

Wells stayed in Russia five months and saw much of the vast
country and met most of its leaders. He concluded that they had
deserted Marx for Bakunin, the communist anarchist — "from
each according to his ability, to each according to his need."
Wells, who considered himself in former years as aligned with
the left wing of the Socialist Party, was surprised to find in
Russia how many socialists were still further to the left. His own
conception of socialism envisaged extension of public control to
the basic industries and services, leaving the social system to
change gradually in accordance with the new economic foundation. Accordingly, the then current communist appeal to workers in the Western countries to arise in revolution as the only
guarantee of the success of the Russian revolution hardly was
the kind to win Wells's support. Upon his return he threw himself into the work of the Russian Famine Relief and helped to
raise several thousand dollars in the Puget Sound country.
Ironically, some ten years later he was again addressing meetings

in Seattle for famine relief, but this time it was to feed hungry Americans, not Russians.

Reaction in Seattle was not through with Wells. The Bar Association had him disbarred for moral turpitude — his opposition to the war was found to be "morally foul, base, vile and depraved." The disbarment did not affect him financially at all as he had always disdained the practice of law as an exercise in defense of capitalist property relationships and he had studied it only to help him in his labor activities. Very likely he could easily have been chosen as a business agent for a local union, but he preferred, independently, to win his living from his own manual work. A lonely man in adversity, stamped as a felon and deprived of the right to vote, denied employment of course in his former jobs with the post office and the city, he and his family endured harsh privation in the long years to 1933.*

Persecution of the I.W.W. from 1917 on, rising to a climax in Centralia, decimated its ranks. For a time it remained a force in western Washington. In 1920 the annual picnic at People's Park near Renton, owned by radical organizations, was the largest affair of the kind ever held in the Pacific Northwest with 6,000 present. George Vanderveer spoke on behalf of the Centralia prisoners while Frank Turco of the Metal Trades Council presided. Turco was a coal and hard-rock miner who had had to leave Butte during one of the recurring outbreaks of violence there. Short and stocky, he had lost a leg in a mine accident and the story was that he kept a can of lubricating oil for his artificial leg in all the various halls and rendezvous he frequented as he limped from engagement to engagement. After the shipyards closed, he sold newspapers on a busy corner for the next 40 years, during which his great shock of black hair turned to snowy white. As perpetual head of the newsboys union he maintained his credentials during all the years in the Central Labor Council, becoming toward the end one of the few, if not the only surviving leader of general strike days in the Council.

*In 1934 Wells was released from his status as a felon and went to Washington, D.C., as assistant to Congressman Marion Zioncheck.

As the depression deepened in 1921, the 9- and 10-hour day crept back into the logging camps and with it many of the old evils of bad food and lodging. In 1923 the Wobblies rallied for their final general strike in the woods for the eight-hour day. Using all the old techniques which had served so well in 1917, the strike failed to become general. Lumber Workers Industrial Union 500 was finished in the camps. The "gyppo" system came in, by which logging operations were contracted out to gangs. In the beginning, by working harder for themselves, as it were, than they would have for a boss, their pay was high. The union having been extinguished, the contract rates were lowered until by 1933 the logger was worse off than ever. What the boss was unable to do in the way of a coup de grâce to the Wobblies, they accomplished themselves. In 1924 dissension tore them in twain. Thereafter many a Wobbly hall kept open, but they were the refuges of "hall cats," men who clung to the memories of great times and came to be known as "three-star patriots," from the famous three stars standing for Education, Agitation, and Organization, on the Wobbly button. The police forgot about them; after the Centralia prisoners were freed there were few victims longer for the terror which in the Turbulent Teens had sent thousands of them to jail.

The depression of 1921 removed the issue of labor capitalism as a cause of dissension in the Central Labor Council by removing, through insolvency, labor's capitalistic enterprises. The Council's continued support of the Farmer-Labor Party in 1922, against the wishes of President William Short of the State Federation of Labor and of the national A.F. of L., produced the final flare-up of Seattle insurgency in 1923. For years the Council had been a thorn in the side of the A.F. of L. as fiery, red-headed Jimmy Duncan rose to puncture the unanimity of President Gompers' inevitable re-elections, and to plead the cause of industrial unionism. After the general strike Duncan had outlined a plan, backed by the Council, for the reorganization of the A.F. of L. through the consolidation of international unions into twelve general industrial units. By June of 1919 endorsements had been won from 30 central labor bodies in 22 states. The plan did not appeal to the craft internationals which dominated the A.F. of L. and never got off first base.

Spurred by President Short of the State Federation, who conducted incessant warfare against the recalcitrant Seattle, Tacoma, and Everett central bodies, and by C. O. (Dad) Young, the aged representative of the A.F. of L. in the state, the national organization on April 10, 1923, demanded that the Seattle Council capitulate or face revocation of its charter. The parent body's indictment included these points:

The Seattle Council devoted more time to urging recognition of Russia and the independence of India than to union affairs.

It has supported the Farmer-Labor Party.

It has antagonized groups of citizens in Seattle.

It sent Hulet Wells to the red union convention in Moscow and published his favorable report.

It seated delegates from unions not affiliated with the A.F. of L.

When the Seattle Council insisted it had violated no rules of the national body and pleaded the cases of the three local unions to which objection had been made, the A.F. of L. on May 14 categorically demanded compliance with its orders. On June 6 the Council replied, acceding to the demand for the unseating of the blacksmiths, shipyard laborers, and lady barbers unions. The blacksmiths local was in a dispute with its international and the shipyard laborers had been unable to find an international which would charter them. The plight of the lady barbers showed the A.F. of L. at its worst. The barbers international was "for men only" and had denied a charter to the Seattle union when it was organized in 1918 with the cooperation of the local men's barbers union. Efforts to obtain a federal labor union charter directly from the A.F. of L. were rebuffed, despite the national constitution's fine words about no discrimination on account of sex in the organization of labor. Nineteen delegates

voted against compliance with the A.F. of L. order, largely on
the basis of loyalty to the lady barbers union.

To the A.F. of L. demand that the Seattle Council "repudiate"
the I.W.W., it replied that it had never endorsed dual unionism.
Asked to repudiate its approval of soviet dictatorship and the
principles of communism, the Council said it had nothing to
repudiate, never having endorsed them in the first place. On the
sticky issue of the Farmer-Labor Party, the Council stood by its
guns. Pointing out that both the Republican and Democratic
conventions in 1920 had turned down the A.F. of L.'s "bill of
rights," and that only the Farmer-Labor Party had incorporated
it in the party platform, the Council reminded the parent body
of its own preamble stating that "a struggle is going on in all
nations of the civilized world between the oppressors and the
oppressed of all countries, a struggle between the capitalist and
the laborer." The preamble had been adopted back in the 1880's
when the A.F. of L. was formed, but Samuel Gompers had
changed his attitude toward oppressors and capitalists quite
substantially since then. Indeed it was something of an oddity
that the Seattle Council should have remembered that the
quaint words still persisted in the A.F. of L. preamble.

Having yielded on the strictly constitutional issues and par-
ried the political questions, the Seattle Council preserved its
charter. The rise of Dave Beck and his lieutenants in the Seattle
movement eventually took care of the other issues. In 1924,
Secretary Duncan, seeing the hopelessness of a continued fight,
retired as secretary of the Central Council and devoted himself
to organizing a promising new field, that of auto mechanics.
Just as Anna Louise Strong's departure from the *Union Record*
marked the end of an era for that paper in 1921, so Duncan's
withdrawal marked an end, in 1924, to the dramatic era in the
Central Labor Council's annals.

The farmers had an even worse time with the National
Grange than the unions with the A.F. of L. Having weathered a
sedition charge by the Department of Justice, Master William
Bouck and the state Grange incurred the displeasure of the

National Grange, an increasingly conservative body whose main strength lay in the northeastern part of the country where it had become largely a social and fraternal organization. The Grange long since had lost its hold on the progressive midwest farmers to the Nonpartisan League and the Farmers Union.

Master Bouck and his fellow farmers combined a moral antipathy to war as essentially un-Christian with a political antipathy to the monopolists who profited from war. When to add insult to injury, farm income was slashed in the depression of 1921, Master Bouck concluded, in his presidential address to the annual state convention in June, that "we are in much worse state than ever before in our history."

"During the war just passed, brought on with the design of preventing the further growth of democratic ideas, during which the opponents of democracy under the guise of patriotism, sought to imprison and hound to death progressive leaders and thinkers," said Bouck, "we had an abiding trust that somehow, someway, simon-pure democracy was to be handed down to us from above. But democracy is never handed down—citizens establish it. They do not receive it. The reign of greed, and the subjection of the producer has been fastened upon the people with iron shackles. Our state and nation are in the iron grip of a 'dollarocracy' more greedy, more relentless than any autocracy of modern or ancient history."

But it was his denunciation of militarism that brought Master Bouck and the state Grange up on charges from the national organization. "Let's organize," he cried, "against this terror of capitalism — its tool in fact. Let's agree to pay no taxes — to lend no aid — to refuse to serve as soldiers for our government or any other to carry on war." In wartime such ideas, expressed in more muted terms, had earned Bouck a federal indictment under the Espionage Act; in peacetime the National Grange took the place of the Department of Justice and placed him on trial. In November, 1921, the National Grange expelled Bouck and four others, who proceeded to form the Western Progressive Farmers. This was proclaimed to be the first "non-

capitalist organization of producers." "This excludes, of course,
bankers, commission men, real estate speculators and all those
whose functions are purely parasitical," the Progressive Farmers
declared. "We are working and planning for the elimination of
capitalism and a substitution of a cooperative commonwealth
where service — not profit — shall be our recompense."

The aims of the new organization included state development
of water power and public ownership of all natural resources
and utilities; a state bank; manufacture of raw products produced by farmers for farmers' use; political action through the
Farmer-Labor Party; a better land tenure system; and "ultimately, to plan a constructive rebuilding of society on the
crumbling ruins of capitalism." The organization published the
Western Progressive Farmer and urged its members to read
the *Farmer-Labor Voice,* organ of the Federated Farmer-Labor
Party, and a new paper just published in Chicago, the *Daily
Worker.* The Progressive Farmers expired in the Hooverian era.

After the depression ended in 1922 America marched forward
on the ever-ascending plateau of normalcy toward the brink of
1929. Meetings of the Central Labor Council returned to the
normal dullness of the earlier 1900's, broken only by a flurry in
1925 when charges were brought against several delegates of
being members of the Communist Party. Among them was
Joseph Havel, head accountant for the *Union Record,* the son
of a proprietor of a Tacoma workingmen's hotel, the Rhine,
which in the old days had been the scene of many a lively
Hungarian dance or radical gathering. Although the temper of
the Seattle Council by then was conservative, many delegates
fought bitterly against the idea of rejecting delegates for their
political opinions, and expulsion was carried by only 78 votes to
71. Thereafter political matters were banned from the Council
floor and a coming leader of the American working class, Dave
Beck, business agent for the laundry drivers, rose to head the
teaming trades, first in Seattle, then in the Pacific Northwest and
on the Coast, and finally as president of his international union,
the Teamsters. Beck's theory of labor relations differed sharply

from those of his predecessors who believed in strikes and militant action. Strikes, he held, did nobody any good, neither the
worker nor the employer. If both sides would sit down together
amicably and organize the industry for their joint profit, class
conflict would end. Beck's theory worked well in the Seattle
laundry industry and was applied in ever-widening circles. But
it never did appeal to employers on the waterfront or in the
woods.

The Central Labor Council under such leadership saw little
need for a daily newspaper, and the *Union Record* was sold to a
corporation headed by Ault in 1924. The "Union" in the masthead was lowered to small type on a shield of stars and stripes
between *Seattle* and *Record* and the dying paper strove hard in
its own way to bring the new message of labor peace to the city's
hard-bitten Chamber of Commerce. In 1928 it expired. Harry
Ault opened a small printing shop but barely survived the
Great Depression. With the New Deal he won an appointment
as a deputy marshal in Tacoma. As such his main functions were
to serve subpoenas and warrants and to conduct prisoners to
federal penitentiaries. An ironic end to the life of the young
printer at Equality's socialist colony, but as his widow remarked
bitterly, those final years were the only years of his life when he
knew when and where the next paycheck was coming from.

In a letter to an old friend, Ault wrote in 1957: "It was hard
going but the only regret I have is that I did not work harder
and more consistently on the paper instead of getting mixed up
in various get-rich-quick schemes which I hoped would help the
paper but only destroyed my own effectiveness." The old socialist in him reappeared in the unfinished manuscript of his
autobiography which he entitled "Thirty Years of Saving the
World." Since his youth there had been great material gains for
workers, he concluded, but an even greater loss of freedom. He
deplored the "slavish devotion to the edicts of a power elite
respecting no authority but their own and so firmly entrenched
that any attempt to rout them appears hopeless." In evident
allusion to Dave Beck, he wrote: "Even our labor leaders have

become a part of this gruesome crew. With enormous salaries
and personal investments running into the millions, they have
lost all touch with the rank and file and look upon them as so
many chattels they may retail or wholesale to the highest
bidder."

After the decease of the Socialist Party, Mark Litchman, the
stocky devoted little socialist lawyer who had defended the
Union Record in the sedition case, organized with other old-
time socialists a Marxist club, to provide a forum for lectures
and discussion. John C. Kennedy, at one time on the faculty of
the University of Chicago and a former socialist alderman in
that city, came to Seattle after the war to serve as secretary of the
state Farmer-Labor Party. In 1922, with Litchman and others he
helped to set up the Seattle Labor College, which enjoyed the
benediction of the Central Labor Council and had quarters in
the Labor Temple. The Labor College featured the usual
courses in labor history, public speaking, parliamentary law, and
current events as well as Marxist theory, and lectures by professors from the University of Washington. At forums the issues
of the day, such as A.F. of L. vs. I.W.W., were debated, and
visiting lecturers such as Scott Nearing were given the platform.
The Labor College Players ranked among the best amateur
groups in Seattle, giving plays by Shaw, Gorki, Tolstoi, Ibsen,
and other social dramatists, and the college sponsored a labor
chorus and maintained a library. A newcomer to Seattle, Carl
Brannin, a representative of the railwaymen's national paper
Labor, taught current events and a workers' correspondence
course. Eventually the labor council withdrew its patronage;
the search for truth among the various ideologies became distasteful to the exponents of business unionism. When Kennedy
left to join the staff of Brookwood Labor College in the East,
headed by A. J. Muste, Brannin became director of the Seattle
Labor College.

By the middle of 1931 the Great Depression into which the
entire nation had dropped claimed some 20,000-30,000 unemployed in Seattle alone. With their dependents they probably

accounted for a third of the people in the city; perhaps another third had only partial employment or reduced incomes. As the last savings disappeared, hunger visited thousands of homes. President Hoover had appealed to the rich to succor the poor, but the response was faltering. Cities and counties were just as broke as most of their taxpayers. In this desperate situation, Carl Brannin of the Labor College, a resident of West Seattle, used to drop in on his old friend, Hulet Wells, a neighbor whose table was as bare as those of tens of thousands of Seattleites. It was one thing to deplore the economic system whose breakdown had been so confidently predicted by socialists for a generation; it was quite another to sit by helplessly while multitudes hungered. To both men came the idea that the unemployed should organize to help themselves inasmuch as no one else seemed inclined to do so. Mrs. Wells, listening to the discussions, asked simply: "Well, then, why don't you organize them?" The three called a meeting for July 23, 1931, in a community clubhouse. They posted notices in stores and public places, talked to neighbors, and awaited the first meeting with some trepidation. West Seattle was a working-class district of small home owners, most of whom had been self-supporting all their lives. The idea of charity handouts was repugnant, and to many it seemed shameful to admit that they had reached the end of their rope and needed help. Rather hesitantly a score or so attended the first meeting to see what hope there might be. Wells and Brannin advanced the idea that the city appropriate $1,000,000 to complete a highway between West Seattle and the main part of the city. The plan appealed to the meeting and the Olympic Heights Unemployed Citizens League was organized to back the plan and to bring up some real facts and figures on the extent of unemployment and need in the neighborhood. So started the first self-help organization of the unemployed in the United States. Brannin offered the columns of the *Vanguard,* publication of the Labor College, as a publicity medium. Within a few weeks other branches of the Unemployed Citizens League were formed in West Seattle and the idea jumped across the tideflats to the rest of the city. By September there were 22 locals functioning, Brannin had become executive secretary of the central federation and the Labor College offices the city headquarters. A young West Seattle lawyer, Marion Zioncheck, volunteered his legal services.

The League stressed the need of employment furnished by city and county, self-help, unemployment insurance, and direct relief, in that order of importance. "In the absence of insurance legislation," proclaimed the League, "we condemn unreservedly all forms of private charity for this purpose. Relief, whether by insurance benefits or direct rations, should come from the public treasury and be borne by the beneficiaries of the prevailing industrial system. We declare that the state owes its citizens the opportunity to earn a livelihood and that every man who stands ready to work is entitled to maintenance as a civic right." The League drafted one of the first unemployment insurance bills and a 30-hour week ordinance for the city.

The city politicians cheerfully enough accepted the idea of a $1,000,000 public works project, but alas, they said, there was no such cash in the city's coffers. The unemployed, seeing that little help was coming from City Hall and desperate in their need, turned to self-help. They got permission to cut useless timber into 10,000 cords of fuel and to distribute 60 tons of unsold fish on the city docks. Each local established a commissary into which went supplies they could locate. Unsold fruit and vegetables offered by Yakima farmers were driven over the Cascades in old trucks owned by League members; crews went across the mountains to dig potatoes which farmers had left in the ground for lack of a cash market and these were shipped by the carload into Seattle. In neighborhood centers the League locals set up canning and preserving kitchens, while unemployed tailors, barbers, shoe repairers, and others went to work two days each week serving other unemployed in return for rations. That was in the desperate winter of 1931. The League's "Republic of the Penniless" attracted nation-wide attention as the first effort of the unemployed to meet a hopeless situation by their own efforts.

Said one of the League's founders: "A spirit of brotherhood prevailed, breaking down barriers of race and creed. It justified the effort, in that it proved the heart of society to be sound, and searching for a constructive way out of the chaotic society of the present. It was a self-motivating experience, never to be forgotten by one who gave to it a year's best effort. It was an education transcending anything to be learned in orthodox institutions, an excursion into the sacred precincts of a future society." But self-help worked both ways, in the opinion of Jimmy Duncan. "It has tended to mitigate the sufferings of the victims of this inexcusable condition," he said, "and at the same time kept the unemployed preoccupied so that they had less time to think about the real solutions to their problems."

Former leaders of the Central Labor Council such as Duncan and Phil Pearl joined with Brannin and Wells to urge the unemployed to force the public authorities to assume their responsibilities. The League then entered politics and was responsible in large measure for a complete overthrow of city and county officials. The dress rehearsal for the 1932 Democratic landslide which virtually swept the Republicans out of office came in the winter of 1930-1931 in the recall campaign against Mayor Frank Edwards of Seattle, a wealthy theater chain owner. He had been elected on a public power platform, but once in office he fired J. D. Ross, revered head of City Light and "Mr. Public Ownership" in the state of Washington. Marion Zioncheck was co-chairman of the committee which campaigned successfully for Mayor Edwards' recall in July, 1931. In this campaign — that colored politics all during the New Deal period — arose the coalition of workers in the cities with farmers in the countryside on the issue of public vs. privately-owned electric power, and against the extortions of the private utility companies. The issue was particularly acute in Washington, with its vast supply of potential hydroelectric power centered in the streams hurtling down from the Cascades and the

Olympics. That Nature's gift to the people should be turned to private profit for Eastern corporations seemed particularly revolting to most workers and farmers.

In the 1932 Presidential election, the Democrats got 353,000 votes to 208,000 for the Republicans, 17,000 for the Socialist Party, 3,000 for the Communist, and 1,000 for the ancient Socialist Labor Party. Homer Bone, who had led the fight for public power in Tacoma, was elected to the U.S. Senate and Zioncheck went to Congress from Seattle in a state Congressional delegation that was solidly Democratic. Democrats held overwhelming majorities in both houses of the state legislature and enacted the state's first old age pension, at $30 a month, and unemployment insurance. Early in the campaign the Commonwealth Builders, forerunner of the Commonwealth Federation, launched an initiative campaign for production for use, and Lewis B. Schwellenbach, later to be a U.S. Senator and Secretary of Labor, campaigned for governor on this issue.

Counterparts of the Unemployed Citizens League sprang up across the state and came together May 29, 1932, in a convention, chaired by Wells, which formed the United Producers of Washington. Paul Haffer of the Tacoma Unemployed Citizens League, who had also served time on McNeil Island for opposition to the First World War, was named secretary. The convention recommended adequate relief, socialization of banking, disarmament, pardons for Mooney and the Centralia I.W.W., and release of the Scottsboro, Alabama, Negro prisoners. The United Producers hoped to encourage the exchange of commodities between communities, such as Yakima fruit for Puget Sound fence posts, and the production of commodities by the unemployed in their own factories. The coming of federal relief dampened the efforts of the United Producers.

Zioncheck, who had performed admirably in Washington as an advanced spokesman for unemployment insurance and social legislation, was re-elected in 1934. He first asked Brannin, and then Wells to come to Washington to serve as his secretary. Wells had just been released from his status as a felon by

Presidential pardon. He had asked Hoover for pardons for all the I.W.W. and other political prisoners, pleading that "the wrongs wreaked by a war-crazed majority were inflicted on a group. The reparation I suggest should be made to the group." Hoover did not bother to answer, despite Washington Senator Dill's supporting statement that the men were convicted because "they disagreed over a war that everybody now knows was the greatest curse the world ever endured." Pardoned by Roosevelt, Wells was reinstated on the post office substitute list, but the Seattle postmaster was in no hurry to give him a permanent job, so he went to Washington as Zioncheck's assistant. After the Congressman became mentally unbalanced and committed suicide, Wells got a job in the Washington post office, where he returned to the postal cases for mail sorting after an absence of some 25 years. In 1945 he retired and returned to the home in West Seattle that he had built himself in the early 1920's.

For Wells, as for many moderate socialists of early times, the New Deal with its labor and social legislation was an adequate answer to his dreams. Rather typical of the thinking of such men was Wells's summary of the new economic order: "The old arrogant capitalism against which I had once enlisted in the socialist crusade had undergone a drastic change. The freebooting system of free enterprise was haltered and hobbled by many laws and taxed until it was groggy. Conversely, the unions grew into giants, and old theories of class exploitation lost much of their validity." For Wells as for Duncan and others of the older generation, their years of retirement were years of modest comfort under social security, and the hectic times through which they had lived became memories of an evil past. As for the future which encompassed nuclear annihilation as a possibility in a world which weltered in brushfire wars and the unceasing indecencies of the cold war . . . well, those were concerns of the new generation.

Alongside the Unemployed Citizens League arose the Unemployed Councils, part of a nation-wide movement. Scorning self-help, the Councils sought to mobilize the unemployed in direct action to gain public relief through demonstrations, picket lines, resistance to evictions, and a constant propaganda for a national security system embracing unemployment and old age benefits. After the League dissolved, the Councils continued their activity and became known as the Workers Alliance. A new political alignment arose, combining the unemployed, those beyond 50 for whom employment had become a mirage, and others shocked at the continued paralysis of the economic system in the 1930's despite NRA and the New Deal's best efforts.

Many of the oldsters remembered well the radicalism of the 1910's, culminating in the general strike, but the new movement was to be dominated by young people whose memories went back at most to the last years of Hoover prosperity and to the catastrophic collapse of the system in 1930-1931. Seared by the shock, they were ready to travel down any of the avenues that led to social redemption. And there were many. Howard Scott's Technocracy, that comet-like apparition that promised to engineer the way to abundance; the Townsend movement which was to ease the plight of the aged by an ingenious turnover-tax scheme; the Commonwealth Builders who saw a roseate future in the common effort of producers to build a social system based on use and not on profit; the various radical parties such as the Communist which used the Russian experience to build a pattern for a Soviet America. As the Unemployed Citizens League withered before the coming of federal relief that undercut their self-help program, these various movements searched for common ground on which to build unity, and founded the Washington Commonwealth Federation in 1935. From this the Central Labor Council, under the domination of Dave Beck of the Teamsters, held aloof, but many local unions and particularly those on the waterfront gave their enthusiasm to the new movement.

The Commonwealth Federation cohorts descended on the 1936 convention of the Democratic Party in Aberdeen and took it away from the astonished and outraged state machine. When the convention ended, the Democratic Party stood committed to nationalization of the banks, public ownership of utilities and natural resources, and production for use. The convention omitted an endorsement of Roosevelt's re-election. It was at this point that Postmaster-General Farley is said to have uttered his famous toast to "the American Union — 47 states and the Soviet of Washington." Many an old-time radical gasped in astonishment too. The old Socialist Party had never come within sight of electoral success; the Farmer-Labor Party of 1920-1922 won no important victories; but the Commonwealth Federation within a year seemed within hailing distance of its goal of a state devoted to production for use — the dream of the old socialists who had colonized Washington to make it a socialist commonwealth. Here was a genuine people's movement, built by the hard work of the old-timers and the hopes of the newcomers on the debris of a faltering economic system — perhaps the most genuine people's movement the United States had seen since its Revolutionary days.

In 1935 the CIO Woodworkers Union swept through the forests as did the Wobblies in 1917 with a general strike that brought out the National Guard and claimed a hundred thousand members. This prodded the A.F. of L. once again to try its hand in the woods, with the Carpenters given sole jurisdiction. The longshoremen's union in 1934 and 1936 tied up the waterfront, winning the six-hour day and hiring through the union hall. The fishermen and the cannery workers joined in the winning union parade, largely under the inspiration of the new CIO. In 1936 the Newspaper Guild struck the ancient *Post-Intelligencer,* the morning paper whose destinies had been taken over by William Randolph Hearst, in a monumental struggle that united, even though briefly, the Seattle union movement; Dave Beck's teamsters refused to haul newsprint to the stricken plant. After three months the Guild scored one of its first and most important victories on the national scene. In this period, too, the Washington Pension Union won the nation's first comprehensive health program. All pensioners received full medical, dental, and hospital care, along with medicines and appliances, and could choose their own physicians. This program was expanded later to all categories of assistance and is still in operation.

In the state capital an impressive bloc of Commonwealth Federation legislators fought courageously on a wide front for improved social security and labor legislation and secured the repeal of the hateful criminal syndicalism law under which the I.W.W. had been harried. It appeared likely that if the Commonwealth Federation could preserve cohesion against the onslaughts of the daily press and the old-line political machines, Washington indeed might become some kind of a cooperative commonwealth. And then came the Russo-Finnish war in 1939 and the Soviet-Hitler pact. The Federation was torn by dissension over these foreign issues and eventually dissolved in 1945. The cooperative commonwealth would have to wait awhile on world events.

By 1944 the divisive events of 1939-1940 had been forgotten in the throes of the Second World War, when Seattle resumed its role as shipbuilder and also, in this new age, as airplane builder for the nation. When the new CIO decided to go into politics and set up its Political Action Committee, it won wide support among perhaps the majority of A.F. of L. members, to judge by the election results. In 1944 former Congressman Jerry O'Connell of Butte became state director of CIO-PAC and was elected soon after as secretary of the state Democratic central committee. Hugh DeLacy, a Seattle councilman, was sent to Congress from Seattle despite the opposition of Dave Beck and old-line Democrats and Republicans. The defection in labor ranks from Beck domination reflected growing distaste for the pudgy, blue-eyed millionaire who had once been a laundry driver. His own predilection in labor-employer affairs could be deduced from his statement: "Why should truck drivers and bottle washers be allowed to make decisions affecting policy? No corporation would allow it." The Chamber of Commerce held him to be the very model of a model labor leader, and Beck, who never finished high school, became a regent and later president of the board of regents of the University of Washington. By then the raiding proclivities of his union had alienated even the conservative Central Labor Council and the State Federation of Labor.

In 1945, through the efforts of CIO-PAC and the Washington Pension Union, the state pension was lifted to a minimum of $50 a month. Crying that such munificence would bankrupt the state treasury, the Republicans and conservative Democrats united and the Republicans won the 1946 election. Jerry O'Connell was displaced by the Democrats. Undeterred, the Pension Union pressed on for a $60 minimum and sponsored two marches on Olympia, the state capital, the second of which urged adoption as well of a program for better social security, more aid to schools, fair employment practices legislation, and a veterans bonus. In reply the legislature eliminated the $50 minimum which the Pension Union had already won, tightened up the law, and took away the right of the aged to pick their own physicians.

At this juncture reaction abandoned its frontal attack and began waving the Red Flag, in the fashion of Ole Hanson back in 1919. It spread rumors that the Pension Union, the CIO-PAC, and the University of Washington were all infiltrated by Reds. Forever in the lead, as it were, the state of Washington was the first to see a concerted attack on academic freedom in that era and to get a foretaste of McCarthyism. The old parties claimed that the leaders of the Pension Union and friendly groups "know that the power to tax is the power to destroy. They are trying to lay the foundation for revolution." Republicans and Democrats joined in 1947 to set up a state Un-American Activities Committee, known as the Canwell Committee. Using the well-worn tactics of the national Un-American Activities Committee and of a parallel committee in California, the Canwell Committee conducted investigations in Seattle into communist infiltration of the Pension Union and the University. The Commonwealth Federation, the Pension Union, and other groups, through their election successes, had attracted quite a

lot of people whose eyes were ever on the main chance. Now
that the winds were blowing the other way, they found it con-
venient to turn on former friends and associates and unburden
themselves to the Canwell Committee.

When the Committee ended its two-year foray into political
beliefs and associations, it could boast that it had obtained the
discharge of three outstanding professors, Joseph Butterworth,
Herbert Phillips, and Ralph Gundlach, had had several others
placed on probation, and terrorized the University into intellectual numbness — "an intellectual concentration camp" —
with the eager support of President Dave Beck of the board of
regents. The Pension Union, while it held together admirably,
lost some measure of support. The Seattle Repertory Theater
was destroyed. Against these successes, the Committee suffered
defeats. The legislature ignored its prescriptions for police-
state legislation and, even worse, most of the members of the
Committee were defeated when they stood for re-election, including Canwell. Sobered by this, the legislature was not eager
to renew the Committee's life, and it expired in 1949.

By then the civic life of Seattle was dominated by the Boeing
airplane plants employing 60,000 workers. Seattle, always a
hotspot in hot wars, became a hotspot in the cold one, too, its
prosperity dependent on stirring the embers of world hostility.
The once-powerful Central Labor Council now played second
fiddle to the men in the gleaming headquarters of the Teamsters,
and to the Machinists Union, which held bargaining rights at
Boeing.

Now, with well-oiled machinery run by international unions,
there appeared to be little point to local union militancy. Truck
drivers and bottle washers, and airplane mechanics as well, as
Beck had said, had no business interfering in matters of policy.
Unions should be run as businesses, and if the officials brought
packages of wage increases and fringe benefits, it was proof that
business unionism paid off. There was nothing for union members to do, not even to bother going to the union office to pay
dues, for these were deducted at the source to save them the

trouble. In only one regard was Seattle like the old days — one of the prominent leaders of labor was on McNeil Island. This time it was no socialist — they had vanished — but the spokesman of business unionism, Dave Beck himself. In mixing business and unionism he had run afoul of the law and was a guest of Uncle Sam, as Hulet Wells, Sam Sadler, and the Pass brothers had been of yore.

Appendixes

Appendix One

The Lives of Radicals

Friends of those years — and these — have helped profoundly in writing this book. Their vivid memories of the period in which they were in the front line of the labor movement have contributed much which has been incorporated in the various chapters. But their own personal experiences and reflections give a deeper feeling of the exuberance and drive of those days than a mere account of events can hope to reveal. I have included three of these accounts in this appendix, although some of the subject matter touched upon is treated in the main part of the book. For various reasons the contributors wish to remain anonymous.

I

I was just a kid when we went to Tacoma, in 1901. We lived, as most people did, in a two-story frame house on a 50x100-foot lot, with grass and morning glories in front and garden and chicken yard in back, and of course a woodshed.

From the day we arrived, it seemed to me, there was an unending stream of "tramps," unemployed men looking for something to eat, at our back door, and my father issued orders never to turn anyone away — even if we had only a slice of bread ourselves, which happened pretty often. We always had coffee for them. It brings to mind Joe Hill's "The Tramp" with the words, "May I chop some wood for you?" We never asked them to do such things. There were kids enough around to do the family chores. Well, it was this stream of hungry men, and the horde of hungry people in the lower end of town, that always held my attention. We are accustomed nowadays to read — with lifted eyebrow — government statistics that there are only 5, or 5.9

percent, or some such fiction, of the labor force unemployed. In those days they never counted the unemployed; just tried to keep them on the run from town to town and from state to state with a "floater," the common sentence for being out of a job. "I'll give you till sundown to be out of this city," said the Jedge, or else — the jail house for 30 days.

Things got much worse during Teddy Roosevelt's argument with Morgan in 1907 about Tennessee Coal & Iron when Morgan shut off the country's credit and we were reduced to living on scrip for some weeks. The Northwest was poor country — workingman's country — where most people had mighty little and even the rich weren't so rich. But during the panic nobody had anything. The Chamber of Commerce printed money for the occasion — a slight deviation from the law but nobody cared — and the employers paid off in the stuff, the merchants took it for groceries, and somehow or other we got along without any genuine money, until Teddy gave Morgan what he wanted. We were neither richer nor poorer for the experience but it left an indelible impression on me that money is merely what people say it is — the gold and silver content doesn't cut much ice and needn't wear holes in our pockets.

Then came the Great White Fleet steaming around the world to show how big was "our stick," after which Teddy stole Panama to dig a canal. The canal got dug and sailing ships were a thing of the past, which was hard on Tacoma, because it had a good sailing ship harbor, but not so good for steamers. I remember the sailing ships used to moor across Commencement Bay under the lee of Brown's Point, dozens of them, waiting for the white wheat to come rolling in from east of the Cascades. While awaiting cargo the sailors were generally driven ashore, to save money for the ship owners, and they joined the unemployed looking for work, but they found none.

The whole thing came to a climax in 1913 with the first real depression of my experience. In Tacoma we were getting 19 cents an hour if we had jobs, in Saint Ole's (St. Paul & Tacoma Lumber Company) sawmill, cutting lumber that sold for $55 a thousand feet right before the war. It was in 1913 that the working stiffs in the Puget Sound area made a real dent in things.

They put on such a show that Seattle started a famous Hotel de Gink for the unemployed to sleep in and get a bite to eat.

Both Tacoma and Seattle had skid roads where the unemployed congregated to be near the slave market. Along the skid road streets they peddled cheap rotgut liquor and worse rotgut food, such as flapjacks and doughnuts and "a full meal — 15 cents." It would fill you up all right, if you could hold it down. In the crumb joints men could rent a place to sleep for 10 or 15 cents a night. There were pretty good rooms for four bits. And there were some good working class hotels, such as the Havels' Rhine Hotel on lower Pacific Avenue — a big wooden structure with a dining room and saloon, and a friendly, socially-conscious landlord and his family.

A bitter literature grew up about jobs and joblessness. There was the old story about the sawmill hand, walking along the road, who came to a millpond where the boom man had fallen into the water and was drowning. He yelled for help and the man on the bank said: "Where do you work?" "In that mill, there," came the answer. The man on the bank dashed away to the mill and told the straw boss, "How about a job?" "There isn't any job." "Go on, I just saw your boom man drowning." "Oh, the guy who pushed him in got that job."

There was leaven in the dough — the Wobblies, the socialists, anarchists, and rebels. Men took their struggles and their hunger with a grin and a determination to change things. The waitresses in Seattle went on strike in 1914, and won. They won because they got help from the men who didn't have enough money to eat in restaurants. But at a quarter of noon, the seats of the big restaurants suddenly filled up with men who said, "Give me a cup of coffee" and sat there drinking it till half past one. Two days of that and the bosses called the cops. The cops couldn't do anything. Another day, and there were cries for quarter from the bosses. The waitresses won. I remember one waitress who told a Wob she didn't have anything else to give him for helping them, and he said: "We don't want that kind of pay. We want you to organize." For a long time afterward, known left-wing organizers got small checks in some of the more expensive restaurants.

When spring came the unemployed got out of town into the jungles simply because it was more comfortable. They rode the rods and brake beams, the tops and the blinds, and inside box-cars and gondolas. Many train crews let them ride — after all, the crew didn't own the road or its freight either, and they weren't paid enough to turn cop. The unemployed rode until they found a job, and the drift was fairly stable and seasonal, from woods to construction jobs to harvest fields; from hay to wheat to southern crops.

My first acquaintance with a real live radical was by chance. Sam Hammersmark, with two comely daughters, lived across the street from us. I was a little appalled to learn that he was an anarchist. Sam ran a tobacco shop which carried a lot of Marxist literature. Another Tacoma radical was Frans Bostrom, who for years was state secretary of the Socialist Party. He ran a book-store on Pacific Avenue near the City Hall and had a big So-cialist Party emblem — hands clasped across the globe — on his window. Later when I joined the Wobs I would drop in at the book store, which also carried a stock of Marxist literature. Frans talked to everyone, always trying to get them to learn a little more than they already knew. He introduced me to a few milder items on socialism such as Marx's *Value, Price and Profit*.

My first direct memory of socialist activity, as a callow high school youth, came when a piece was printed in the local socialist paper about a scandal at the high school — one of the graduating girls was pregnant. The author was Paul Haffer, and later they threw him into Pierce County jail for "defaming the dead" — he wrote that George Washington was a slave-owner. I was work-ing then after school hours as a page in the public library and part of my job was to carry books up to the county jail. Some of the prisoners knew what they wanted to read, and it wasn't "crime" stuff by a long shot. The library had all the socialist classics in it — Hillquit and Spargo and others of the milk-and-water gang, as well as Marx and Engels. I found the milk-and-water stuff pretty poor reading. I think I absorbed most of my intransigence from reading U.S. history rather than from the socialists, but the application of past history to current events became quite obvious, when I began to think about it.

Any account of the Pacific Northwest should have something about that strange animal, the snake farmer. He led such a life as nobody ever tried to lead before. He came along after the lumber companies had stripped the land of trees, leaving stumps about six to ten feet above ground. The snake rancher, after paying the company for the land, tried to make a living off it. It was a double deal. He had to work in the woods nine months a year or so to have enough money to meet payments and to spend three months grubbing stumps. For that reason he was also known as a stump rancher. After some years he might have burned, grubbed, and snaked out enough stumps to plant a bit of oats, barley, or wheat, and maybe a spud. If so he would have something to eat the next year. And if he couldn't pay his taxes, the State was glad to relieve him of his few acres and return them to the lumber company. The snake farmers were a hardy breed to tackle such a life, and they eventually found that farming wasn't quite the sure thing the song said it was. A lot of them just drifted back to the skid road and to the camps and mills. As a result most of them weren't very loyal to the lumber companies. But some could be depended on to be the backbone of anti-labor campaigns to defend the system against the Reds.

Vagrancy laws were a factor in the early years of the century. In the early 1920's I did a study of vagrancy laws running back to New Hampshire's for "runaway" servants, which included factory workers — laws little changed from the 1700's. If jobless for ten days, the man was eligible for jail unless he had visible means of support. The jails of the period were built primarily to house "vagrants" arrested for "mopery with intent to gawk," as the boys used to wisecrack. The judge could just about throw away the key, but the general rule was a 30-day floater. The floater system and vagrancy laws were used in strikes, along with the National Guard. Strike leaders were pulled off the picket lines and given floaters — and if they refused, the usual 30 days.

I suppose there was some excuse for the small towns using the floater method to keep free of people for whom they had no jobs. Even the townspeople were apt to be out of work a good part of the time and they didn't want strangers camping on them — except when the heavy work periods came. During harvest time there was not much "vagrancy" although the jungle outside town might have several hundred men waiting for the wheat to ripen. I remember Connell in 1916 — there were about

300 stiffs waiting for jobs, and the town was only 200 people altogether. Some of them were scared, and to be sure, some of the harvest hands looked pretty scary — one fellow had a heavy eastern overcoat on, just because that was his "blanket" and it was easier to wear than to carry. The combines had not hit that part of the state yet — it was awfully heavy wheat and they worked it with reaper, header box, and thresher. Men forked the heavy stuff and sweated — then lay down to sleep where they could, still damp with the day's work. They got a bath when they came to a river, between jobs.

Radicals didn't neglect the cultural aspects of their movement. The Yipsel (Young People's Socialist League) dances usually started out with an hour's study of Marxist topics, with teachers about as green as their students. After the dance there might be a bit of a stage show on a class struggle theme, or local talent singing songs from working class culture. I remember an Englishman who had a fairly good baritone voice and a repertoire of working class (not Marxist or socialist) songs and poems he loved to recite. And I remember efforts to teach young Scandinavians the mysteries of the English "J" sound. All this was part of the effort to win the world for the workers. In between there was dancing, for boy to meet girl, and the rest of it. And there were literary efforts by the young fellows, some of which brought surprising results such as the young Yipsel who felt that the reason the Russians won their revolution was because they *sang*. He was so enthusiastic about his theory that he wrote a piece for a socialist paper on The Afterbirth of the Russian Revolution, which required a little editing.

And there were enormous meetings, in Swedish, Norwegian, Jewish, as well as English, where people spoke their hearts out. Socialism was at the bottom of these meetings, along with temperance, which was a crying need, and a general cultural growth. There was writing, singing, studying, everywhere. There must have been scores of people who wrote "poems" — parodies of hymns or of poems they knew — trying to express their ideals and their emotions about what was going on around them. And they succeeded, within reasonable limits, which is as good as most people ever do.

About 1919 I was working as a printer's apprentice in the

Equity print shop, where we published the I.W.W. and socialist papers, and considerable stuff for A.F. of L. unions and other outfits such as the Private Soldiers and Sailors Legion. It was right after the general strike and the cops were rounding us up and closing down the shop, when Art Shields walked innocently in. Walker Smith, the manager of Equity, grabbed a package of leaflets and said, "Here is your bundle," and waved him to the door. He took it and his bland smile and his Army uniform got him past the army of cops without trouble. The rest of us went to jail and the cops put a big padlock on the door. The shop was owned by workers' organizations and by individuals who had put a few dollars of hard-earned money into it so as to have a place to print what they wanted to — "freedom of the press," they called it. When we got out of jail a few days later, we opened the place again. The editor of the socialist paper, the *International Weekly*, had very wisely departed these areas, and another editor took his place.

"We" opened the place? That is wrong. The cops opened it for us at 8:00 A.M. and one of them stood around until noon. Then he locked us out for lunch. We came back at 1:00 P.M. and another cop unlocked the door for us to go in again. He stood by until 5:00, when he locked us out for the night. This went on for some weeks.

The Morning Cop was a martinet, a member of the ruling clique in the police department, and very much a labor-hater. The Afternoon Cop was one of the opposition and he didn't care much for the job of spying on our affairs. The shop had a deep gully behind it. We used to set type and make up forms in the morning and print them in the afternoon. Things that we didn't think the Morning Cop would approve were just passed down into the gully where the owner picked them up. Thus we avoided police censorship.

When the new editor, Dan Ronald, came on the scene, he decided that the socialist paper should be called *Freedom*. He wrote reams of copy for that first edition. He was a Socialist Party of Canada man — a Marxist of the old school who could argue for hours on which came first, the State or exploitation. He also believed that "you could teach any worker" and he took it into his head that a cop is a worker — especially the Morning

Cop. While we were setting up his paper, he was busy explaining the class struggle to the Morning Cop. Noontime came, and the Morning Cop locked us out and we went up to the Swedish restaurant in the IOGT hall for lunch. One o'clock. We came back. The Afternoon Cop was not there. Instead there were four other cops, with a lieutenant and the Morning Cop. The Morning Cop unlocked the door. We went in. The lieutenant walked over to the form we had been working on. Four newspaper pages, all locked up and ready to go.

"Give me a proof of that," he ordered. We got out the roller, the wet paper and the mallet and pounded out a proof. He took a hard look at it. "Break it up! Break the whole thing up," he said, although he had looked only at the first page. Gene Travaglio, the printer, started unlocking the form, to throw the type into the hellbox. The lieutenant looked at me and said:

"You ought to be ashamed of yourself, printing things like that in a country where you have free speech." "Yeah," I said, and smiled. Since then I have never had any doubts about what free speech means, or the First Amendment.

Douglas Browett and Jack McVeagh also worked on *Freedom,* as volunteers. Browett refused to take anything but a pick and shovel job because he didn't want the boss to exploit his mind. He could think what he pleased while shoveling, but would have to think of his job if he worked at a skilled trade. These two and many more used to gather at the home of Mark Litchman, the socialist lawyer, and debate through the night the more abstruse angles of Marxist doctrine. Mark, an East Side boy, went West to do hard work before becoming a lawyer. His wife, Sophie, was a lot sharper on the class struggle. She had felt the teeth of the harrow. Of course, so had Mark, and he never went over, as so many did.

II

Madison Avenue propaganda in recent years has hammered away at the theme that socialism-communism is an imported commodity, foreign to our way of life. We know how economic exploitation wheels the worker in certain directions. But how does he come to know socialism? From a picket line, a meeting, or from a friend comes a pamphlet, a newspaper, a magazine, a book. In my own case the economic angle made me receptive. When the $15 monthly rent fell due, there was always a family conference in the kitchen. We peddled Sunday papers — we called it Landlord's Day. But actually, how did I come to a mature understanding of socialism?

I recall the time when I was 13 or 14. I had read avidly the Leach and Spaulding sports annuals, as well as the baseball and detective novels with their bright-colored paper covers. I had read Mark Twain and the Alcott books, but beyond Alcott our teachers did not direct or encourage us. Until — O, happy day! — I strolled into our neighborhood library where I was attracted by the steel engravings and woodcuts of some old magazines. I liked those pictures of a bygone age. A thoughtful and kind human being had bequeathed to the library bound volumes of magazines dating back to the 1870's. What a find! Now I realize that good growing seed was planted in me. For in these old volumes I found the road to the books which made democracy an ever-growing, ever-blooming tree of life for me.

From the pictures, the 13-year-old boy trotted on to the text. To this day I recall the stories, poems, and names of these writers, although some of them are rarely mentioned in our literature today — Sarah Orne Jewett, William Sharp, Emma Lazarus, Emerson, Thoreau, William Dean Howells, Whittier, Mary Wilkins Freeman, Thomas Hardy, Louise Imogene Guiney, Henry James, Mary Austin, Robert Herrick.

Don't let anyone ever tell me again that socialism, expanding democracy, and faith in the people is an imported commodity. These are the writers who led the 13-year-old boy, by now 16, straight to Shelley, Blake, Whitman, Ibsen, William Morris, Shaw, *The Jungle,* Gorky, *The Iron Heel,* Debs, Marx, Engels, and to *Men and Mules,* the first simple socialist pamphlet I ever read. There are many roads to socialism, but it is always the printed word that leads the way, clearing the mind of Madison Avenue propaganda.

In 1915 there was no Left and Right. Life was more colorful — Yellow and Red. And what a bitter struggle followed the 1912 convention of the Socialist Party! My heroes were Debs and Haywood; my villains, Hillquit and Berger. What youthful anger possessed me was stimulated by life in the interior of Alaska where at the age of 18 I met up with ever so many miners, my seniors and teachers, wonderful human beings, many from the Western Federation of Miners — all on the Red side. Returning to Puget Sound in 1914, I found the Yellow and Red factions were at each other with hammer and poison. Ideological fist fights, and on one occasion I witnessed a heavyweight match for the skid road championship. The Reds seemed to be in the majority. The Yellow faction was led by some unscrupulous, shrewd, experienced politicians, some of whom rose to be mayor and councilmen in later years. Debs once refused to go on the platform in Dreamland Rink, with more than 4,000 present, until an extreme Right Winger had been removed as chairman. The Reds supported the Wobblies in all strikes and free-speech fights, although at odds politically. The Yellow faction balked, sabotaged, and referred to the Reds as anarchists.

The Yellows had a model — the German Social Democratic Party. Full dress respectability; municipal ownership socialism; the day to day struggles you leave to Gompers and his piecard artists; picket lines and militant demonstrations are for roughnecks; votes for women? — yes, but the ideal place for the distaff is in the kitchen; to defend the working class against physical violence by the ruling class and their Pinkertons, elect a socialist sheriff! As I see it now, years later, the Reds had their hearts in the right place and were brave and militant. If one considers the democratic process as occurring only on a certain Tuesday in November, then the Yellows were right. But if there are 364 more days a year and 364 ways and roads to a better life, then the Reds were right.

In those days we read Austin Lewis, Louis B. Boudin, the *International Socialist Review,* and to some of us, the so-called Seattle intelligentsia, the old *Masses* (later the *Liberator*) was the one great magazine in the USA. What a magazine the *Liberator* was! In Raymer's bookstore piles of the magazine reached counter high, on the skid road up to the knees. A literary agent sold it from union hall to union hall and from mass meeting to mass meeting. More than 3,000 copies came into Seattle each month. The working stiffs liked the magazine; it was theirs. It was for labor, pro-Red, for socialism, for the Russian Revolution, and defended the Wobblies.

While I never crossed any Reds with wings, their contribution to the labor movement was basic. The first time I heard Debs his subject was industrial unionism, and the very first time I laid eyes on Big Bill Haywood, it was a dramatic soapbox lecture on Sam Gompers, craft unionism, and socialism.

Was there ever really another period in our lifetime when two factions in the same organization, Left and Right, could both publish weekly newspapers, without trials and expulsions? I was in a Socialist Party branch with 500 members when a decision was made to publish a weekly paper in opposition to the right-wing *Herald*. Came the *Socialist World* where I ran a Yipsel column. There were no financial angels; the paper was supported by Puget Sound workers. There was no living wage, unfortunately, for the editor, and when his weekly stipend dropped to $7, Paul Bickel and I took over the job for awhile. When Walker Smith joined the staff, things began to hum. We hit hard, perhaps too hard at times, but there was poetry in the air, a promise and a hope, and the Puget Sound country, from the A.F. of L. to the extreme Left, was moving forward.

What a shame no copy exists of the *Socialist World* in which we covered the Everett Massacre. That was a Walker Smith masterpiece. I was politically a novice. Paul after a few drinks was ready to shoot the works. Walker held us to our tasks; the front page was done on a Monday night, 24 hours after the massacre, and the paper was on the streets Tuesday, mobilizing not only Left and Center, but whipping the Right first into submission and then support.

The soapbox was the proletarian lecture platform, the street corner and the skid road the living school. Tom Lewis, Tom Hickey, James P. Thompson, Gurley Flynn, Kate Sadler, "Red" Doran, all held chairs in that university. The workers listened, asked questions, bought pamphlets. Free Speech, the right of assembly and organization, were the Holy Bible in the Puget Sound and the entire Northwest. Kate Sadler was its flaming embodiment. Her anger at injustice was a beautiful sight; her sense of humor a delight. Her elementary lessons in socialism struck deep. I heard her often, and was always amazed at the simplicity of her technique. The workers loved her. Kate was the flame and the practical brains.

There were "characters" in Seattle in those days. Old Charles

D. Raymer, the atheist, in his cavernous, musty, old bookstore preaching municipal socialism but selling the *Masses* and later the *Liberator* by the hundreds every month, and thousands of socialist pamphlets and books. John McGivney, the labor editor, who after a hot discussion on Ruskin, William Morris, Oscar Wilde, and others, sent me next morning a three-page single-spaced letter on the subject. Bert Carpenter, a top investigator under George Vanderveer in labor cases. Later he did invaluable work in the Sacco-Vanzetti case around Boston. Jack Lawson, the philosophical anarchist, drinking Peruna when broke, reciting gypsy poetry and singing labor songs old and new. Dozens come to mind — socialists, anarchists, Wobblies, rebels, all for Labor, all hating capitalism, the boss, and the status quo.

I remember being chairman at a socialist meeting called to hear John Spargo, who was seeking support for his pro-war position before the St. Louis convention in 1917. Smart enough not to attack the Debs faction in Seattle, he concentrated on the Hillquit-Berger group. During the question period he was showered with ideological rotten eggs. Turning to me, he said that I was giving the floor to only one side. The truth was that there was only one side there — the Seattle labor movement from left to right was anti-war. Spargo left the meeting in a huff.

The Russian Revolution moved us all, from extreme Left to Right, as no other event did. Capitalism, exploitation, done with. No more war. The working class in control. When the names of the leaders came over the wires, well, *we* had never heard of them. Lenin, Trotsky, Rykov, Lunacharsky, Stalin, all of the first cabinet. Who were they? And how strange the terminology — Bolshevik, Menshevik, soviet, commissar! But we knew this was a socialist revolution. The workers took over the factories, the peasants the land, the soldiers were marching home from the trenches, the people were fighting for their freedom. The Seattle labor movement greeted them as brothers and sisters.

III

My father was a cook on one of the transcontinental railroads from St. Paul to the Coast; he boasted that he was on the first diner that came over the Cascades after the tunnel replaced the switchbacks. The kitchen crew worked from six in the morning until ten at night with a couple of hours off in the afternoon. In the cramped quarters of the narrow kitchen, my father used to burn out the seat of his pants every few trips. At night they put thin pallets on the tables and slept there. After 20 years of this, he developed tuberculosis and when no longer able to stand the heat of the kitchen, he was transferred to a commissary car. These cars supplied the restaurants at the stations along the route — in those days important because few passengers could afford the luxury of the diner. When too weak for that job, he was fired. No pension, severance pay, or social security in those days. When my father saw that he was becoming a drag on the family, he went back East where he died of pneumonia in an alley.

My mother opened a rooming house, after having pawned the few valuables she had accumulated in her married life. It was in the early 1910's and depression hung like a pall over the city. The roomers were nearly as poor as the widow; I went to work delivering for a bakery after school hours and on weekends. My $5 a week supplied the food while the roomers' rent met the monthly bill to the landlord. On Saturday nights we went down to the public market where there were bargains on vegetables and fruits that would not keep over the weekend. As the sparse furniture accommodated only the roomers, the family sat on apple boxes. At the time I hardly understood my mother's sacrifices to keep me in school — most poor boys worked, or looked for work. High schools were for the upper strata of society; for most working class parents it meant real hardship to send their children to high school, still more for a widow.

Poverty and the curse of unemployment were so prevalent that I accepted them as the natural order of the world, a fate to be endured by those not favored by fortune. Then in high school — I always had the highest praise for that school for it capped my formal education — I fell upon socialism. The debating club picked that as one of its subjects and I boned up on the theme with a book of John Spargo entitled *Elements of Socialism,* or some such title, a rather dry approach to the subject. My mother had a great fear of radicalism and unions;

once my father had been tempted to join a newly organized
union of dining car workers and she was frightened out of her
boots for fear he would be fired. As she was a strong-willed
woman, he yielded. Sure enough she was right — the organizers
were fired. So when her oldest son marched home from school
with the red-covered *Elements of Socialism* under his arm, she
said: "Young man, you turn right around and take that book
back where you got it and never bring another book on socialism
into this house!" The book was dull, but my curiosity was
whetted by the idea that I had come across a forbidden fruit.
Some time after the debate, I noticed a socialist hall on my
delivery route and dropped in to talk to the secretary. That
genial scholarly old Swede opened my eyes by a human practical
approach to socialism, miles away from Spargo's academic milk-
and-water parliamentarism. Poverty and unemployment, I
learned, were not necessarily a foreordained order of Nature; a
better system could be fought for. I was soon initiated into the
Young People's Socialist League and later the Industrial Workers of the World.

What a contrast the education afforded in socialist and
Wobbly halls, and in the logging camps, was to the sterile
political hoaxes of the day. In 1912 the big political issue the
old parties were arguing about was the tariff — free trade vs.
protectionism; in 1916 "he kept us out of war" — but a few
months after the majority had voted for that, Wilson took us
right in. The difficulty of the people getting what they wanted
by voting was burned in on my mind in those formative years
and the parliamentary farce deepened into tragedy in later
years, as the people voted but got the same old run-around after
every election, except for a few of the Roosevelt terms. Inci-
dentally my mother changed her mind about unions and
radicalism after her son had gotten in trouble following the
Seattle general strike; she became as militantly critical of Mayor
Ole Hanson, who claimed he had quelled a revolution, as was
her boy.

Years later I was reproached by an associate who had defected
from radicalism. "Only fools or knaves don't change their
minds," I was told. I was not impressed. "In my own lifetime I
have seen two world wars, with their debasement of humanity,

and I see no end to it as long as the drive for profits is the chief motive force in society," I said. "In the first world war soldiers were forced to take potshots at each other and the slaughter in the trenches was barbarous enough, but still somewhat on a man-to-man basis. Now demoniac button-pushers have the power to blot out entire nations and destroy the planet. Certainly socialism has something better than that to offer. Nor am I impressed with the welfare state. True, my parents might not have died in poverty of tuberculosis under the welfare state; but have workers as a class gained much by exchanging a little comfort and a little — very little — security, at the expense of being helots in a warfare state? The 60,000 Boeing workers in Seattle, most of them employed in turning out murderous instruments of mass destruction — what kind of a job is this for civilized man? No, I see little reason to change my views on society fundamentally; the system if anything is more barbarous than ever it was, although its stench may have had a bit of perfume sprayed around."

Appendix Two

One Woman's Resistance

BY JESSIE LLOYD

The case of Louise Olivereau is described here in detail, not because it is the most important, but because letters are still available which give the live flavor of the times. Today's conformists can read, incredulously no doubt, the thoughts of a loving, peaceful person, devoted to American ideals of freedom, who believed that the majority of the people should stage a non-violent revolution against the powerful interests who used the controls of government to line their own pockets; and who dared to say so, war or no war.

She was a gentle, warm-hearted young woman of about thirty who in 1917 had a job typing in a Wobbly local hall. Formerly a cook in resort camps, she was evidently well educated: she never failed to write "shall" when grammar demanded it, even in letters to close friends. She had left her parents somewhere, geographically or spiritually, for she told nothing about them except that her father was French and her mother was German.

Strongly imaginative, she felt the war as a personal pain, and could not bear that the youth of our country should follow Europe into the meat-grinder without a protest. She had long taken a motherly interest in the high school youngsters who sought out the Wobbly hall looking for adventure in the great task of improving conditions. A little foursome of them used to spend evenings together, near the lakes, in the hills, or in a modest room, reading poetry and philosophy aloud, or discussing beliefs, economics, and the future of the human race.

When the draft calls began to hit Seattle, Louise took money

248

from her meager salary (surely not over $15 a week), bought paper and postage, mimeographed leaflets, and mailed one to each draftee. "We assume since you are not a volunteer that you are a conscientious objector," began one; and she then quoted from the great anti-war and libertarian writings of Thoreau, Lincoln, or Tolstoy. "If you are not carried away by emotional appeals, you can resist your government when it would play the tyrant."

On September 5, 1917, federal authorities raided the Wobbly hall. Two days later Louise went to the office of the Department of Justice investigator, Mr. Wright, to ask for a package of literature she had ordered from New York, and not even read yet, which had been confiscated with the I.W.W. material. It was ten copies of "Backwash of War" and several hundred leaflets entitled "Shambles." Instead, Mr. Wright showed her one of her mimeographed circulars and asked if it was done by the I.W.W. He and District Attorney Allen could not believe that Louise personally had given the time and money to do them.

She reported later, "I said that if out of 2,000 circulars I could get five men to consider the connection of the individual with government and war, I would consider myself quite successful." Louise was a philosophical anarchist, of the kind who had such faith in human decency that she believed people would manage better without the force of government. This force she, like the Wobblies, saw used mostly to frustrate efforts of working people to better their conditions. As to the war, she was sure that the ordinary people of Germany and the Allies both would emerge worse off, but that the very wealthy would make money out of it; and the same thing would happen to Americans. Her conclusion was, therefore, that to be loyal to the working class — the vast majority of the United States — one should oppose the war and try to stop it as soon as possible.

"Mr. Allen said he didn't know if I was harmless, sentimental or dangerous. A Mr. Perkins said I was a very dangerous woman and after a conference, I was arrested. They asked if I had more circulars, and I said yes. We went to the house and I gave them over; also a copy of a letter to a lady explaining that I had no

desire to dissuade any one who had seriously thought it his duty
to enlist."

Ironically, a woman who was so open and honest in her opposition to the government that she disdained to use any mis-
statement, or even silence, to avoid prosecution, was indicted
under the new "Espionage Act." Of course this act was not
directed mainly against spies, but was a catch-all to discourage
Americans from expressing their widely felt opposition to the
war, and was vigorously so used. The counts against Louise
were nine: chiefly, attempting to cause disobedience in military
forces, obstruction of the recruiting of the United States, and
use of the mails for any matter urging insurrection or any other
offense under the two previous counts.

For lack of bail money Louise spent the next two months in
jail awaiting trial. She still wrote to her young friends, and they
wrote back and wrote to each other about her. "My mother read
Louise's letter and fell in love with her immediately," says
beautiful red-headed Hannah. And in another letter, "I have
had that same all-empty feeling that I had the day of her arrest,
all day today." Later, "I can feel Louise closer than before. . . .
I hope for her sake that they find some one that can read French
so that they will allow her to have those French books. She does
want very much to learn French. It eased my mind greatly to
hear that she is well and — happy. It seems almost an im-
possibility."

Louise wrote to another of her "family" October 13: "This is
the life, believe me. We have two new prisoners, and my ears
need washing all the time as a result." She expressed concern
over a friend who lost his job, congratulated an editor on his
poems, complained that the Wobbly paper was not arriving.
She commented:

Housecleaning operations in both Seattle and Tacoma seem to
be occupying quite a large place in the sun just now. Curious thing
about that. Military training and in fact the whole business of
soldiering is superlatively good for the youth of our country: it
inculcates all the highest and most manly virtues — and yet, and yet!
wherever soldiers are, there too flourish most amazingly, even like
unto a whole grove of green bay trees, all the vices of sex and intemperance. I suppose it's my lamentable inability to make distinctions, which the good Commissioner deplored, which makes me pre-

fer the normal and milder viciousness of the civilian. . . . We hear
much of the "spiritual revival" which this war has caused, but after
all, what we are concerned about are the material possessions of the
nation — its territory and trade — rather than its ideals of equality
and fraternity and justice. . . .

I wish you could have been here when the lawyer was giving me
good advice. He says I should plead not guilty and argue that I
never meant to break the law . . . that I have respect for and desire
to keep within the law at all times. He used the old old argument
which almost makes me despair when it comes from the lips of
radicals — "Think how much more you can do if you are on the
Outside" — that specious argument which rots the backbone of so
many of us and makes us crawl in the dust and lick the boots of our
oppressors — What would "freedom" be worth, gained in such a
way?

"Freedom of body is an empty shell
Wherein men crawl whose souls are bound with gyves."

At all costs I must keep the inner freedom without which life is
worse than worthless. — That sounds almost as selfish as the Christian's concern for the spotlessness of his own soul, doesn't it? However, I'm not a fanatic on the subject: simply *my own* skin isn't
worth that price.

She asks about other friends and a gay song one sang:

"Who then shall sing of the springtime" — and again we go quick-
stepping to its gleeful rhythm along the friendly, dusky streets.
Love to all the good friends and rebels,
For Freedom,
Louise

P.S. Thank you for the books. I read about half of Steinmetz
last night — it's elementary economics of the most extremely mate-
rialistic variety — the sort that argues that just because wars always
have been, therefore there could have been no other possible way
to settle financial supremacy between France and Germany — depressing if like Mr. Dooley I didn't comfort myself with the reflection that it's not true. . . . Just read Oppenheim's "Laughter" —
it's great stuff.
For Happiness,
Louise

On November 3 Louise wrote to Hannah's boy friend,

I am glad you so often know when I am with you — for you are
quite right, I go from my cell, from the "soiled and sacrificed" ones,
out into the clean sweet world, to you and to the other dear ones,
very, very often. And I try always to take you my strength, not my

weakness. May the Ever-Living Spirit of Humanity, at whose mercy
Life holds us all, grant you always to gain strength from me. I think
sometimes that even as the best thoughts can be communicated only
in silence, so the most intimate comradeship can be developed only
in separation. At any rate, I know this particular separation has
brought us into closer communion than we enjoyed before.

I received today a message of strength and cheer from E.G. She
approves of my attitude towards lawyers who "sacrifice their clients'
ideals to the safety of the client." . . . I shall no doubt make but a
clumsy defense: but at least there will be in it none of the lawyer's
"expediency." . . . I shall have served rather a severe sentence before
ever I come to trial — fifty-six days today. All for lack of money.
Eh? — who said "free and equal"? . . . I am returning "Splendid
Futility" . . . inconsistent and rather unhealthy in spots. It is not
in the great natural forces that futility resides, but in us, or even
more, in our enemies the Conservatives, when we or they try to "progress" in a manner contrary to natural law. Both "Cons" and "Rads"
are sinners in that respect, sometimes. . . .

The inscrutable Providence has moved again, and yesterday I got
a copy of the "Call." It looks good, and any time you want a "character" as editor of a great metropolitan daily, I shall be pleased to
give you one. . . . Seriously, you will get more real education out of
this winter's work and associations than if you were at the University, I think.

I shall look forward to reading the work of the young poet who
has not yet entered upon the "great adventure." Excellent poetry
can be written without that spur — and some of us find such poems
restful. . . .

Greetings to A.L.S. and love to the "Family."
For Freedom,
Louise

Louise conducted her own defense, including the questioning
of prospective jurors, fully reported in a contemporary booklet
published by a friend, of which only one copy is now known.

"Have you any prejudice against a declared anarchist?" she
asked one propertied gentleman.

"I certainly have."

"Then withdraw."

The judge interposed, "All we want to know is can you give
her a fair trial. Anarchism is not an issue."

The prosecutor: "Maybe the newspapers have declared her an
anarchist. Or does she declare it?"

"Both," replied Louise.

Of another juror, she inquired, "Do you believe the minority should be silenced in wartime, including anarchists? Do you believe the people have a right, in war as in peace, to express themselves?"

Again the judge interposed: "The jurors' opinions of the law are irrelevant in a criminal case. *I* instruct them what the law is."

Louise challenged one juror on the ground that he was not well informed on public questions: "Am I not entitled to a jury of my peers?" The court ruled against her.

"Do you know," Louise asked another, "that our state constitution declares that citizens have the right to institute a revolution?"

"This is not a proper inquiry!" exclaimed the judge.

"Have you any prejudice," she asked, "against individuals who advocate that the conscription of money be made at least as extensive and forceful as the conscription of men in support of this war?"

The prosecutor: "We object!" The judge: "Sustained."

"Do you believe that the laws always perfectly reflect the will of the people of the United States?" Objection again, also sustained.

As her limited peremptory challenges became exhausted, the jury was gradually completed. The prosecutor repeated the counts against her, and declared that when people intrigue and strike at the very foundations of government, it is time to punish them.

"I have never advocated lawbreaking or forcible resistance to the draft," said Louise in opening her defense. "The only suggestion of violence in my circulars was what I quoted from Elihu Root, where he urged people to stop thinking and just fight." She continued:

My purpose in these circulars was to call the attention of drafted men to the fact that they are ordered to resign the right to think for themselves what was the best good of the country . . . on a question upon which they were given no opportunity to vote: the right to dispose of their own lives. . . . A large part of the material in my circulars was copied from books in the Public Library. The rest is a frank discussion by a conscientious objector with men who have a right to know his position.

If this material was so seditious, why did the government continue to permit it to circulate? I had known that my letter to Mr. Leach in Bellingham, containing one of the circulars, was known to the authorities a few days after it was sent. Knowing that the government was aware of the circulars and could stop them and did not, I continued to prepare and send them out. And I was not arrested until more than a week after the last lot was mailed. . . .

I have to explain what I mean by anarchy. It comes from the Greek: *arche* is force, power, violence; an-arche means a condition without force or violence. Violence breeds violence; war breeds hatreds; suppression within a nation or community results in rebellion, revolution. Mutual aid, a social sense, a recognition of a common interest among individuals is the greatest factor in the world's progress. The struggle for supremacy is a reactionary, destructive force.

What is necessary for progress is perfect freedom of discussion and perfect freedom of experiment. Ideas occur to single individuals oftener than to masses of people. Therefore the right of the minority to propagate their ideas must be inviolate if we are to have a progressive society. In most matters, it is right that the majority should determine the policy of the nation; in almost none is it safe to *silence* the minority or prevent it from attempting to become a majority.

Repression now exists not only against the anarchists, but against freedom of speech, assembly, and press — against our Constitution, which tries to guarantee those freedoms. No country except Czarist Russia has so sternly silenced minorities as the U.S. The immediate cause of my sending out the circulars was the speech of Elihu Root. They were aimed only at men subject to the draft — not those who enlisted. . . .

The real issue in the case is: have citizens the right to think of their relation to war and government in any terms except compliant acceptance? Are we an autocracy like Czarist Russia or like the Germany we hate so much we entered the war to destroy it?

If we take President Wilson literally, on May 18 he said this was in no sense a conscription of the unwilling. The conscientious objector is unwilling, so, by the President's explanation, he should be exempt. Wilson goes on saying the law provides for selection from a nation which has volunteered in mass. The nation has not volunteered in mass; the nation has not volunteered at all. If the nation had volunteered it would never have been necessary to pass conscription.

Louise pointed out that Wilson was elected on an anti-war platform. The government, she said, should carry out the national will — if not, it is not a democracy, but a despotism. Wilson himself pointed out in his book, *The New Freedom,* that we have a government of interests. He said we must reorganize our economic life, even as we once reorganized our national political life — and that the way to do it is to take counsel together and form opinions, and make those opinions known. "The jails of this country today are full," she said, "of people who have attempted to act upon President Wilson's advice." She noted:

Even before the war declaration, citizens were forbidden to hold peace demonstrations and parades, but "preparedness" parades were encouraged and protected. Hulet Wells and Sam Sadler were prosecuted for opposing conscription even before it was passed. Members of the People's Council for Democracy and Terms of Peace have been hunted around the country; people have been arrested for reading the Declaration of Independence, or quoting the Bible. . . .

Meanwhile, in 1916, 40 corporations made $677,000,000 more than the 3-year prewar average. Wage advances have not kept pace with the cost of living. All attempts by the workers to better conditions have been bitterly opposed as unpatriotic. And the employers did not confine themselves to peaceful methods. At Bisbee, Arizona, 1500 strikers were taken out to starve in the desert; men seeking freedom of speech were shot on the Verona; organizer Frank Little was lynched; all the I.W.W. halls have been raided, their property confiscated, men jailed, often without charge for three months. And the government has not investigated or prosecuted the illegal mob violence and interference. . . . No, the U.S. Government today is not a means for expressing the will of the people. . . .

Yet I never counselled any man to forcibly resist the government in any way whatsoever. I fear violence, because what might be gained by any forcible overthrow is less, and less enduring, than by organized efforts for great economic and social changes without violence. Wars never settle anything. In the days of chattel slavery, people of Negro blood were enslaved. Today practically the whole nation is in economic slavery, and since the war, military slavery as well. My circulars recommended the patriotic duty to analyze the situation; the good of the country was placed above obedience to law. The prosecutor says this is treason, disloyalty, anarchy. It is not treason to the best good of the people, whatever it may be to the established government. When the government deliberately violates the will of the nation . . . and the necessity is urgent for making our opinions known, what course is left but for citizens to remain loyal to the principles of freedom for the perpetuation of which this nation is supposed to have been founded, even at the expense of breaking a law in the making of which the people had no part? Is it ever to the interest of the nation that citizens should resign their freedom of conscience? No. There are thousands, yes millions of citi-

zens whose conception of patriotism immeasurably transcends mere
obedience to law. . . .

They realize the interdependence of all nations. Just as a family
conserves the interests of its members, just so a nation conserves, or
should conserve, the interests of its states; and so a world state, a
recognition by all people of all countries of their common interest,
is necessary to conserve the best interests of the separate nations.
Wars do not help. The workers will not gain no matter who wins.
And all will do atrocities. . . .

The United States has now thrown away the greatest opportunity
to make the world safe for democracy that any nation ever had.
Unlimited resources, freedom from rigid tradition, immigrants with
a strong love of liberty and desire for a world nation — all these we
had, and have not used them wisely to avoid the horrible degradation and slavery into which we have fallen today. I love America, and
other countries, but I hate the forces keeping us from freedom. . . .

Industrial government has moved in, and its iron hand is our
present ruling force. The only way the people can regain control
is to gain the ownership and control of industry. Then our government will still be industrial, but will be the expression of the necessities and desires of the whole people. . . .

The circulars show plainly that I didn't advocate forcible resistance. War will settle nothing. The struggle for industrial supremacy will go on. It will be settled by superior industrial efficiency.
. . . Ultimately the highest efficiency will be seen to be incompatible
with production for profit. Then competition between nations will
cease and production for use take its place . . . and the greatest of
all causes for war will be eliminated. The best brains of all the
nations will be set free for labors of science, art and culture of all
sorts. Then we may perhaps attain a civilization of which mankind
need not be ashamed.

The prosecutor pointed out to the jury that to find the
defendant guilty it was not necessary to prove she advocated
force; if her action tended to cause disloyalty or refusal of duty,
that was enough. The jury was out half an hour and found her
guilty.

The booklet reporting this trial, which sold for 25 cents in
1918, also included two of the leaflets Louise sent out. After
citing Root's advice to quit thinking and fight, Louise
commented:

In other words, since the financial masters of the nation have succeeded in plunging the country into war against its will, our patriotic duty is to help them to as great a benefit as possible, even at the

expense of "our lives, our fortunes and our sacred honor" — this doesn't sound sensible, but isn't it really what it means? But aren't we traitors, not only to ourselves but also to our country, when we go to war in the justice of which we don't believe?

At epithets like "traitor" and "slacker" we can be calm, knowing that we never owed allegiance to the powers which plunged us into war; therefore we can't be traitors to them. Slackers? Only if we refuse to keep firm for our principles. Cowards? No, this is braver than fighting. . . . Read the article in the American Magazine on the psychology of a soldier in training; read LaFollette's Magazine, and judge your position.

In the second circular Louise said the government was organized for the protection of property; that to the worker it was

only a method of oppression by which he is made to work for the benefit of another class, from which he receives nothing, not even an adequate living. It is this thing which you are asked to protect with your life, for which you are ordered to go into the worst hell imaginable. . . . If you want to die to perpetuate this monster, for continuation of the power that oppresses you, and makes you slave your life away so others may live in luxury, why go ahead. Make yourself into fertilizer for the sunny fields of France. But if you are opposed, then resist, refuse to go, stay away. They can't do more than kill you — and it is better to die for truth and your ideals than for ideals you hate.

George Washington said "Government is not reason, not eloquence — it is force — like fire, a dangerous servant and a fearful master — never for a moment should it be left to irresponsible action." If it is constructed to be of, by and for the people, we are much to blame for leaving it to irresponsible action. Thoreau said: "We have used up all our inherited Freedom. If we believe in freedom we must make it." Also "The law will never make men free; it is men who have got to make the law free. They are the lovers of law who observe the law when the government breaks it."

She also quoted from the speech of Senator Robert LaFollette on April 4, 1917:

Are the people of this country so well represented in the war movement that we need to go abroad to give another people control of their government? Will the President and his supporters submit it to a vote of the people before the declaration of war goes into effect? If not, it ill behooves us to use as an excuse for entering the war the claim that war was forced upon the Germans by their government without their previous knowledge or approval.

Encouraging draftees to be independent, Louise wrote, "There are too many 'wooden men'; most legislators, politicians, lawyers, officeholders rarely make any moral distinctions: they are as likely to serve the devil as God. A very few, such as heroes, patriots, martyrs, reformers in the great sense, and *men* serve the state with their conscience also, and necessarily resist it for the most part, and are commonly treated as enemies by it." She closed with a quotation from Thoreau: "There will never be a really free and enlightened State until the State comes to recognize the individual as a higher and independent power, from which all its own authority is derived, and treats him accordingly."

The day Louise was found guilty was December 1, 1917, and her bail was increased to $15,000. On December 4 the judge pronounced sentence: ten years imprisonment at Cañon City, Colorado.

Wrote young Hannah to her boy friend next day:

Tell Louise that she made a splendid plea, and that the news of her sentence has made me angry enough at the system that I can make a decent talk tomorrow [at 18 she was organizing for the I.W.W.]. Mamma is awfully sorry she didn't have me stay with Louise till the trial — to atone for that she says she will send me to Cañon City next summer — if Uncle Sammy don't beat her to it. If I continue organizing she says he most assuredly will. . . . I have the utmost faith in Louise's ability to accept her imprisonment with a smile — as she does everything.

Yours for Liberty of the Masses,
Hannah

From the jail, almost a year after she went in, Louise sent a picture of herself which is printed in the little booklet. With a smile? So it appears: a round, bright, cheerful face, like a sensible and conscientious nurse, with much humor in the eyes and mouth.

In 1918 and 1919 she was full of vigorous optimism, or at least, that is what she expressed to friends. One had admired some poetry of withdrawal from the world, and Louise exploded:

To me, denied for two years now any active participation in the world's life — hearing innumerable calls to work, to laughter, to love, to joy, to sorrow — to me, forced to sit with folded hands and silent lips, it is almost inconceivable that a healthy young man in possession of all his senses should loll against Lady Antrim's knees, or any other knees — and be weary of the vast horizon and all the marvelous life it comprises. If the rose is too red, the ivy too black, leave 'em and go to cutting cabbages and digging potatoes. Whatever may have been true, for other peoples, in other times, for us, in these times, Love must open our lives to let in the world, not shut it out. — Here are four lines of Jean Starr Untermeyer's that I like better than a whole bushel of "decayed poetry":

> "I would rather work in stubborn rock
> All the years of my life
> And make one strong thing
> And set it in a high clean place."

Yet Louise had gloomy moments too, as her poem in the booklet shows.

> In the stark hours
> Before dawn
> I waken.
> Like a great Bird
> The unquiet Spirit of the jail
> Broods close above me
> Till I gasp for breath
> And now it settles,
> Beak and claws upon my heart,
> Its evil, searching eyes within my soul.

Other verses etched the pain of her fellow prisoners.

Her jailer wrote her friends in November, 1918 that she "is really doing good work in the way of teaching physical culture exercises and also stenography . . . is well liked by officials here. . . . Her life is not at all uninteresting." Louise, on the other hand, wrote Emma Goldman, "You will understand that any happiness I have comes from outside." There was evidently not enough work assigned to absorb her energy for she constantly begged her friends for patterns, needles, and thread to knit and embroider. In letters she said little about conditions; after she was out, she reported in a talk at the Seattle Labor Temple that the matron took delight in keeping the prisoners under tension, and was mentally cruel to another particularly sensitive prisoner.

Because of good behavior, and perhaps because the war was over, Louise was released in March, 1920, and hurried to Seattle. Ten days after her arrival she wrote to a member of the little foursome that had called themselves "the family" and spent so many hours reading and discussing together before her arrest:

I returned to Seattle March 29, but as far as the conduct of some of my friends is concerned, I might as well have remained in exile. . . . This note is chiefly to ask you whether you have yet got Jim's address . . . I wish to write to him. Perhaps I may seem impatient, but I've looked forward for two years and a half to resuming the very pleasant friendships which seemed pretty well established, and that can seem a terribly long time. . . . I have a good many unengaged evenings still on hand. . . . Be a good boy and ask me out to meet your new friend, and do all the other things a good son should.

Affectionately as always —

By the end of April, 1920, Louise was staying with a friend in Portland, Oregon. She was quite active, speaking at union meetings and women's clubs, visiting the Oregon state prison, writing to and about Wobs still in jail, and distributing pamphlets on deportation and prison cases to the bookstores and unions that would sell them, meanwhile doing secretarial work by the day to support herself. She was invited to speak on May Day in Seattle, and also for the Finns in Portland: she flipped a coin and stayed with the Finns, for which her Seattle friends severely scolded her, since she had been scheduled for an important part of the program.

May 5 she wrote, "I mean to use half the proceeds of all my meetings to start a fund for Magón" (Ricardo Flores Magón, the Mexican anarchist who later died in Leavenworth — forgotten here but still named on many streets of Mexico). "That gives me about $40 now on hand, not much, when a thousand is to be raised, but yet a beginning."

By June 11 she had a full time job at $125 a month — explaining that she "bought a hat and had to go to work to pay for it." Yet she still asked for shipments of pamphlets to distribute.

Her last known letter, August 26, 1920, said she had wearied of "the fantastic," namely, an anarchist spending eight hours a day typing a book on "The Law of Accounts," and got fired after suggesting that the boss pay all his help better. She then had a chance either to go into the delicatessen business or an 8-stool lunch counter that did a $60 to $80 daily business.

"I've not seen anybody 'in the movement' for so long I don't know are they all alive or dead, nor whether I myself am dead or alive; dead, I think, though. I know I'd like to be. . . ." Yet just before that, she had mentioned "I could get rid of Lille Sarnoff's 50 pamphlets in one fell swoop."

She was an intense nature and had a good deal of trouble sleeping — she even said that might explain her desire for death — "it would be like a sound sleep." More poignantly she had written before, "I wish God would pull in his moon, or else send me somebody who likes moons as well as I do to walk with me as long as the moon shines. . . . Once more I wish God had made me 'two little dogs so I could play together.' "

The last letter closes with the news that

I have found a sympathetic listener. . . . Oh no, it's not a case — only I discovered he liked to read a lot of the same things I do, and he had never had anybody to talk about books with, he being a conservative and merely happening, by some strange freak, to get hold of some more or less radical books. . . . Drop me a line, but don't expect any proper letters from me. . . . I never did have much sense, and I seem to have lost what I was born with. Too bad!

Lovingly,
Louise

Years afterward, a Seattle friend reported seeing her in California married to a conservative and determined to cut all her radical connections.

"What hurt Louise the most after she came out of prison," explained another friend, "was the bitter divisions she found among men and women who had been so united in working for a better world for labor when she was taken away in 1917. People had had their own ideas before, and would argue vigorously for them — the I.W.W. with the Federation of Labor, the Socialists with the Anarchists — but when it came to a struggle for free speech, or the 8-hour day, or wage increases to meet the cost of living, they would all work together, usually in a jolly, bantering comradeship." By 1920 the A. F. of L. had cut their Seattle locals away from working with the I.W.W., which had been decimated and scattered anyway, bearing the brunt of government wartime prosecution. The Communists had entered the picture, two varieties, and the Socialists were disorganized. Legal and vigilante persecution, fanned by the war spirit, had also discouraged many, and growing unemployment suggested that each should look to his own skin. It was far from the climate of robust hope and idealism that Louise had left.

Notes

A complete list of works referred to in these Notes will be found beginning on page 283.

Chapter 1

The founding of the Brotherhood of the Cooperative Commonwealth is recounted in *Henry Demarest Lloyd*, a two-volume biography by his sister, Caro Lloyd, pp. 45-67 of Vol. II. Nathan Fine's *Labor and Farmer Parties in the United States* and Ray Ginger's *The Bending Cross* also deal with this period. Debs's letter to Rockefeller is reproduced on page 201 of *The Bending Cross*.

E. B. Ault's manuscript autobiography gives the most complete account of Equality Colony. In Marvin Sanford's amateur journal, the *Searchlight,* William McDevitt, an Equality colonist, wrote a series of articles on Equality appearing in the issues of March, 1950, to April, 1951. Articles on Home and other colonies, by Sanford, appeared in issues of September, 1949, to April, 1950, of the *Searchlight*. A memorial issue of the *San Francisco Evening Lamp* of June, 1957, was devoted to DeForest Sanford, the Freeland colonist.

Skid Road, by Murray Morgan, is a lively history of Seattle. He devotes a chapter to Mary Kenworthy and the anti-Chinese riots. George Kinnear, a participant, gave a pamphlet account of the affair in *Anti-Chinese Riots.* Mary W. Avery in *History and Government of the State of Washington* discusses the anti-Chinese and Populist movements, as does Calvin F. Schmid in *Social Trends in Seattle. Washington: A Guide to the Evergreen State* describes the state in the early days. Melvin Gardner De Shazo in his master's thesis at the University of Washington entitled "Radical Tendencies in the Seattle Labor Movement," sketches the early history of the Seattle unions.

The University of Washington Library has an incomplete file of the early *Seattle Daily Call,* with accounts of V. Smith and his Port Angeles colony. Many issues of the *Socialist,* edited by Dr. Titus, are in the Sanford Collection of the University of Washington. A sketch of Dr. Titus and his Four-Hour Day movement appeared in Sanford's *Searchlight*, May-June, 1950. Hulet Wells's manuscript, "I Wanted To Work," sheds much light on the early socialist movement.

The Terrible Truth About Marriage was published as a pamphlet in Seattle in 1907. Its author, Vincent Harper, for a time was on the staff of the *Socialist*.

The early history of the I.W.W. is told in the official history, *The I.W.W.*, by Fred Thompson. Paul F. Brissenden's *The I.W.W.* is the classic work on the early years of the organization.

William Z. Foster in *Pages From a Worker's Life* records memories of the Wage Workers Party of Dr. Titus, Home Colony, and soapboxing in Seattle. His book is valuable for insight into the lives of migratory workers.

Page 1, line 10. James A. Farley's famous toast appears in Richard L. Neuberger's *Our Promised Land* and in Morgan's *Skid Road*, p. 247.

Page 2, line 2. The Lloyd quotation is from Vol. II, p. 46, of the biography.

Page 3, line 22. Debs at the 1898 convention of the Social Democracy said: "Give me 10,000 men, aye, 10,000 in a western state with access to the sources of production, and we will convince the people of that state, win their hearts and their intelligence. We will lay hold upon the reins of government and plant the flag of Socialism upon the State House." (*The Forging of American Socialism* by Howard H. Quint.)

Page 7, line 9. Dr. Theodor Hertzka, a Viennese economist, published *Freeland* in 1890.

Page 8, line 6. The colonies in the state of Washington were by no means isolated incidents in American life. Several hundred colonies, all the way from New England to Oregon, flourished in the 19th Century. Many had religious inspiration such as those of the Shakers, but the remarkable influence of Robert Owen and Charles Fourier, the early Utopian socialists, had a powerful influence in establishing the New Harmony, Yellow Springs, Brook Farm, Nashoba, and other colonies. Emerson, Thoreau, George Ripley, Margaret Fuller, Thomas Wentworth Higginson, James Russell Lowell, Albert Brisbane, and Horace Greeley were among proponents of the colony idea. Richard T. Ely's *The Labor Movement in America* and John H. Noyes' *History of American Socialisms* deal with aspects of the Utopian colonies.

Page 18, line 10. The *Commonwealth*, the socialist paper published in Everett, sketched the life of George E. Boomer in its issue of July 24, 1913.

Page 22, line 5. The story of the "Blethen riots" is given in Morgan's *Skid Road,* p. 188 ff., and in Wells's memoirs, "I Wanted To Work." Wells's little drama, *The Colonel and His Friends,* was a 3-act play in which the third act was a verbatim report of the trial itself, a fantastic piece of judicial nonsense which beggared satire. Wells's collection of newspaper accounts of the riots from the *Times* and other Seattle papers is in the University of Washington Library.

Chapter 2

The best account of the troubles in Everett is contained in Walker C. Smith's *The Everett Massacre,* the 302-page book published by the I.W.W. Smith, as editor of the *Industrial Worker,* the official I.W.W. weekly in Seattle, had intimate knowledge of the events.

The I.W.W., the official history by Fred Thompson, records the growth of I.W.W. influence in the woods, the Spokane free-speech fight, and the Everett Massacre. Brissenden's *The I.W.W.* also details the early growth of the Wobblies but ends before the Everett episode. Ralph Chaplin in *Wobbly* gives a vivid account of the I.W.W. and the nature of their organization. On p. 202 ff., he tells of his part in handling publicity on the Everett case.

The Bloodstained Trail, by Ed. Delaney and M. T. Rice, in Chapter XVII reports on Bloody Sunday at Everett. David C. Botting, Jr., in "Bloody Sunday" gives a balanced account of the massacre. The role of George F. Vanderveer as counsel for the Everett prisoners is told in *Counsel for the Damned,* a biography by Lowell S. Hawley and Ralph Bushnell Potts. Elizabeth Gurley Flynn in her autobiography *I Speak My Own Piece* has several pages on the Spokane free-speech fight.

Page 30, line 32. The description of work in a shingle mill is from *Sunset Magazine,* February, 1917.

Page 32, line 21. The life of Maynard Shipley has been told by his widow, Miriam Allen De Ford, in *Up-Hill All The Way.* He edited the *Commonwealth,* the socialist weekly in Everett, from 1913 but had left that city before the I.W.W. free-speech fight.

Page 35, line 3. Stewart H. Holbrook in *Holy Old Mackinaw* has retold the story of the Spokane free-speech fight.

Page 35, line 36. Elizabeth Gurley Flynn in her autobiography, *I Speak My Own Piece,* relates: "When I came to Spokane, Washington, in December, 1909, to the free speech fight there, the all-male committee was somewhat disconcerted to be told that I was pregnant. . . . I felt fine, but my co-workers were disturbed about having me appear in public. In those days pregnant women usually concealed themselves from public view. 'It don't look nice. Besides, Gurley'll have that baby right on the platform if she's not careful!', one fussy old guy protested." After five editors of the *Industrial*

Worker had been jailed, Miss Flynn was put in charge of the paper.

Page 36, line 35. The quotation from Roger N. Baldwin appeared in *25 Years of Industrial Unionism,* a 124-page booklet published by the I.W.W.

Page 37, line 21. The description of the lumber operators' control in Everett is by G. O. Williams in the November, 1950, issue of the *Sheriff and Police Reporter,* published in Seattle.

Page 42, line 32. The Sergeant's story is condensed from Walker Smith's account in *The Everett Massacre.*

Page 46, line 28. The *Northwest Worker* (formerly the *Commonwealth*), the Everett socialist weekly, carried a graphic account of the massacre in its issue of November 23, 1917. A file of the *Northwest Worker* is in the University of Washington Library. The *Socialist World* in Seattle also carried firsthand reports. A file is in the Washington State University Library at Pullman.

Page 47, line 24. The quotation from the *Union Record* on the massacre appeared in Smith's *The Everett Massacre,* p. 98.

Page 55, line 12. The description of the funeral parade by Minnie Rimer appeared in *Mother Earth,* June, 1917.

Page 56, line 5. Robert L. Tyler's "Rebels of the Woods" sketches the history of the I.W.W. in the woods.

Page 57, line 28. The poem by Charles Ashleigh, "Everett, November Fifth," was published in Smith's *The Everett Massacre.*

Chapter 3

Walker C. Smith's *The Everett Massacre* has an interesting review of the development of the lumber industy in Washington. The early history of Seattle and of the lumber industry is recounted by George R. Leighton in *Five Cities.* Also valuable are Holbrook's *Holy Old Mackinaw* and two pamphlets published by the I.W.W., *The Lumber Industry and Its Workers* and *Evidence and Cross-Examination of J. T. (Red) Doran.* Matthea Thorseth has written a novel, *The Color of Ripening,* dealing with a Norwegian family and covering various incidents in the lives of lumber workers, including the Everett Massacre.

Page 61, line 22. The description of logging camps and the Seattle skid road is from the writer's own memory, based on several years working in some three dozen camps. Chaplin's *Wobbly* and Morgan's *Skid Road* offer valuable insights into life in the camps and on the skid roads.

Page 64, line 12. The origin of the word "wobbly" is in doubt. The official I.W.W. history says the term first appeared about 1912-1913 and gives the legend that a Chinese restaurateur had arranged to feed I.W.W. strikers on the Grand Trunk and Canadian

Northern Railroads, then building into British Columbia. He is said to have asked his customers: "All loo Eye Wobble Wobble?" from whence came the word "wobbly." *The Dictionary of American Slang* by Harold Wentworth and Stuart Berg Flexner gives this version: "In Vancouver, in 1911, we [the I.W.W.] had a number of Chinese members, and one restaurant keeper would trust any member for meals. He could not pronounce the letter 'w,' but called it 'wobble,' and would ask: 'You I. Wobble Wobble?' . . . Thereafter the laughing term among us was 'I Wobbly Wobbly'." This version is credited to *Business Week*, May 19, 1956, in an article, "Labor's Special Language from Many Sources."

Page 65, line 25. The Little Red Songbook, usually titled *I.W.W. Songs*, is a pocketbook-size pamphlet with a red cover, usually 64 pages. By 1956 it had run through 29 editions.

Page 66, line 36. Reporting Ralph Chaplin's death, the *New York Herald Tribune* of March 28, 1961, declared he was a leading figure in the "International Workers of the World" (the tautology involved in the title should alert any competent copyreader). The *New York Times* and other papers frequently use the same perversion of the I.W.W.'s name. The *Herald Tribune* article also commented that "Solidarity Forever" was sung by members of "the Congress of Industrial Workers"—a new title for the CIO.

Page 68, line 35. The early history of the I.W.W. lumber workers' union is recounted in *The I.W.W.*, the official history, and also in Brissenden's *The I.W.W.*

Page 70, line 22. The I.W.W.'s declaration of opposition to war is reported in the *International Socialist Review*, April, 1917. The June, 1917, issue reported the Spokane loggers' convention.

Page 70, line 29. Chaplin tells of the Wobbly stickers on page 205 ff. of *Wobbly*. Among the 3½ by 2¼ inch stickers, red ink on white paper, were these: "One big union—we want the earth —I.W.W. Universal"; picture of an owl saying, "Hoo hoo, you—line up! LWIU 500"; "Fellow Worker—why worry about halls? Organize on the job, and use the parks for recreation and education," in reference to the closing of Wobbly halls; "Industrial Democracy: The masters fear it, we need it, the I.W.W. will get it!"; picture of a man chained to a log, "The I.W.W. holds the key"; "Now this place runs you. If you want to run this place, line up now. I.W.W."

Page 71, line 20. The report on the general strike in the woods is based on articles in the *Industrial Worker* and *New Solidarity* of the period. Incomplete files of both papers are available in the New York Public Library. Robert L. Tyler reviews the strike in "Rebels of the Woods."

Page 73, line 8. The quotation from President Brown of the Shingle Weavers appeared in the *Union Record* of August 25, 1917.

Page 73, line 19. The background of the metal miners' strike is given in *The I.W.W.*, the official history.

Page 74, line 14. William Preston, Jr., in *Aliens and Dissenters,* pp. 96-108, outlines the preposterous opinion held by many influential people in the Government, local and federal, that deportation would decapitate the I.W.W. movement. Quoting from extensive research into files of the Department of Justice, the Labor Department's Immigration Bureau, and other federal and local sources, Preston emphasizes the unconstitutional methods used by the authorities against the I.W.W., including the first use of federal troops in a strike since the railroad strikes of 1877 and 1894.

Page 77, line 4. Eldridge Foster Dowell in *History of Criminal Syndicalism Legislation in the United States* asserts that there is no case available in the court records anywhere of an I.W.W. member caught practicing sabotage or convicted of it.

Page 77, line 32. I am indebted to Terry Pettus, then a Tacoma newspaperman, for the report on George Fishburne's investigation.

Page 78, line 13. Secretary Duncan's report on the I.W.W. strike appears in the *Industrial Worker* of December 8, 1917.

Page 78, line 20. Cornelia S. Parker's *An American Idyll* recounts her husband's role in the general lumber strike, p. 136 ff. "It is," wrote Parker, "a strike to better conditions. The I.W.W. are only the display feature. The main body of opinion is from a lot of unskilled workers who are sick of the filthy bunk-houses and rotten grub." Later he wrote of a conference with the big lumbermen who "roared over the I.W.W. I told them that condemnation was not a solution, or businesslike, but what we wanted was a statement of how they were to open their plants. More roars. More demands for troops, etc. I said I was a college man, not used to business; but if business men had as much trouble as this keeping to the real points involved, give me a faculty analysis. They laughed over this and got down to business, and in an hour lined up the affair in mighty good shape."

However "the affair" was not lined up and Parker was in continuous conferences for weeks more. His proposal for the eight-hour day was turned down by the operators. "The whole situation is drifting into a state of incipient sympathetic strikes." Later he wrote his wife: "This is the most bull-headed affair and I don't think it is going to get anywhere." Later: "Things are not going wonderfully in our mediation. Employers demanding everything and men granting much but not that." Parker, as head of the Department of Economics and dean of the College of Commerce at the University of Washington, adopted a "psychological" approach to the I.W.W., declaring that their lack of patriotism, hostility to employers, and advocacy of sabotage were not the result of original sin, but of their own experiences in industry and life. Soon after the lumber strike Carleton Parker died, the victim of overwork in carrying on his university teaching and mediation for the Government in various strikes.

Page 78, line 38. The Government's efforts to organize the 4 L's are related in Robert L. Tyler's "The U.S. Government as Union Organizer: The Loyal Legion of Loggers and Lumbermen."

Page 79, line 21. Carleton Parker's biography, *An American Idyll,* gives a presumed quotation from an I.W.W. member: "You ask me why the I.W.W. is not patriotic to the United States. If you were a bum without a blanket, if you had left your wife and kids when you went West and have never located them since; if your job has never kept you long enough in one place to qualify you to vote; if you slept in a lousy, sour bunkhouse and ate food just as rotten as they could give you and get by with it; if deputy sheriffs shot your cook cans full of holes and spilled the grub on the ground; if your wages were lowered only when the bosses thought they have you down; if there was one law for Ford, Suhr and Mooney, and another for Harry Thaw; if every person who represents law and order and the nation beat you up, railroaded you to jail and the good Christian people cheered and told them to go to it, how in hell do you expect a man to be patriotic? This war is a business man's war and we do not see why we should go out and get shot in order to save the lovely state of affairs we now enjoy."

Chapter 4

Much of the material in this chapter comes from my own memory of events and from correspondence with many who were active during the period. Hulet M. Wells's autobiography, "I Wanted To Work," is especially valuable in recounting incidents in the fight against the war and conscription.

Page 81, line 21. The Everett socialist resolution against the war appeared in the *Washington Socialist* of March 11, 1915, published in Everett.

Page 82, line 28. The Seattle Central Labor Council resolution against the war, voted in March, 1917, is reported in De Shazo's thesis, "Radical Tendencies in the Seattle Labor Movement."

Page 84, line 6. The May 28, 1916, peace meeting is reported in Wells's autobiography.

Page 85, line 11. Anna Louise Strong in *I Change Worlds* describes, pp. 55-57, the activities of the Seattle peace movement. The quotation from General Hugh S. Johnson appears in Wells's autobiography, p. 189, and in an undated newspaper clipping in the Wells Collection at the University of Washington Library.

Page 85, line 18. Bruce Rogers was one of the most colorful figures in the Seattle radical movement. After a brawl in an Indian Territory town in which a man was shot, he left on the lam on the next freight and enlisted under an assumed name for the Spanish-American War. Years later he appealed to Senator Morris Sheppard of Texas, who had been a classmate of his at the University of Texas, to correct his military record, presumably to receive a pension. He died in September, 1934, at the Veterans Hospital at Sawtelle, California.

Page 87, line 22. Nathan Fine's history of socialist parties reproduces the St. Louis anti-war resolution of the Socialist Party, p. 310. James Weinstein's monograph, *Anti-War Sentiment in the Socialist Party, 1917-1918,* is valuable in reporting the extent of opposition to the war.

Page 89, line 36. Anna Louise Strong's reaction to the founding of the *Seattle Daily Call* is recounted in *I Change Worlds,* pp. 58-61.

Page 90, line 5. Mauritzen, the founder of the *Call,* reviewed his role in his amateur journal, *Welcome News,* June-August, 1949, later reprinted in a pamphlet, *Printer's Ink on a Shoestring,* in 1950.

Page 91, line 22. Hulet Wells's reaction to the founding of the *Call* is from his autobiography, "I Wanted To Work."

Page 92, line 21. The only complete file of the *Seattle Daily Call* is in the University of Washington Library. Much of the detail about the *Call's* existence comes from the writer's memory, as a staff member. "Bertuccio Dantino's" name appeared in *Gale's Magazine,* in Mexico City, in 1919-1921.

Page 93, line 33. John McGivney later became editor of the *Tacoma Labor Advocate,* the official A.F. of L. weekly. He helped Tacoma newspapermen organize the Guild and stood by them when they joined the CIO in 1937. Soon afterward McGivney was eased out of his job and replaced by Ralph Chaplin who by that time had become a rabid anti-Communist and opponent of industrial unionism.

Page 95, line 26. The raid on the *Call* is related in the *Call* of January 7, 1918, and also in a magazine article in the *New York Call* of February 3, 1919, by Joseph Pass.

Page 99, line 3. Kate Sadler, who later became Mrs. Charles Greenhalgh, died in Tacoma, November 6, 1939.

Page 99, line 31. The arrest and trial of Louise Olivereau were reported in the *Call,* September 8, December 1, and December 4, 1917.

Page 101, line 27. Miss Strong's first publications were *Bible Hero Classics in Words of the Scripture* (1906-1908), *Biographical Studies in the Bible* (1912), and *Boys and Girls in the Bible* (1911). Her doctor's degree at the University of Chicago was granted for the thesis, "Consideration of Prayer from the Standpoint of Social Psychology," later published as *The Psychology of Prayer* (University of Chicago Press, 1909). In 1904 she wrote *Storm Songs and Fables*, and in 1906 a book of verse, *The Song of the City.*

Page 102, line 25. Miss Strong's account of the school board incident appears in *I Change Worlds*, pp. 61-66. The *Call* of October 24, October 27, and November 9, 1917, reported the campaign.

Page 104, line 26. The "Shilka" incident is reported in the *Union Record* of December 29, 1917, and January 5, 1918, and in the *Call* of December 24, 1917, and January 9, 1918. An interview with the crew appeared in the *Industrial Worker* of December 29, 1917, and January 12, 1918.

Page 105, line 20. Paul Haffer, imprisoned for resistance to the conscription law, maintained his militancy throughout life. He was active on the picket lines in the 1935 lumber strike. While Tacoma was under martial law and the militia were gassing the strikers, Haffer showed the pickets that a leather-faced glove was useful in picking up the hot tear-gas and nausea shells and tossing them back to the militia. He burned an Army truck that way right in front of a department store on Pacific Avenue.

Chapter 5

Page 109, line 12. The description of shipyard work is from Wells's autobiography, "I Wanted To Work."

Page 109, line 35. The old Labor Temple was torn down in 1963 to make way for a parking lot of the Washington Athletic Club. Years before the unions had built a new Labor Temple.

Page 110, line 21. The Council's denunciation of the Pigott raid appeared in the *Call* of January 10, 1918.

Page 110, line 36. Jay Fox made his comment on newspapers in the *Union Record* of February 16, 1918.

Page 111, line 27. The early history of the Central Labor Council has been related by De Shazo in his thesis. The history of the Grange is related in Harriet Ann Crawford's *The Washington State Grange.*

Page 112, line 35. The *Union Record*'s editorial on the war appeared April 7, 1917; that on the Supreme Court decision, December 15, 1917; and on the Chamber of Commerce, May 11, 1918. Some of the *Union Record* citations refer to the weekly edition, which carried highlights from the daily edition.

Page 113, line 33. The difficulties in the early period of the daily *Union Record* are recounted by Editor Ault in private correspondence in the Ault Papers, University of Washington Library.

Page 114, line 21. The *Union Record*'s views on industrial democracy were expressed in the issue of February 17, 1917.

Page 115, line 3. The *Union Record*'s comment on the police strike appeared July 28, 1917.

Page 115, line 7. *Aliens and Dissenters* gives a detailed description of Naval Intelligence operations on the Seattle waterfront.

Page 117, line 32. The Machinists' resolution on the jury system appeared in the *Union Record* of March 21, 1918.

Page 119, line 18. The *Union Record* edition of Lenin's speech is contained in a pamphlet *The Soviets At Work,* published in 1919.

Page 120, line 20. The *Union Record's* estimate of the international situation appeared in the issue of November 16, 1918.

Page 120, line 35. Captain Bunn's remarks were reported in the *Union Record* of March 31, 1917.

Page 121, line 22. The *Union Record's* comment on the Council of Workers, Soldiers and Sailors appeared in the issue of November 16, 1918.

Page 123, line 2. The Chicago Mooney convention was reported in the *Liberator* of March, 1919, and the *Union Record* of January 25, February 1, and February 22, 1919.

Chapter 6

The most authoritative account of the origin and conduct of the general strike is contained in the Central Labor Council's official report, *The Seattle General Strike,* issued by the History Committee of the General Strike Committee and published in 1919 by the *Union Record* as a 63-page pamphlet. The report was prepared by Anna Louise Strong and approved by the strike committee.

Lewin's "The Seattle Labor Movement and the General Strike of 1919" and George R. Furber's term paper at the University of Washington, March 8, 1949, "The Seattle General Strike," give detailed quotations from the Seattle press of the period. "Seattle Class Rebellion," by Joseph Pass in the *New York Call* magazine of March 2, 1919, gives an on-the-spot review of the strike. De Shazo's thesis, "Radical Tendencies in the Seattle Labor Movement," deals extensively with the general strike. Robert L. Friedheim has written a scholarly account, "The Seattle General Strike of 1919." Ole Hanson's version of the strike appears in his book, *Americanism vs. Bolshevism.* Robert K. Murray in *Red Scare* places the general strike in its historical perspective. William Simmons in the *Fourth International,* December, 1945, has a useful commentary entitled "Lessons of the 1919 Seattle General Strike."

Page 126, line 15. Anna Louise Strong's estimate of Seattle's position appeared in the *Union Record* of February 1, 1919.

Page 134, line 33. The letter to the Kiwanians is reproduced in De Shazo's thesis.

Page 135, line 11. The *Union Record* editorial disclaiming rumors of violent revolution appeared in the issue of February 6, 1919.

Page 135, line 24. Selvin's editorial appeared in the *Business Chronicle* of January 25, 1919, and as an advertisement in the *P-I* of January 28. These lurid charges of subversion seeped through to Washington. President Wilson wrote Attorney-General Gregory: "It is thoroughly worth our while to consider what, if anything, should and could be done about the influences proceeding from Seattle." The quotation is from Preston's *Aliens and Dissenters,* page 153.

Page 138, line 2. The notion that the Seattle general strike was violent seems to be accepted by many historians and writers, despite the evidence to the contrary. Theodore Draper, for instance, in *The Roots of American Communism* describes the general strike as one in "a series of big, unusually violent strikes [that] erupted all over the country." He cites the Lawrence, Massachusetts, textile strike and the Butte miners' strike as other examples.

Page 139, line 15. The *P-I* editorial appeared in the issue of February 6, 1919.

Page 139, line 20. The quotation from the *Star* appeared in the issue of February 7, 1919.

Page 143, line 6. Many Seattleites were convinced that Ole Hanson's "revolution" served as a smokescreen veiling the notorious purchase by the city of the broken-down Stone & Webster street car system.

Page 143, line 13. The police officer's statement appeared in an article, "The History of the Seattle Police Department," in the *Sheriff and Police Reporter,* published in Seattle.

Page 143, line 18. The *Saturday Evening Post* article, by Edgar Lloyd Hampton, appeared in the issue of April 12, 1919.

Page 144, line 2. An interesting sidelight on the *Saturday Evening Post's* weird story is given by Preston in *Aliens and Dissenters,* p. 152. He found in the Department of Justice files a letter from pistol-packing Dr. Mark A. Matthews of Seattle's First Presbyterian Church to Attorney-General Gregory which claimed that "the Kerensky overthrow . . . [had been] largely planned, schemed and executed in the city of Seattle." Seattle, said the minister, had fallen into the hands of "the pro-German forces, the I.W.W. fiends, and the vice syndicate agents of this country." As these elements controlled all the juries, Dr. Matthews urged amendment of the Espionage Act so that the military authorities could "arrest these fiends, court martial and shoot them." He also asked for appointment as provost marshal general in the Pacific Northwest with authority to shoot all violators of the law.

Colonel M. E. Saville, head of the military police at Camp Lewis, the big cantonment outside Tacoma, reported that Seattle was run by Mayor Hi Gill, George F. Vanderveer, and the Seattle National Bank, "the Vatican's instrument in the West." Thus the old "Rome,

rum and rebellion" unholy trinity was recreated. Saville said that
the Russian consul in Seattle was manipulating this gigantic plot,
as a German agent, using the I.W.W. (p. 159).

Page 145, line 2. The *Union Record* editorial on "the Great
Change coming" appeared about February 8, 1919. The comments
of *World's Work* and *Sunset* magazines appeared in their issues of
April, 1919. The *P-I* editorial was in the issue of February 11, 1919.

Chapter 7

Page 147, line 2. The leaflet, which I wrote, had a modest circulation of 20,000 copies but it was later reproduced in magazines with
circulation mounting into the millions to sustain the Seattle "Revolution" contention. *Business Chronicle* of February 1, 1919, reprinted the leaflet.

Page 147, line 32. The newsboy never went to trial, the issue being
resolved by the acquittal in the Bruce case (see pp. 153-154).

Page 148, line 23. Editorials of the *International Weekly* were reproduced in the Senate Judiciary Sub-Committee *Report on the
Brewing and Liquor Interests and German and Bolshevik Propaganda* (Government Printing Office, February 11, 1919).

Page 148, line 37. The editorial theme of "Agitate, Organize,
Emancipate," was inspired by the I.W.W. watchwords symbolized
by the three stars of the Wobbly emblem.

Page 149, line 5. "The Revolution is on" quotation is from the
January 17, 1919, *International Weekly*.

Page 149, line 14. Christmas greetings were in the issue of December 27, 1918, of the *International Weekly*.

Page 150, line 2. The Seattle socialist convention was reported
in the January 3, 1919, issue of the *International Weekly*.

Page 150, line 5. The number on trial in the Chicago case varies,
as some were released during the trial.

Page 151, line 1. Debs's Canton speech is reported in Ginger's
The Bending Cross, p. 358. The quotation from the September 14
speech, made before imposition of sentence, is reported on page 376.

Page 151, line 15. Reports on the repeated raids on the I.W.W.
hall and the arrests appeared in *New Solidarity* of February 15,
March 1, March 15, April 5, April 19, May 21, June 7, and June 21,
1919.

Page 151, line 23. Prosecutor Brown's statement and reports on
the case appeared in the *Union Record* of February 14, February 15,
and February 17, 1919. The *Union Record* statement on the indictment appeared February 15, 1919.

Page 153, line 23. The *Union Record* statement on the shipyards
appeared in the issue of March 6, 1919.

Page 153, line 27. The Bruce trial was reported in the *Seattle Times* from May 19 to June 5, 1919.

Page 154, line 32. Details about the Red Special and the raids were reported in *New Solidarity* of October 18, 1919. Preston in *Aliens and Dissenters* reveals much material hitherto unpublished in connection with the Red raids which had their start in Seattle and then spread across the nation in 1919-1920. He discovered a brief by the Immigration Bureau of the Department of Labor which declared that the I.W.W. "and its members should be handled without gloves." Most I.W.W. were "yeggs and tramps, men . . . lying idle as long as they can get sufficient to eat without working." "The scum of the earth . . . a landless and lawless mob, who, having no property themselves, recognize no rights or property . . . no law, and no authority save the policeman's night stick or physical violence." (p. 165)

Preston reported that the Seattle detention station was overcrowded and Bureau officials were appealing to Washington for funds to build stockades in which they expected to lodge 3,000–5,000 aliens pending deportation (a forerunner of the detention camps for Japanese-Americans in the Second World War and the plans for immense concentration camps for Reds in case of a third). (p. 167) By the spring of 1918, Preston reported, 150 aliens had been rounded up in the Seattle region. There they were subjected to utterly illegal procedures, denied habeas corpus, and subjected to incessant questioning. (p. 180)

The U.S. District Attorney wired the Department of Justice on the eve of the Seattle general strike that "intention of strike is revolution led by extreme element openly advocating overthrow of Government." Preston states that 36 aliens were on the Red Special sent from Seattle to Ellis Island and he gives a moving account of their trip across the country and their treatment at Ellis Island. (p. 180 ff.)

According to Preston, George F. Vanderveer outlined the defense strategy for the foreign-born in 1919-1920 of refusing to answer all Immigration Bureau questions, including names, dates of birth, and country of origin. Thus the Bureau would have no data on which to base deportation. This was a forerunner of the use of the Fifth Amendment in the McCarthy era. While most of the foreign-born were later released for lack of evidence, they had spent 8 to 15 months in detention, Preston records. In Seattle alone, he estimates, more than 150 I.W.W. were arrested and 27 deported (pp. 180-215)

Spurred partly by persecution in this country and partly by their desire to take part in the building of socialism in Soviet Russia, many Finns in the Puget Sound area emigrated in a group to build a commune in Russia. In 1925 while touring Russia, Carl Brannin visited the "Seattle Commune" near Rostov in the Don Cossack region. The Seattle Commune had been in operation then for three years. Brannin reported that the members of the Commune endured the hardest kind of pioneer life, were working in harmony, and were hoping that the worst was over.

Page 156, line 32. The demand of the *Times* and the *Star* for the purge appeared in their issues of February 10, 1919.

Page 157, line 18. The Labor Council's declaration against cleaning house was made March 6, 1919.

Page 158, line 14. The Associated Industries' account of labor unrest appeared in a pamphlet, *Revolution: Wholesale Strikes; Boycotts*. The unions' rejoinder appeared in a 69-page pamphlet, apparently prepared by President William Short of the State Federation of Labor, and dated November 28, 1919. Its title was *History of the Activities of the Seattle Labor Movement and Conspiracy of Employers to Destroy It and Attempted Suppression of Labor's Daily Newspaper, the Seattle Union Record*.

Page 159, line 13. The Kolchak arms shipment was reported in the *Union Record* of September 20, 1919. The munitions shipment later was handled by soldiers but thanks to the delay, the "S.S. Delight" arrived in Vladivostok after the Red Army had occupied the city, and the arms were gratefully received by the Bolsheviks, according to a story much relished by C. B. Irish, a Seattle longshoreman.

Page 159, line 24. The *Union Record* statement on Americanism appeared in the issue of October 11, 1919.

Page 159, line 34. The Kickapoo Indian Sagwa ad appeared in *New Solidarity* of July 12, 1919.

Page 160, line 6. Paul Bickel's statement appeared in the *Times* of February 14, 1919.

Page 160, line 22. The *P-I* editorial on Niederhauser appeared in the issue of February 17, 1919. The *Union Record* commented in the issue of March 3, 1919.

Page 161, line 17. Copies of the *Forge* are in the Sanford Collection at the University of Washington Library.

Page 161, line 36. The papers of Roy John Kinnear of the Associated Industries are in the University of Washington Library.

Page 162, line 18. After his release from McNeil Island, Morris Pass went to New York where later he became cartoonist for the *Daily Freiheit*.

Page 163, line 19. Details of imprisonment on McNeil Island appear in Hulet Wells's autobiography and from memories of another prisoner. "Sean" is the pseudonym for the Irish patriot who is still active in his home country.

The case of Emil Herman is recounted in *Opponents of War* by H. C. Peterson and Gilbert C. Fite. Herman was arrested after he

appeared as a defense witness for another Everett socialist arrested
for violation of the Espionage Act. Books and stickers found in
Herman's state Socialist Party office were used as evidence against
him. One sticker, falsely attributed to Jack London, read: "Young
man! The lowest aim in your life is to be a good soldier. The 'good
soldier' never tries to distinguish right from wrong. He never thinks,
never reasons; he only obeys. . . . A good soldier is a blind, heartless,
murderous machine. . . . No man can fall lower than a soldier — it
is a depth beneath which we cannot go. Young Man, Don't Be a
Soldier, Be a Man." Herman got ten years.

Page 167, line 10. The Council's protest against continued imprisonment appeared in the *Union Record* of September 6, 1919.

Clemens J. France later took part in writing the constitution of
the Irish Free State. Afterward he became director of public welfare
in Rhode Island and ran for governor on the Progressive ticket in
1948. Royal W. France's autobiography *My Native Grounds* tells of
the family.

President Wilson's visit to Seattle was reported in the *Union
Record* on September 6, September 13, and September 20, 1919.

Page 168, line 24. The political prisoners of the First World War
still in jail were freed by President Coolidge on December 15, 1923.

Page 169, line 12. Winston Churchill's comment appeared in a
column by John T. Flynn, undated. Hugh Johnson's comment is
from his syndicated column. Both clippings, in the Wells Collection
at the University of Washington Library, are undated, but Johnson's
was written apparently in 1940 during the Roosevelt presidential
campaign.

Chapter 8

The Armistice Day tragedy and the events leading up to it are
related in Walker C. Smith's *Was It Murder?*, a 47-page pamphlet
published by the I.W.W. in Seattle. Ralph Chaplin's 80-page pamphlet, *The Centralia Conspiracy*, also published by the I.W.W., is
illustrated and reviews operations in the lumber industry as a pre-
lude to the events in Centralia. *The Centralia Case,* a 50-page pamphlet published by departments of the Federal Council of Churches,
the National Catholic Welfare Conference, and the Central Conference of American Rabbis in 1930, gives an objective view of the
case and of the efforts to win release of the prisoners. Robert L.
Tyler's "Violence at Centralia, 1919" is a scholarly presentation of
the facts.

The Mark Litchman Papers in the University of Washington
Library give a running account of the *Union Record* case arising
from the Centralia tragedy. Litchman was an attorney for the *Union*

Record. The *Nation* of December 13, 1919, published an article by Anna Louise Strong on the seizure of the *Union Record.* President William Short's pamphlet *History of Activities of the Seattle Labor Movement* reviews extensively the press hysteria against organized labor arising from the Centralia events.

Page 170, line 13. The Lumber Workers' votes were reported in *New Solidarity* of November 8, 1919.

Page 171, line 10. Litchman's defense of the Wobblies is recorded in his Papers at the University of Washington Library.

Page 171, line 37. *New Solidarity's* account of the job market appeared in the issue of November 1, 1919. *New Solidarity* was the successor to *Solidarity,* the I.W.W.'s eastern weekly, after its suppression during the September, 1917, raids.

Page 172, line 14. No effort is made to annotate the various facts concerning the events leading up to the tragedy itself, as they are not in dispute, aside from the central issue of the timing of the attack on the Wobbly hall. The various authorities cited above are in substantial agreement about the events.

Page 173, line 36. The Tacoma *News-Tribune* commented in its issue of November 7, 1919.

Page 177, line 13. Many of the colorful or euphonious place names in western Washington come from the Siwash (Chinook) language. Skookumchuck could mean good food. Other place names include: Humptulips, Tulalip, Puyallup (Pew-AL-lup), Mukilteo, Nisqually, Snohomish, Skykomish, Snoqualmie, Kamilche, Lilliwaup, Ducka-bush, Sequim (Skwim), Quilcene, Issaquah, Kapowsin, Clallam, Quillayute, Chehalis (She-HAY-lis). Seattle is a corruption of Sealth, name of an Indian chief; Tacoma for Tahoma, Indian name of Mt. Rainier.

Page 179, line 22. Mrs. Anne Cloud of Richmond, California, recalls that while she was serving as an I.W.W. delegate in 1919 in Aberdeen no active member knew from one day to the next when he would be taken into custody. The branch secretary for Lumber Workers Industrial Union 500, realizing that his days were numbered, brought the organization records to Mrs. Cloud's home and was arrested shortly thereafter, tried and sentenced to two years under the catch-all criminal syndicalism law. In Seattle a man was given a year and a day for having a copy of the *Industrial Worker* in his pocket.

The *Industrial Worker* was delivered in bundles of 100 to Mrs. Cloud's home. One day, after receiving the parcel, she noticed a policeman at the front door. Hurriedly she dumped the bundle in the oven of her kitchen stove, turned on the gas a bit, and remarked to the policeman, who was prowling through the house, that she had supper cooking in the oven. He didn't find the *Industrial Workers.*

Page 181, line 10. Commander Bassett's comment appears in *The Centralia Conspiracy*, p. 69.

Page 182, line 29. The *Times*'s editorial on terrorizing the Bolsheviki appeared in the issue of November 12, 1919.

Page 183, line 19. The *Union Record*'s editorial "Reason Will Triumph" appeared in the issue of November 13, 1919.

Page 184, line 3. Editor Selvin's incendiary editorial appeared in the *Business Chornicle* of November 15, 1919, and the *P-I* of November 18, 1919.

Page 186, line 20. Copies of the federal indictment and other legal papers in the *Union Record* case are preserved in the Litchman Papers at the University of Washington Library.

Page 188, line 22. Vanderveer's defense of the I.W.W. is recorded in *Counsel for the Damned*, pp. 273-285.

Page 192, line 15. Attorney Vanderveer, after the Centralia trial, organized a legal bureau for the Seattle Central Labor Council to handle workmen's compensation and other cases. In the early 1920's this bureau had a corps of young lawyers working under Vanderveer's direction.

Page 193, line 34. The *Industrial Worker*'s comment on John Lamb appeared in the issue of December 26, 1962.

Page 195, line 26. Facts about Elmer Smith's later life were given by relatives and friends, including William Smith, a brother, now living in Gresham, Oregon, and Mrs. Cloud.

Page 197, line 17. The *Industrial Worker* of December 12, 1962, reported a proposal to establish a Wesley Everest memorial hall in Chehalis. That the memory of the Centralia tragedy still lives is attested by a column-long Associated Press article in the *New York Times* of November 11, 1962, recounting the story.

The trial documents in the Centralia case, File 16354, are in boxes in a back room of the office of the Clerk of the Washington State Supreme Court in Olympia. These include newspapers, affidavits, handbills, and other evidence used during and after the trial.

Chapter 9

Page 198, line 3. The report of the labor jury appeared in Chaplin's *The Centralia Conspiracy*, p. 79.

Page 199, line 17. The Great Red Scare of 1919-1920 has been recorded in Murray's *Red Scare*.

Page 202, line 10. David Rodgers' plan is recorded in the Spy Reports in the University of Washington Library.

Page 203, line 16. Efforts to build a Labor Party in 1919-1920 are recorded in Fine's *Labor and Farmer Parties*, p. 378 ff. *Winning Washington for the Producers*, a pamphlet by John C. Kennedy, published by the Farmer-Labor Party of Washington, outlines the program of that organization.

Page 203, line 29. The *Union Record*'s report on the State Federation program appeared in the issue of December 21, 1918.

Page 204, line 20. The O.B.U. movement was reported in the *Union Record* of June 28, 1919, and August 16, 1919. *The Winnipeg General Sympathetic Strike*, a 276-page book, was prepared by the Defense Committee in Winnipeg.

Page 205, line 5. The Civic Federation's letter appeared in the *National Civic Federation Review*, March 5, 1919.

Page 206, line 8. The collapse of the radical movement coincided with the deep depression of 1920-1921. Labor, which had been scarce in the war years, became a drug on the market and employers mounted a savage assault which robbed the unions of the gains so recently made. The split in the Socialist Party weakened that organization by depriving it of many of its militant members, who either joined the new Communist parties or else withdrew, like Kate Sadler and many others, from active political life. Socialist propaganda, as such, practically disappeared. Increasingly the Communist Party found its main interest in internal power struggles for leadership which were resolved from time to time in Moscow. Not until the Great Depression of 1929 ended the period of industrial stability under Coolidge and Hoover were American radicals to focus their main attention again on domestic issues. Another factor in the sudden decline of radicalism of course was the massive repression unleashed by the federal and state governments.

Page 207, line 30. The statement on the aims of Listman Service appeared in the *Union Record* of January 18, 1919.

Page 208, line 25. The fight on "labor capitalism" is recorded extensively in the Litchman Papers at the University of Washington Library. De Shazo's "Radical Tendencies in the Seattle Labor Movement" also deals with this period.

Page 209, line 9. Anna Louise Strong's disillusionment is recorded in *I Change Worlds*, p. 86 ff.

Page 209, line 31. Hulet Wells recorded his Russian trip in his autobiography.

Page 212, line 36. Duncan's proposal for reorganization of the A. F. of L. is contained in a four-page printed "Letter to All Organizations Affiliated With the A. F. of L." dated March 12, 1919.

Page 213, line 18. The Seattle Council's fight to retain its charter is recounted in a 12-page pamphlet *Statement of the Seattle Central Labor Council Relative to Its Controversy With the Executive Council of the American Federation of Labor*.

Page 216, line 17. The Grange – Western Progressive Farmers conflict is recorded in *Master's Address* by William Bouck and *Prin-*

ciples and Purposes, Western Progressive Farmers of Washington, a 63-page booklet.

Page 216, line 23. De Shazo records the Council's anti-communist stand in "Radical Tendencies in the Seattle Labor Movement."

Page 217, line 28. Harry Ault's comment was made in a letter to me, February 21, 1957.

Page 218, line 33. Activities of the Labor College are recorded in "Seattle Labor College News," a small four-page brochure issued intermittently in the 1920's. Senator Paul Douglas of Illinois, while on the faculty of the University of Washington, taught at the Labor College.

Page 221, line 2. Hulet Wells records the rise of the Unemployed League in his autobiography. *The Unemployed Citizens' League of Seattle* is the most complete study of the league. "The Republic of the Penniless" article appeared in the *Atlantic Monthly* of October, 1932. Carl Brannin has been most helpful in his memories of this period.

Page 222, line 31. Terry Pettus, a labor newspaperman during this period, has furnished me with a wealth of detail on the political upheaval in Washington State in the 1930's and 1940's. At the time he worked closely with the Washington Commonwealth Federation and kindred organizations. Hulet Wells in his autobiography tells of Congressman Zioncheck's rise and fall. *Washington: A Guide to the Evergreen State* has a useful survey of radical movements in this era.

Page 227, line 2. Morgan's *Skid Road* has an exhilarating chapter on Dave Beck's influence in Seattle, pp. 220-271.

Page 228, line 4. Activities of the Canwell Committee, with a review of radical activities in the 1930's and 1940's, are recorded in Vern Countryman's *Un-American Activities in the State of Washington.* Schmid's *Social Trends in Seattle* also is useful for the period of the 1930's.

Appendix Two

The chief source is a booklet, *The Louise Olivereau Case,* published in late 1918 or 1919 by Minnie Parkhurst in Seattle. Other sources are the *Mother Earth Bulletins* for January and March, 1918, brief mentions in the American Civil Liberties Union Files (LXII, 81) and in *Opponents of War* by Peterson and Fite, and letters from and about Miss Olivereau preserved by friends, as well as their reminiscences.

In a letter to Louise Olivereau from Leavenworth Penitentiary, May 29, 1920, Charles Ashleigh in discussing the prospects for release from prison wrote: "I am quite prepared to put in my remaining five years with cheerfulness and equanimity. It is one of the risks of war; and I knew it was, when I entered this war; so one should take it as one of the unavoidable episodes of the game. When people join the active labor movement, they should be prepared for this kind of thing. Of course, we all would like to be out . . . but . . . !"

List of Works Cited

In recent years historians and journalists have shown a marked interest in the dramatic 1915-1920 period of Seattle's annals. They have written mainly of the outstanding conflicts of that period, the Everett and Centralia trials and the Seattle General Strike; the role of the lumber industry, basic in the economy of the Pacific Northwest; and the relation of the radical movement in the Puget Sound country to the development of the national anti-Red hysteria of 1919-1920. The more important books and articles have been noted in the following list of publications, referred to in Notes.

Associated Industries. *Revolution: Wholesale Strikes; Boycotts.* 1919?

Ault, E. B. "Thirty Years of Saving the World." Unpublished manuscript, University of Washington Library.

Avery, Mary W. *History and Government of the State of Washington.* Seattle: University of Washington Press, 1961.

Botting, David C., Jr. "Bloody Sunday," *Pacific Northwest Quarterly* (October, 1958).

Bouck, William. *Master's Address.* Washington State Grange, 1921.

Brissenden, Paul F. *The I.W.W.* New York: Russell & Russell, 1920.

The Centralia Case. Federal Council of Churches, National Catholic Welfare Conference, and Central Conference of American Rabbis. 1930.

Chaplin, Ralph. *The Centralia Conspiracy.* I.W.W., 1920.

———. *Wobbly.* Chicago: University of Chicago Press, 1948.

Countryman, Vern. *Un-American Activities in the State of Washington.* Ithaca: Cornell University Press, 1951.

Crawford, Harriet Ann. *The Washington State Grange.* Portland: Binfords & Mort, 1940.

De Ford, Miriam Allen. *Up-Hill All The Way.* Yellow Springs: Antioch Press, 1956.

Delaney, Ed. and M. T. Rice. *The Bloodstained Trail.* Seattle: Industrial Worker, 1927.

De Shazo, Melvin Gardner. "Radical Tendencies in the Seattle Labor

Movement." Unpublished Master's thesis, University of Washington, 1925.

Dowell, Eldridge Foster. *History of Criminal Syndicalism Legislation in the United States.* Baltimore: Johns Hopkins Press, 1939.

Draper, Theodore. *The Roots of American Communism.* New York: Viking, 1957.

Ely, Richard T. *The Labor Movement in America.* New York: Crowell, 1886.

Evidence and Cross-Examination of J. T. (Red) Doran. Chicago: I.W.W., 1918?

Fine, Nathan. *Labor and Farmer Parties in the United States.* New York: Rand School, 1928.

Flynn, Elizabeth Gurley. *I Speak My Own Piece.* New York: Masses and Mainstream, 1955.

Foster, William Z. *Pages From a Worker's Life.* New York: International Publishers, 1939.

France, Royal W. *My Native Grounds.* New York: Cameron Associates, 1957.

Friedheim, Robert L. "The Seattle General Strike of 1919," *Pacific Northwest Quarterly* (July, 1961).

Furber, George R. "The Seattle General Strike." Unpublished term paper, University of Washington, March 8, 1949.

Ginger, Ray. *The Bending Cross.* New Brunswick: Rutgers University Press, 1949.

Hanson, Ole. *Americanism vs. Bolshevism.* New York: Doubleday Page, 1920.

Harper, Vincent. *The Terrible Truth About Marriage.* Seattle: 1907.

Hawley, Lowell S. and Ralph Bushnell Potts. *Counsel for the Damned.* Philadelphia and New York: J. B. Lippincott, 1953.

Hillman, A. H. *The Unemployed Citizens' League of Seattle.* Seattle: University of Washington Press, 1934.

Holbrook, Stewart H. *Holy Old Mackinaw.* New York: Macmillan, 1956.

Kennedy, John C. *Winning Washington for the Producers.* Washington Farmer-Labor Party, 1921.

Kinnear, George. *Anti-Chinese Riots.* Seattle: 1911.

Leighton, George R. *Five Cities.* New York: Harper, 1939.

Lewin, Edward B. "The Seattle Labor Movement and the General Strike of 1919." Unpublished Master's thesis, Princeton University, 1962.

Lloyd, Caro. *Henry Demarest Lloyd.* 2 vols. New York: G. P. Putnam's Sons, 1912.

The Louise Olivereau Case. Seattle: Minnie Parkhurst, 1918 or 1919.

The Lumber Industry and Its Workers. Chicago: I.W.W., 1919?

Mauritzen, Thorwald G. *Printers Ink on a Shoestring.* 1950.

Morgan, Murray. *Skid Road.* New York: Viking, 1951.

Murray, Robert K. *Red Scare*. Minneapolis: University of Minnesota Press, 1955.

Neuberger, Richard L. *Our Promised Land*. New York: Macmillan, 1938.

Noyes, John H. *History of American Socialisms*. New York: Hillary House, 1961.

Parker, Cornelia S. *An American Idyll*. Boston: Atlantic Monthly Press, 1919.

Pass, Joseph. "Seattle Class Rebellion," *New York Call* (March 2, 1919).

Peterson, H. C. and Gilbert C. Fite. *Opponents of War*. Madison: University of Wisconsin Press, 1957.

Preston, William, Jr. *Aliens and Dissenters*. Cambridge: Harvard University Press, 1963.

Principles and Purposes, Western Progressive Farmers of Washington. 1922?

Quint, Howard H. *The Forging of American Socialism*. Columbia: University of South Carolina Press, 1953.

Schmid, Calvin F. *Social Trends in Seattle*. Seattle: University of Washington Press, 1944.

Seattle Central Labor Council. *The Seattle General Strike*. Seattle: *Union Record*, 1919.

———. *Statement of the Seattle Central Labor Council Relative to Its Controversy With the Executive Council of the American Federation of Labor*. Seattle: 1923.

Short, William. *History of the Activities of the Seattle Labor Movement and Conspiracy of Employers to Destroy It and Attempted Suppression of Labor's Daily Newspaper, the Seattle Union Record*. Seattle: Washington Federation of Labor, 1919.

Simmons, William. "Lessons of the 1919 Seattle General Strike," *Fourth International* (December, 1945).

Smith, Walker C. *The Everett Massacre*. Chicago: I.W.W., 1917?

———. *Was It Murder?* Seattle: I.W.W., 1922.

Strong, Anna Louise. *I Change Worlds*. New York: Garden City Publishing Co., 1937.

Thompson, Fred. *The I.W.W.* Chicago: I.W.W., 1955.

Thorseth, Matthea. *The Color of Ripening*. Seattle: Superior Publishing Company, 1949.

25 Years of Industrial Unionism. Chicago: I.W.W., 1930.

Tyler, Robert L. "Rebels of the Woods," *Oregon Historical Quarterly* (March, 1954).

———. "The U.S. Government as Union Organizer: The Loyal Legion of Loggers and Lumbermen," *Mississippi Valley Historical Review* (December, 1960).

———. "Violence at Centralia, 1919," *Pacific Northwest Quarterly* (October, 1954).

286

Weinstein, James. *Anti-War Sentiment in the Socialist Party, 1917-1918.* New York: Academy of Political Science, 1959.

Wells, Hulet. "I Wanted To Work." Unpublished manuscript, University of Washington Library.

————. *The Colonel and His Friends.*

Wentworth, Harold and Stuart Berg Flexner. *The Dictionary of American Slang.* New York: Thomas Y. Crowell Co., 1960.

Williams, G. O. "The History of the Seattle Police Department," *Sheriff and Police Reporter* (Seattle: November, 1950).

Winnipeg Defense Committee. *The Winnipeg General Sympathetic Strike,* 1920?

Writer's Program, W.P.A. *Washington: A Guide to the Evergreen State.* Portland: Binfords & Mort, 1941.

Checklist of Radical Papers in the State of Washington (1898–1920)

This checklist has been prepared with the cooperation of Marvin Sanford of San Francisco. Sanford, a union printer and amateur journalist, accumulated the largest collection of Washington State radical publications extant, now housed at the University of Washington.

The checklist notes the first year of publication, title, place of publication, years of publication, editors and main contributors, and political orientation. Most of the earlier papers were privately owned but from about 1910 the more prominent papers were official organs. Exact dates of publication for most of the papers are not known; in some cases no copy of the paper is known to exist. Even the years of publication in some cases are conjectural. The University of Washington has in addition to the Sanford Collection, files of the *Seattle Daily Call* of 1885-1886, that of 1917-1918, and of the *Northwest Worker*.

1898   *Cooperator,* Olalla, Burley, 1892-1906, socialist.

1898   *Spirit of '76,* Tacoma, 1898-1899, George E. Boomer, socialist.

1898   *Whidby Islander,* Langley (Free Land Colony), 1898-1903, DeForest and Ethel Brooke Sanford, cooperative.

1898   *Industrial Freedom* (later *Freedom*), Edison (Equality Colony), May 7, 1898-February, 1901, weekly, then monthly until December 1902, William McDevitt, David Burgess, George E. Boomer, E. B. Ault, socialist.

1899   *Young Socialist,* Edison (Equality Colony) and elsewhere, November, 1899-1903, E. B. Ault, socialist.

1900   *New Light,* Port Angeles, daily, E. E. Vail, merged with *Socialist* of Seattle, December 23, 1900.

1900   *Socialist,* Seattle, August 12, 1900-1910, Dr. Hermon Franklin Titus, William Mailley, Vincent Harper, A. B. Callaham, Edwin J. Brown, Emil Herman. Published in Toledo, Ohio, 1905, and in Caldwell, Idaho, 1906, by E. B. Ault; name changed to *Next* for few issues about 1905 and to *Workingman's Paper,* 1910, socialist.

1900   *Discontent,* Lakebay (Home Colony), 1900-1902, anarchist.

1902   *New Time,* Spokane, January 21, 1902-April 1, 1905, Joseph Gilbert, socialist.

1902   *Soundview,* Olalla, October, 1902, radical.

1902?   *Tacoma Sun,* Tacoma, George E. Boomer, socialist. This may have been published in 1908.

1903   *Prosser Record,* Prosser, 1903-1909, George E. Boomer, socialist.

1903   *Demonstrator,* Lakebay (Home Colony), 1903-1904, anarchist.

1904   *Next,* Seattle, 1904-1905, Dr. Hermon F. Titus, E. B. Ault, socialist.

1907   *Saturday Evening Tribune,* Seattle, 1907-1908, Walter Thomas Mills, E. Backus, socialist.

1909   *Industrial Worker,* Spokane, March 18, 1909-September, 1913, James Wilson, Fred W. Heslewood, I.W.W.

1909   *Suppressed Facts,* Seattle, Dr. Edwin J. Brown, socialist.

1909   *World's Referee,* Seattle, 1909-1910, monthly, Edwin J. Brown, David Burgess, socialist.

1909? *Northwest Forum,* Sunnyside, 1909-1910?, H. D. Jory, socialist.

1910   *Agitator,* Lakebay (Home Colony), 1910-1913, semi-monthly, Jay Fox, anarchist. Became the *Syndicalist* in Chicago in January, 1913.

1910   *Workingman's Paper,* Seattle, 1909-1910?, Hermon F. Titus, E. B. Ault, William Z. Foster, socialist.

1910   *Socialist Voice (Voice of Labor),* Seattle, 1910-1912, William P. Parks, Bruce Rogers, David Burgess, O. M. Thomasson, Hulet M. Wells, Socialist Party organ.

1910   *Wage Worker,* Seattle, "only 3-color 'roughneck' revolutionary monthly on earth," George E. Boomer, Emil Herman, Joseph Biscay, socialist, Wage Workers Party official organ.

1911   *Commonwealth,* Everett, 1911-1917, (known also as *Washington Socialist,* 1914-1915, *Northwest Worker,* 1915-1916, *Cooperative News,* 1917), O. L. Anderson, J. T. Hazard, Alfred Wagenknecht, James M. Salter, Maynard Shipley, H. M. Watts, Peter Husby, Socialist Party of Washington official organ.

1911   *Political Socialist,* Seattle, 1911-1912, Edwin J. Brown, socialist.

1911   *Socialist News,* Kelso, 1911-1926?, Logan S. Ellis, William Marston, socialist.

1911   *Three-Hour Day,* Seattle, November, 1911-1912, semi-monthly, E. B. Ault, John Downie, Arthur Jensen, socialist.

1912   *Four-Hour Day,* Seattle, Hermon F. Titus, socialist.

1912   *Lewis County Clarion,* Centralia, M. D. Wood, W. H. Stackhouse, socialist.

1912   *Kitsap County Leader,* Bremerton, George E. Boomer, M. E. Giles, socialist.

1912   *Truth,* Tacoma, 1912-1914, Walter E. Reynolds, socialist.

1912   *Socialist Worker,* Tacoma, 1912-1913, Walter E. Reynolds, Leslie Aller, E. L. Currier, socialist.

1912   *Revolution,* Seattle, 1912-1913, William P. Parks, socialist.

1913   *Barbarian,* Seattle, weekly, George E. Boomer, Bruce Rogers, socialist.

1913   *Eye-Opener,* Orting, socialist.

1913   *New Era,* Aberdeen, V. T. Evans, socialist.

1913   *Socialist Herald,* Seattle, 1912-1916, Joseph Gilbert, O. L. Anderson, Edwin J. Brown, Glenn Hoover, Hulet M. Wells, socialist.

1914   *Washington Socialist* (see *Commonwealth,* 1911).

1914   *Peninsula Free Press,* Port Angeles, George E. Boomer, socialist.

1915   *Northwest Worker* (see *Commonwealth,* 1911).

1915   *Spokane Socialist,* Spokane.

1916   *Industrial Worker,* Seattle, April 1, 1916-May, 1918, also 1918-—, J. A. MacDonald, Walker C. Smith, I.W.W.

1916   *Red Feather,* Seattle, monthly, Bruce Rogers, socialist.
1916   *Socialist World,* Seattle, 1916-1917, Walker C. Smith, Scott Bennett, Joseph Pass, Paul Bickel, Marius Hansome, Socialist Party organ.
1917   *Cooperative News* (See *Commonwealth,* 1911).
1917   *Seattle Daily Call,* Seattle, 1917-1918, John McGivney, Lena Morrow Lewis, Joseph Pass, Anna Louise Strong, Paul Bickel, Harvey O'Connor, Hays Jones, Thorwald G. Mauritzen, business manager, Socialist Party organ.
1918   *International Weekly,* Seattle, 1918-1919, Harvey O'Connor, Hays Jones, Socialist Party organ.
1918   *Industrial Unionist,* Everett-Seattle, replaced *Industrial Worker* during its suppression.
1918   *Party Builder,* Everett, 1918-1919, Emil Herman, Socialist Party organ.
1919   *Freedom,* Seattle, Socialist Party organ.
1919   *Forge,* Seattle, 1919-1920, Arne Swabeck, Workers, Soldiers and Sailors Council organ, socialist-syndicalist.
1920   *Farmer-Labor Call,* Centralia, 1920-1921, Harvey O'Connor, Farmer-Labor Party.

Index

Index

293